SAM TORRANCE

OUT OF BOUNDS

Legendary Tales from the 19th Hole

SIMON & SCHUSTER

London · New York · Sydney · Toronto · New Delhi

A CBS COMPANY

First published in Great Britain by Simon & Schuster UK Ltd, 2012
This paperback edition published by Simon & Schuster UK Ltd, 2013

A CBS company

Copyright © 2012 by Sam Torrance

1 3 5 7 9 10 8 6 4 2

Simon & Schuster UK Ltd
1st Floor
222 Gray's Inn Road
London WC1X 8HB

www.simonandschuster.co.uk

Simon & Schuster Australia,
Sydney

Simon & Schuster India,
New Delhi

A CIP catalogue record for this book is available from the British Library

ISBN: 978-1-84983-722-4
Ebook ISBN: 978-1-84983-723-1

Typeset in the UK by Hewer Text
Printed in the UK by CPI Group (UK) Ltd, Croydon, CR0 4YY

To Suzanne, Daniel, Phoebe and Anouska,
with thanks for your constant love and support.

Contents

Introduction

E ver since Mary, Queen of Scots pitched up at St Andrews for 18 holes and James VI of Scotland threw a bag of clubs into his boot for the trip south to become James I of England, golf has produced a rich vein of stories.

The same might be said of most sports, but only golf added an area to the pitch, as it were, for the specific purpose of telling tales and sinking pints. You rarely have one without the other when golfers gather, glass in hand and yarns ready to weave. We are talking about the 19th hole.

Now this is a subject about which I can claim a certain expertise. Very rarely would I play golf without washing the glorious experience down with a beer. Ideally, the drink would be coupled with companionship, which in turn would generate the kind of laughter that is always the best medicine. Where better than the 19th hole and when better than after a round of golf to exchange both the latest jokes and the oldest anecdotes? Or the newest anecdotes and the most ancient jokes?

Husband: We had a terrible day at the course, darling. Charlie had a heart attack on the 2nd.

Wife: That's awful.

Husband: You're telling me. All day long it was hit the ball, drag Charlie, hit the ball, drag Charlie.

Trevino: Have you seen the amazing golf ball that comes equipped with beeps and flashing lights so that it simply can't be lost?
Torrance: That's fantastic, where did you get it?
Trevino: Oh, I found it.

Bob Hope: Arnold Palmer told me how to cut eight strokes off my score – miss out one of the par threes.

It is not generally known that Bernhard Langer had been literally struck dumb by lightning as a toddler. One day his mother served soup for lunch, whereupon the boy said, 'Mummy, the soup is cold.'

'Gott im Himmel,' his mother said, sounding like a racial stereotype. 'For seven years you have never spoken, never complained about anything.'

'Up to now everything has been perfect.'

That's a joke I like to tell about Langer, the perfectionist.

This is not a book of golfing jokes, though. This is a book of golfing tales, most of which are true, some of which started out life as fact and may have become exaggerated in the telling, and some of which would be apocryphal were they not such obvious invention. Actually, that last bit is not the case. I believe that the stories in this book, brought to me by word of mouth or dredged from the reservoirs of a lifetime spent in the 19th hole, are true. And if they're not quite true, then they certainly ought to be.

Introduction

I cannot vouch for the veracity of those so kindly and freely provided by my fellow professionals and friends. Would you accept a used story from the likes of Ian Botham, Ian Woosnam, Brian Barnes and David Feherty? A rum bunch (and a rum punch) indeed, but all passionate about a sport where camaraderie and comradeship live in perfect harmony with individual endeavour.

The great Jack Nicklaus and that most elegant of swingers Tom Weiskopf found themselves in such perfect harmony during the 1978 Masters that they turned up for the final round, in which they were paired together, wearing exactly the same colour and make of shirt and identical coloured trousers.

Weiskopf immediately swung into action by asking his then wife, Jeanne, to go to the professional shop to buy a different coloured shirt. While Jeanne was away, a security guy approached Weiskopf with some important information about Nicklaus having received a death threat. There would be an FBI presence in the gallery for the round.

Jeanne returned with the shirt just as Weiskopf was walking on to the 1st tee. He ripped off his original shirt to reveal a brown bear of a torso and put on the new one.

'What the hell are you doing?' Nicklaus asked.

'I just want to make sure they don't shoot the wrong guy,' Weiskopf replied.

Both players fell about laughing and proceeded to play pretty diabolically, finishing well down the field.

While the amount of time I have spent in the 19th hole makes me an obvious candidate to become involved in writing a book of yarns, there is one obvious drawback. I have a terrible memory – but only for the who, where, when and why!

Poor Sue Barker and the team from *A Question of Sport* have long since passed the point of ultimate exasperation as I rack my brains for an answer I know but cannot locate. The cameras roll and roll and roll for much longer than the heavily edited version for broadcasting would indicate. I believe my record is in the region of ten minutes before eventually coming up with the correct answer.

'How did you get on at the recording today?' my long-suffering wife, Suzanne, asked on my return from the filming of one *QoS* programme.

So I told her. 'I got stuck on one golf question. I came up with all sorts of names. I went through just about everyone you could imagine. We filmed for about ten minutes. It was terrible, really embarrassing. Eventually, I got it right.'

'What was the question?'

'Who is the only golfer from Europe or the United States to win two major championships and never play in the Ryder Cup?' I told her.

'You mean John Daly,' she said.

I gave her what my mother would call an old-fashioned look. But it showed that Suzanne acquired a greater knowledge of golf than she probably wanted following me up and down the fairways of the world. Not that it was all sunglasses and sundowners. At the 1987 World Cup in Kapalua, Hawaii, during monsoon rain she went head over heels and slid down a hill for about 40 yards like a tobogganist who had lost her sledge. We can laugh now, but we did not know at the time that she was pregnant with Daniel.

One thing I have had confirmed in bringing all the subsequent tales together is that two (sober) people can be involved in the same incident and give two completely contrasting accounts of it.

Take those terrible twins (there were times the European Tour wished someone would) Mark Roe and Robert Lee, and their classic game 'scissors, television cable and fried golfer'. Both agree that Roe took scissors to an electric cable during a late-night dispute in a hotel at Lake Como and lived to replace the wire. But both disagree completely about who was to blame and what the circumstances were that led to Roe blowing not just his own fuse.

Another example – the aforementioned Botham, England cricket's greatest all-rounder and a mad-keen golfer, insists that when I joined him on one of his charity walks I strolled a few yards before climbing into a support vehicle for a drink and a fag. I know for certain that I walked 19 miles suffering from a bad back. You can read both versions.

Explosions feature heavily in this book. Golf can be the most satisfying and pleasurable of sports. But it can also be the most humbling, the most humiliating and the most infuriating. While golfers are encouraged to maintain their equilibrium, even the best crack. If you think Tiger Woods slamming his club into the ground is bad, consider the golfer who broke his toe when smashing a putter into his foot; the players who headbutted trees; the Ryder Cup captain (not me) who cracked a bone in his hand punching his hotel bedroom wall; and the American pro who threw his clubs, his caddie and himself into a pond.

We have stories of great golfers, calamitous golfers, drunk golfers, naked golfers, injured golfers, crazy golfers, eccentric golfers and superstitious golfers. We have tales of famous singers, famous actors, famous sportspeople, famous comedians and notorious gangsters. We have presidents and we have royalty.

We have drinking, gambling, misbehaving, club throwing, caddie throwing (no dwarf throwing), three-putting, four-putting and more putting. We have holes-in-one and a hole in 17.

We have sporting triumph and we have sporting disaster.

We have nicknames. Boy, do we have nicknames. El Gato, El Nino and El Pato, alias Eduardo Romero, Sergio Garcia and Angel Cabrera; The King, The Golden Bear and The Black Knight, The Big Three – Arnold Palmer, Jack Nicklaus and Gary Player; Double D, Chippie and Slippery, aka David Duval, Paul Lawrie and Paul Eales; Junior and Senior, or Gordon Brand and Peter Senior. And that's only the players.

What about The Seagull, The Lip, The Brain, The Ferret, The Elbow, The Professor and The Russian? All caddies who need – and prefer – no other introduction. Cornflake, Crunchy Nut Cornflake, Yorkie Bill, Jungle Jim, Toffy Tim, Edinburgh Jimmy, Staggering Haggerty and Stuttering Stanley. The list could go on.

My mate John O'Leary once loaned Jungle Jim £30 and had a devil of a job getting it back. In fact, he never did. 'Just put it down to experience,' JJ said when asked for the umpteenth time.

I am hugely grateful to the thrity contributors, each of whom provided stories covering all aspects of golf. My intention to make a contribution to the Seve Ballesteros Foundation no doubt helped to persuade some of those who receive countless requests for their time and energy every day.

Some responded swiftly to my request, some were a little slower to come up with the goods. And then there was my great buddy David Feherty, who is a busy man and has an email account that sends messages into spam folders!

The first to reply in the affirmative was Arnold Palmer, who tells some delightful stories about his favourite hole at Bay Hill, the short 17th. The first to submit an offering was Ryder Cup captain par excellence Tony Jacklin, who writes of a memorable practice round with the legendary Ben Hogan. Well done, Arnie and Tony, there is no substitute for class.

Alastair Johnston, one of the top men at IMG and the former chairman of Rangers FC, reveals the Mrs Malaprop inside his great friend Arnold Palmer; Lee Westwood remembers how he mistook me for Manchester United great Peter Schmeichel (or words to that effect); Paul McGinley writes emotionally about the Ryder Cup; and Des Smyth recalls 'the greatest shot' he ever saw from, who else, the great Ballesteros.

Seve very rarely allowed anyone to get the better of him. But Tony Johnstone, though a great admirer of the Spaniard, did. It was one of those occasions when Seve demonstrated his encyclopaedic knowledge of the rules and how he could make this work in his favour. Seve was having one of his wilder days, a round when he sought – and received – relief four times. Johnstone was fed up.

Late on in the round, both players pulled their drives at a semi-blind dogleg left over the brow of a hill into the trees. They arrived to find one ball lying clear to the left of a big tree and the other completely stymied behind the same tree, almost touching the trunk.

Tony asked Seve if he thought a nearby mark was a rabbit scraping. Seve thought not. Tony then addressed the ball in such a convoluted way that his foot just about touched a path. Could he get relief? No, Seve said.

Tony finally questioned whether the area might be GUR (ground under repair). No chance. 'So there's no way you can get relief from here?' Tony asked.

'No, Tony,' Seve replied.

'Good, because it's your ball!' Tony concluded. I think that is what Tim Henman, one of the best British tennis players of the modern era, a terrific golfer and one of the contributors to this book, would call game, set and match.

By the way, lest you doubt some of my meticulous research, Mary, Queen of Scots did play golf at St Andrews and James VI did take his clubs to London when expanding his regal portfolio.

And when Gene Sarazen was prevented from entering the clubhouse at Royal St George's, the then Prince of Wales (the Duke of Windsor) was on hand to assist.

'We were playing [together],' Sarazen recalled. 'After the ninth hole we went for a dish of tea. He walked ahead of me. The head waiter stopped us at the clubhouse door. He said I wasn't allowed in because I was a professional. The prince said: "You either change that rule or I will take the Royal out of Royal St George's."'

Prince Andrew, a former captain of the R&A, is now the royal most associated with golf. His aunt, the late Princess Margaret, was not a golfer, though she found herself socialising in the Greywalls Hotel at Muirfield following the final round of the 1980 Open.

The story goes that Tom Weiskopf was at the next table spouting off about something. His wife Jeanne had been trying to shut him up. Eventually, the unrevealed royal got up to leave the table for a while.

'Do you know who that woman is?' Jeanne is supposed to have asked her husband.

'I give up, she's the queen of England,' Weiskopf replied.

Introduction

'Close, she's her sister, Princess Margaret.'

Weiskopf was apparently mortified. On Princess Margaret's return, she told the American that her father had been a keen golfer.

'That's nice,' Weiskopf remarked. 'What did your father do?'

'He was King of England,' said the princess.

Chapter One

Practical Jokers and Complete Fruitcakes

They say there are no characters in the game these days and they have a point. But what about that lovable Swedish meatball Jarmo Sandelin, who wanted to wear a pair of cowboy boots with spikes in the 1999 Ryder Cup at Brookline?

He had previously been banned by the European Tour from wearing transparent golf shirts. 'I respect the decision,' he declared. 'Nobody wants to see my nipples, do they?'

The same Sandelin, who did not get a game until the singles on the final day of his only Ryder Cup, kept everyone's spirits high with his extravagant entrances. 'I love you here, I love you there, I love you every fucking where,' he would shout every time he burst into the team room.

Ian Poulter is as quiet as a mouse, or David Gilford, by comparison. Poulter, of course, is the 21st-century golfing clotheshorse, albeit a colt to the stallion that was Doug Sanders in the 1960s and 1970s. It was said that Sanders kept in his wardrobe 200 pairs of brightly coloured trousers with matching shoes.

Each generation of golfers has spawned its eccentrics. As Wayne 'Radar' Riley, a whacky Australian pro, once asked rhetorically, 'How long can you live with the constant disappointment before you go a little crazy?'

Take Joe Ezar, the famous American golfer and trick-shot artist, who would play in a camel-hair coat bound at the edges with leather. His caddie–valet removed it for every shot and replaced it in between. Ezar probably needed it at the winter resort of Sestriere when he played one of his more remarkable rounds. He had wowed the local dignitaries with his trick shots and was challenged to break the course record of 67.

'How much for a 66?' he asked.

'One thousand lira,' came the reply.

Ezar repeated the question for both a 65 and a 64, with the promised rewards going up to 2,000 and 4,000 lira respectively.

'Right, I'll do a 64,' he declared.

Whereupon, amid much laughter, the golfer wrote down on a cigarette packet a prediction for his score on each hole. The next day he shot 64 and achieved the correct number at all but two of the eighteen holes!

Canadian Moe Norman, for whom the word eccentric could have been devised, came to the final hole of one tournament needing a par 4 to break the course record. He wondered out loud what the nature of the hole was.

'A drive and a 9-iron,' someone said.

So, contrary as ever, Norman hit a 9-iron from the tee, a wood from the fairway to a foot from the flag and tapped in the tiny putt for a birdie and the record.

Practical Jokers and Complete Fruitcakes

Norman, who never won on the PGA Tour, would often arrive at tournaments wearing strange outfits and proceed to play at breakneck speed. No bad thing in my book. Famously in Toronto in 1969, partnered by the great Sam Snead, he found himself alongside the legend with a 250-yard carry across a stream to the green. Snead laid up and expected Norman to do likewise. Norman, however, prepared to go for it.

'You need to lay up, Moe,' Snead said.

'I am aiming for the bridge,' he replied.

Snead watched in utter amazement as Norman hit a perfect shot across the bridge on to the green. No wonder so many US Tour professionals, for example Vijay Singh, insisted that Norman was the best striker of the ball they ever saw.

It was said that Norman treated money in the oddest way. He kept all his money in his car, stashed away under the front seat, in the boot, any old hideaway. He didn't trust banks at all. The story goes that he would rent a motel room, reverse his car in front of the door and then sleep in the car alongside his money. He would have as much as £40,000 in cash in his glove compartment. His philosophy was to always have enough for a rainy day.

Ky Laffoon, known as The Chief, a tobacco-chewing tumult of a man (and a damn fine player, apparently) and 'Lefty' Stackhouse, a small Texan with Popeye arms, were genuine characters who, like so many of that ilk, could easily have featured prominently in this book in the chapter on temper tantrums.

Laffoon, who played in the 1935 Ryder Cup, once broke a toe while smashing a putter into his foot in anger. On another well-chronicled occasion, his 3-foot putt on the 18th spun round the hole and stopped on the front lip, almost taunting him. At least that is how he viewed just one of many short putts that failed to drop. Those familiar with his temperament could have guessed that his putter was going to get it. What followed was pure Basil Fawlty. Laffoon walked off the green, headed to the nearby car park, opened the boot of his car, removed a pistol and shot his putter three times!

'Take that, you sonofabitch, that's the last time you three-putt on me,' he cried, though the legend may have grown in the telling. One writer, perhaps the great Dan Jenkins, labelled it as the first known example of 'clubicide'.

Laffoon fared better when winning the Cleveland Open, albeit luckily and after considerable drama. He missed a 5-foot putt on the 72nd hole and missed again, prompting him to slam his putter down on top of the ball. It hopped 3 feet in the air and plopped into the hole for a one-stroke victory. And if you believe that . . .

'Lefty' Stackhouse's real name was Wilbur Artist. Both his temper and his thirst were said to be raging. Merely failing to carry a water hazard prompted him to dive into a rocky stream. His reaction to missing one short putt was to stand erect, let out a mighty roar and then run towards a tree, which he headbutted. On another occasion, a wayward drive led to his walking into a rose bush and whipping his right hand back and forth through the thorns. 'That'll teach you to roll on me,' he cried, his hand dripping with blood. And turning to his left hand he added, 'Don't think you are going to get away with it either.' And it didn't.

Once in his native Texas an excellent start to a round was marred when he pushed his drive into a lake. Stackhouse snatched his bag from his caddie's shoulder, threw the clubs into the lake, removed his socks and shoes, rolled up his trouser legs and walked barefoot back to the clubhouse through a field of nettles.

Many of the characters who shared my time on the European Tour tended to be practical jokers rather than complete fruitcakes. People like Mark Roe, Robert Lee and Russell Claydon, the great triumvirate of golf mischief-makers.

Who would have the sort of mind and mentality, for example, to crouch in the corridor outside a hotel room, poised to strike with fire extinguisher in hand, and wait for an hour for a friend and fellow professional to open his door? Mark Roe is the answer. He let Tinkerbell, as Claydon is known on Tour for his fairy-like proportions (not), have it by way of revenge for a previous jape.

David Jagger was from the same mould. One of his jokes took shape at Selby Golf Club, where he was a pro, when Phil Morbey – who as Wobbly went on to caddie for Ian Woosnam in his great Masters' triumph – took a first step towards joining the rake-rats.

Wobbly, then a member at Selby, asked Jagger about the possibility of being a caddie. Jagger offered him a tryout in the Captain & Pro Challenge. It proved something of an ordeal as Wobbly struggled to carry the heavy bag. He barely made it to the 9th green, by which time he was bathed in sweat and out of breath.

'Do you think he's done a good job so far?' Jagger asked the club captain.

'Yes,' came the positive reply.

'Do you still want to caddie?' Jagger asked Wobbly.

He just about managed to nod his head.

'OK, if you are going to carry on, you had better take the bricks out of my bag.'

You would never describe such sober individuals as Warren Humphreys and Ian Mosey as characters, but there is a certain eccentricity in the fact that they travelled together on Tour for years with a television, a VHS player and a stack of videos.

Danny Goodman, who Eamonn Darcy writes about, was a total extrovert. I remember a most glorious summer's evening at the halfway point in the Portuguese Open when Mark James and I came across a despondent Goodman sitting on the balcony. He looked so miserable you wanted to remove his belt and shoelaces.

'Are you all right?' James asked.

'Yeah,' our American friend replied. 'But I don't know what to do. I have just been left twenty million dollars. All I have to do to collect my inheritance is prove my sanity and I don't think I can.'

Eamonn Darcy

Sam on Eamonn: '"Digger" Darcy is one of the best raconteurs known to man and fantastic fun to be around at any time. Darcy won six times on the European Tour, and was a regular near the top of the Order of Merit. His greatest moment came at Muirfield Village in the 1987 Ryder Cup when, shaking all over, he holed a terrifyingly fast downhill 6-foot putt on the final green for a crucial victory over Ben Crenshaw. My father had given him a lesson that week – "set and turn" was the simple message. It worked.

Darcy grew up wanting to be a jockey and now he is combining golf with eventing back in his native Ireland.'

A week or two after I won the Spanish Open in 1983 I came across a likable crazy American called Danny Goodman for the first time. We were drawn to play together in the third round of the Dutch Open. The name was familiar, as was his reputation as the sort of man about whom stories are told. I am sure Sam knows a few. Anyway, he came up to me on the practice putting green and offered a warm greeting.

'Mr Darcy, my name is Danny Goodman,' he said with a smile. 'I have the pleasure of your company today. And what a lucky day it is for you.'

'Why is it my lucky day, Danny?' I enquired with some puzzlement.

'Today you get to play with someone with a worse swing than yours,' he retorted.

Ah, my swing, my idiosyncratic swing, with its notorious flying elbow, a swing that served me pretty well throughout my career but that invariably prompted a sense of incredulity among those seeing it for the first time.

Its genesis was simple enough. That was how you struck the ball in hurling and, though I say so myself, I had been a useful hurler in my youth. When it came to swinging a golf club I could have been wielding a hurley. I was never taught how to swing a golf club and I never much thought about technique. I just did my own thing. And I was not much bothered about what the so-called purists thought and said.

My nickname was almost inevitably going to be linked to my swing. I have been 'Digger' Darcy from my early days on the

Tour on account of the huge divots I dug with my irons when coming in at a steep angle to the ball.

As I said, my swing usually prompted a reaction of some sort. South African John Bland tells a story of Tony Johnstone's first event on the European Tour. Blandie was showing him the ropes, telling him where everything was, outlining the facilities, etc. Eventually, they reached the practice ground.

'There's Eamonn Darcy, the Ryder Cup player,' Bland said to Johnstone as they walked along the range.

'Don't give me that shit, Blandie,' was Johnstone's response.

Johnstone refused to believe that the guy in front of him was a golfer never mind a Ryder Cup player. He insisted that I must be an 18-handicapper friend of Darcy's, who had been given Darcy's bag to hit a few balls. Blandie, perhaps laying it on a bit thick, swears that Johnstone insisted on following me down to the 1st tee just to make sure this was not some elaborate hoax from Bland, a renowned joker. Only when I was announced and hit my opening drive did he accept the truth.

I never really thought about trying to change and fashion a more orthodox swing. As I said, I did it my way. I recall the great Henry Cotton, who ruined a few swings in his time, bringing up the subject during one of my visits to his beloved Penina in Portugal. Henry had taken an interest in me and we got on very well. We had enjoyed our game of golf and were sitting down to a coffee when he volunteered his opinion.

'Laddie,' he pronounced, he always called me laddie, 'do not let anyone change your swing. For you to change would mean having to take two years away from the Tour.'

I was doing well at that time, I was near the top of the Order of Merit several years in a row. In fact, I finished in the top 20 of the Order of Merit nine times in my career. Still, they questioned my method. The attitude of the purist prevailed over here. Over there, in the States, they were less interested in your swing than the number of wins you managed and the amount of money accumulated. Jim Furyk was always regarded as a great player with a great record rather than a freak with a weird swing. We played together a few times but funnily enough, or not, the subject of our swings never arose!

Anyway, as I said, it did not prevent me from playing in the Ryder Cup and enjoying the moment of a lifetime at Muirfield Village in 1987. That was when I holed a putt down a slope as slippery as polished marble on the 18th green to gain a vital singles victory over Ben Crenshaw. The honour of holing the winning putt went to Seve, bless him, but he always said that it was my putt that really secured that famous victory.

The pressure was immense and not just because the Ryder Cup was on the line. I had been 4 up against Crenshaw, who had broken his putter. I would have been crucified if I had let the American off the hook.

Golf was not always so serious. You could not be serious when Simon Hobday was around. He was the character of all characters. My story of him – and there are many – is from the PGA Championship at Wentworth. He could not buy a putt, as usual. I remember him striking a beautiful second shot at the par 5 12th to just a couple of feet from the hole. He missed the short eagle putt and, lo and behold, missed the one coming back. His reaction was typical Hobday. He threw his putter to the ground, took out his wallet and showed the club a yellow card. The gallery loved that.

Just to put a seal on one of his many miserable putting days, Hobday three-putted the last green for a 78, or something like that. He proceeded to take a red card from his wallet and waved it at the club. The crowd loved that even more.

An hour later we were standing at the bar. I had a pint of Guinness, as you do. Simon had two, as he did. But the head of the offending putter was drowning in one of the glasses. Later, as he drove out of the car park, the shaft of the same putter was tied to the back bumper of his car, clattering along the ground.

Years later, I came across Simon at a course in South Africa where he was the club professional. We talked about old times and particularly that day at Wentworth.

'Hang on a minute,' he said, while beginning to rummage around his hire bags. 'No, I can't find it. Some poor bastard is out there with it!'

A final word on the aforementioned Goodman, whom I also met years later. We were in Tunisia, if memory serves me correctly, and we were playing together again. I remember a par 5 where I hit my second shot to the back of the green. Danny landed short of the putting surface in a front bunker. I walked to my ball and waited and waited. Nothing. No sign of his ball appearing, no sign of Danny.

Eventually I walked over to see what was going on. There was Danny hunched up like a little child, lying in the corner of the bunker with a plugged ball at his side. He was a one-off. Golf has thrown up a few one-offs, if you can have such a thing.

Chapter Two

Yips and Shanks

There was a time, not so long ago, when the word 'yips' would not have been mentioned by two consenting golfers, even in the privacy of their own homes. But there it is, bold as carbon fibre, in the opening paragraph of a chapter on putting. I suppose that is only right from a man who, as a sufferer, introduced the broomhandle long putter into Europe more than twenty years ago.

The term, which used to be avoided in much the same way that Shakespeare's *Macbeth* would be spoken about as 'the Scottish Play', is nowadays pretty commonplace in conversation and in print and on television. The 'shank', where the ball darts straight right having come into contact with the hosel of the club, is following suit.

'Let's not beat about the bush, that was a shank,' Colin Montgomerie said of Peter Hanson's tee shot at the 12th during the final-round commentary of the Masters in 2012.

The yips, an involuntary twitch of the wrist that causes the golfer to lose control of the putter, particularly on short putts, go way back to before the word existed.

Old Tom Morris, who won four Opens on his home course between 1861 and 1867, once received a letter addressed to 'Misser of Short Putts, Prestwick'.

The term yips is said to have been coined by Tommy Armour, an Edinburgh-born American immigrant who lost an eye in World War I and who went on to win all three major championships available to him. The Silver Scot, as he was known due to the premature greying of his hair, said famously, 'Once you've had 'em, you've got 'em.'

Some of the greatest golfers in history suffered from the yips, including Ben Hogan, Sam Snead, Bobby Jones, Tom Watson and Johnny Miller.

Hogan, no doubt influenced by his own situation, felt that putting should form a less significant part of the game because success depended too much on it. He argued that superior ball striking was what mattered and advocated a larger hole to reduce the emphasis on putting.

Snead, a fellow yips victim who would go through all sorts of contortions trying to find relief, was something of a pot calling Hogan black when speaking about the latter's affliction.

'Towards the end of his career,' Snead said of Hogan, 'he could hit the ball about as good as ever but he got so he could not even pull the putter back from the ball.'

Hogan, who was known to freeze motionless over the ball, three-putted seven times and four-putted on another occasion in one tournament. It became so bad that back at home with his friends he would play only 'greenies', whereby points would be awarded for hitting greens and putting was banned. When in his seventies, Henry Cotton would pick up his ball within 10 feet of the hole on the strength that in his prime he would have sunk the putt.

My first experience of a bona fide 100 per cent yip came during my Open debut at Muirfield in 1972. As I was walking from a green to a tee, I saw Mr Lu – he of the pork-pie hat and permanent smile who so enchanted Scottish spectators that year – twitch extravagantly on a short putt. 'What the hell was that?' I thought. It was like a wriggling snake. I had never seen anything like it in my life and I did not want to see its like again. Unfortunately, I saw many, eventually at close hand, or rather hands. My hands.

I was playing with Bernhard Langer in a PGA Championship at Hillside in 1982 when he struck a 15-foot putt on a flat green straight off the putting surface. If you are capable of doing that how on earth can you control yourself to win a tournament? Yet Langer – living proof that when you've had 'em you can get rid of 'em, at least temporarily – has won more than sixty tournaments around the world, including two Green Jackets. There can be no greater testament to his mental strength and fortitude.

I had putted badly often in my career without ever accepting that I had a problem. My first inkling that something was seriously wrong came during the 1987 Ryder Cup, with a putt on the final green of my singles match with Larry Mize that 'went off' in my hand and could have gone anywhere. My dad swears I was still shaking ten minutes after striking the putt. Later in the day, Eamonn Darcy found himself gripping tightly on to his putter handle long after holing a putt to defeat Ben Crenshaw on the 18th.

If that was the beginning, then the end came in France early in 1989. I three-putted the 72nd green to finish fifth in the AGF Open at La Grande Motte, Montpellier, a tournament I should have won by 10 strokes such was the quality of my long game. That was it. I had to do something.

I had experimented that winter in Florida with a broom-handle putter, which was being successfully used by Orville Moody on what used to be called the US Seniors Tour. I headed home, lengthened an old Ping putter by two feet on the vice in my garage and climbed on to my snooker table. As you do. In fact, the speed of the green baize proved a perfect place for me to become accustomed to the pendulum motion and the rather alien concept of tucking my left hand under my chin. While others have adapted the method to place the top of the club on their chest, and the belly putter has become the latest fashion, I have stuck to my original method.

Arnold Palmer said the broomhandle putter should only be 'tried in the privacy of the bathroom'. Tom Watson, who has suffered from the yips for many a year, insisted he would rather retire than use it. I tried to persuade Bernhard Langer to use it for years before he eventually adopted it. Who knows how many more tournaments he might have won had he relented?

The change to my results was dramatic. From official winnings of £42,000 in 1988, I jumped to £170,000 in 1989, when I also became the first to use the long putter in the Ryder Cup. I won the German Masters in October 1990, my first tournament success for three years. (Peter Senior beat me to becoming the first using that method to lift a trophy in Europe when taking the European Open at Sunningdale earlier that year.)

Yips and Shanks

Of course, golf has regularly produced great putters who have required neither the latest gimmick nor extensive experimentation to maintain their form on the greens: men like Ben Crenshaw, Bob Charles, Loren 'Boss of the Moss' Roberts, Tiger Woods at the height of his powers, Mark McNulty and many more. South African Bobby Locke, who was renowned for his putting prowess, used the same putter throughout his career and negotiated at least one season without three-putting.

Jack Nicklaus had a love/hate relationship with putting. He loved holing putts, but he hated practising putting. 'I suppose it's a terrible admission for a guy in my business, but ever since my early teens I have found practising putting immensely boring,' he once said. 'It's a necessary chore, of course, but I generally have to push myself to do it and, when at home, have frequently failed in that effort.'

Putting problems are not solely confined to the yips. I remember Lionel Platts missing a putt by 10 yards in South Africa when he mistakenly aimed at the flag that his caddie had removed from the hole and was holding as if tending on a different part of the green.

The yips had nothing to do with a putt that probably cost me the English Open at The Belfry in 1988. I had driven on to the green at the famous par 4 10th and rolled my 20-foot eagle putt to the very edge of the cup. It was so close in fact that I thought it would drop in. It did, but too late as it transpired. I had waited longer than the maximum permitted ten seconds, a rule with which I was not familiar at the time. I was penalised one stroke, significant when you think that I ended up in a play-off with my old mucker Mark James. A play-off I lost at the first extra hole.

The American players know the ten-second stipulation as the January Rule, after Don January waited seven minutes on the final hole of the Phoenix Open in 1963 for his ball to drop. It never did.

But back to the dreaded yips, the condition that all golfers fear no matter what their ability – professional, amateur or hacker.

Mac O'Grady, another of life's eccentrics, suffered so badly that he donated $30,000 to the medical department of the University of California, Los Angeles (UCLA) to study the problem and find a remedy.

No cure was discovered and I don't believe one will be.

Lee Westwood

Sam on Lee: 'Like Gordon Brand, Lee Westwood is Junior to me, a reference to the schoolboy who asked for my autograph many moons ago. I love him to bits. No one was more deserving when he became world number one in October 2010. A great driver and an equally good iron player, he would have added many major championship successes to his considerable achievements but for a slight weakness on the greens.

Westwood has won thirty-nine professional tournaments around the world including twenty-two on the European Tour. He has also contributed greatly to the European Ryder Cup cause, accumulating four and a

half points out of five in the 2004 match and four out of five in 2006. He was a key member of the team I captained to victory in 2002.

He had not been playing his best that year. But I impressed upon him the old saying about talent being forever and form being temporary and I like to think that played a small part in his performing so well. The partnership of him and Sergio Garcia won their first three matches together as the gambler in me played a hunch. They had never hit a ball together in practice that week and had never entered my mind as a possible pairing play that week. I have no idea to this day where it came from. With Sergio King of the Hill at the time I just thought his brashness might blend nicely with Junior's calm demeanour.'

So there we were – me, my wife Laurae and the kids – sunning ourselves on the beach in the Bahamas where we have a house, enjoying the peace and quiet, lapping up the luxury of a Caribbean island.

Along comes not the Bounty girl but Scots Family Torrance, looking like the victims of a shipwreck. Of all the paradise joints, in all the islands, in all the world, they had to walk into ours.

Actually, I am always delighted to see Sam, who has called me Junior since the first day we met. I was fifteen (maybe it was fourteen, though Sam thinks I was nearer nine!) and had been picked by the English Golf Union to attend a junior coaching week at Inverclyde. Inverclyde, now the National Sports Training Centre for Scotland, situated on a wooded hillside behind Largs, the Ayrshire town where Sam was born, is well known for two things – it is where the Scottish international football team prepared for many of its defeats by England, and where Sam's father, Bob, a true coaching guru, has looked after the swings of many a great player. He stands there even now, at the age of eighty, in fair weather and foul, mostly the latter.

Back to my first meeting with Sam. While at Inverclyde, I wandered across to a five-a-side football match, as you do. One of the goalkeepers caught my eye. He was smallish, stocky and pretty tubby in truth, OK fat, less Lev Yashin, more Ferenc Puskas, in terms of size and shape, not ability. It was none other than Sam Torrance, the Ryder Cup golfer. As a keen golfer, I recognised him immediately, even in this footballing environment. I approached him and asked for his autograph. I still have it to this day.

This idyllic day of which I write, under a cloudless azure sky and beside the bluest of seas, suddenly changed. You know when you meet Sam and his family that there is going to be a bit of a party. Out came the beers, down went the sun and it was time for some fun. Golf clubs appeared as if from nowhere and before long we were hitting balls from the sand to an inflatable diving board about 80 yards into the ocean. Fortunately, there was no one else around.

I learned a lesson that day, one that I probably already knew: never play Sam Torrance for money when alcohol is involved. At anything. Not golf, not tiddlywinks, nothing. He could not miss, as he likes to remind me or anyone else within hearing distance.

'It did not matter what the shot was, I hit it first time,' is Sam's recollection. 'Hooky ones, slices, high or low, no matter the club, I could not fail. Hee, hee.'

Yips and Shanks

That's exactly how I remember it. High wedges or bendy 6-irons, he never missed. He hammered me. While I was feeling a bit 'woosie' – no, Ian Woosnam wasn't there – Sam played as if in the zone, as if the Claret Jug was at stake, not just a few bucks.

There is another thing I remember about that day. My son, Sam, and no, he is not named after Torrance, was about six years old at the time. That was the moment he put away his Lego bricks and found out about girls. He is going to hate me for saying this now, but he fell madly in love with Phoebe Torrance who was then eleven or so.

By then, Sam had enjoyed his greatest day in golf as captain of a victorious Ryder Cup team. Despite not playing very well at the time, I qualified for the match due to be played in 2001. The shocking events of 9/11 in New York put the contest back by twelve months. I was struggling with my game in 2002 and, lacking confidence, I approached the match with some trepidation.

Sam came up to me early in the week with a question. 'Would you mind playing with Sergio Garcia?' he asked. Just those words were enough to raise my level of confidence. Would I mind playing with Sergio Garcia? This was the amazingly talented Spaniard who had been a brilliant performer in the previous Ryder Cup. 'Oh, go on then,' I replied.

Our first match pitted us against David Duval and Davis Love III. We won that 4 and 3. We took out Tiger Woods and Mark Calcavecchia by 2 and 1 on the Friday afternoon. We saw off the combination of Stewart Cink and Jim Furyk in the Saturday morning foursomes by the same margin. That left only the Woods–Love pairing standing in the way of us completing a perfect four out of four record. Sadly, we lost the final two holes for a last-green defeat in a match we should have won.

Of course, it all ended well, the cue on Sunday night for one of the biggest parties in Ryder Cup history. The huge bar in The Belfry was packed to capacity. Somehow, it fell to me to act as MC, introducing, from my precarious position on top of a table, each player in turn and leading the community singing. Who could forget Phillip Price, Pontypridd Man of the Year himself, tugging at my trousers, shouting in that distinctive South Wales accent of his, 'Tell them who I beat, tell them who I beat.' He had beaten the great Phil Mickelson, no less.

Prior to that, it had been my responsibility to get all the guys down to the bar. That involved the rather scary task of dragging Jesper Parnevik from the shower. He is always the longest in the shower.

But that's another story.

Chapter Three

It's a Jungle Out There

'Beware the injured golfer' it is often said.

Never was that truer than at Torrey Pines in June 2008, when Tiger Woods won the US Open on one knee, or one leg, or one-and-a-half legs depending on how you viewed the seriousness of his injury that week.

All Woods's flinching and grimacing in pain during four remarkable days did not begin to tell the extent of the injury, the details of which were revealed only after the victory. Everyone knew some knee cartilage had been removed in April, but only those closest to him were aware that he had suffered a double stress fracture of the left leg just two weeks prior to the start of the championship. And for ten months previously he had played on despite a torn knee ligament.

Speaking of winning majors on one leg . . .

Not until the USPGA Championship of 1993 did Jack Nicklaus lament to his wife, Barbara, 'I am tired of playing on one leg.' Jack Nicklaus endured the legacy of a hip injury in 1963 for the duration of his career. After years of suffering from osteo-arthritis, he eventually had his hip joint replaced.

Hips, knees, elbows, shoulders and backs often give golfers problems; especially the back. What club golfer of a certain age does not complain about having a sore back? Lee Trevino had a back; Fred Couples has a back; poor Seve Ballesteros suffered ter-rible pain from a back injury that, probably more than any other reason, led to his loss of form. So painful was it in the early 1990s that he went to a local doctor in Thailand for some treat-ment. The doctor filled a drinking glass with alcohol, set light to it and laid it against Seve's back. It worked to the extent that the pain from burns the size of beer cans dwarfed the agony of the sore back itself. There was no second consultation.

Golfers can be injured in action, as happened to Brett Ogle in the 1990 Australian Open at Royal Melbourne. Ogle thought he could hit a 2-iron recovery shot through a gap in the trees having found trouble from the tee. But his ball struck wood, rebounded from a trunk and shattered his kneecap.

We all remember the case of Sky Sports golf commentator Richard Boxall and the broken leg. Boxy was just three shots behind leader Ian Baker-Finch at the halfway stage of the third round of the Open Championship when calamity struck. As he stood up to the ball on the 9th tee at Royal Birkdale and swung his club spectators heard a loud crack. Playing partner Colin Montgomerie looked around to see Boxall lying on the ground, his face twisted in pain from what turned out to be a shin bone fracture of his left leg. He had been feeling pains for a couple of days but had no idea he was suffering from a stress fracture.

I was 'injured in action', as it were, when tackling a masked intruder. Actually, that's not strictly true. The masked intruder turned out to be a plant pot, albeit a big plant pot. You see, I have had a reputation for sleepwalking, a reputation I allowed the media to develop. I am not sure it was anything more complicated than a sleepy person getting up for a pee, sometimes drunk, sometimes not. The plant pot was located in the middle of my room at The Belfry hotel. During the night I mistook it for a masked intruder and launched myself at it with a flying rugby tackle. That woke me up. There I lay in agony, surrounded by hundreds of pieces of broken pot and shredded shrubbery. For months afterwards every time I hit the ball into the trees a playing partner would come out with something like 'Careful Sam, it's a jungle out there'.

And no, contrary to popular belief, I was sober. The diagnosis was a fractured sternum, not the sort of injury to suffer a few weeks before the Ryder Cup. I recovered from the sternum injury only for an ingrown toenail to cause me problems. It began with a tiny blister in the tip of the nail, which I thought nothing of. Adrenalin kills physical pain during a Ryder Cup. By the eve of the contest, however, it had worsened. That was when I informed Bernard Gallacher, the European captain, while declaring myself fit for the morning foursomes.

I shouldn't have played. It was a difficult call to make when the Ryder Cup had become such an important part of my life, but I didn't play very well. I was hopeless, in fact. From the moment I hit a 5-iron 30 yards right of the 8th green after feeling a sharp pain, I never hit another decent shot. You can't carry a crock in the alternate-shot format of foursomes. Mark James and I lost five holes in a row, four of them to pars, and we were beaten 4 and 3 by Lanny Wadkins and Corey Pavin.

When I took off my shoe at the end there was gunge caked to my sock, pus oozing out of my toe. 'Pus in boots' David Feherty called it.

The nail was removed under local anaesthetic at Birmingham Hospital that evening. I hoped to recover in time for the singles on Sunday. But there was no great change by then. I was desperate to play. I would have taken pills, had injections, anything, but Bernard was not keen on taking a chance with me. I hit a few balls on the range but I already knew my fate. When I struggled to walk back to the team room I had to tell my caddie, Malcolm Mason, that I wouldn't be playing. That was one of the lowest moments of my career. The 'sealed envelope' rule was invoked and Lanny Wadkins – who had volunteered to be the American to stand down should the situation arise – and I were each awarded half a point.

Missing a Ryder Cup match pales into insignificance compared to the misfortune that befell that great Australian character Jack Newton. Newt the Beaut was one of the really good guys on Tour. The Aussie, a three-time winner in Europe, lost the Open in 1975 to Tom Watson after a play-off and tied for second place in the 1980 Masters. His world turned upside down on 24 July 1983. He was heading home from a rugby match in Sydney when he was basically mown down by a light aircraft. A propeller cut off his right arm and took out an eye. He never lost his zest for life and became a brilliant television commentator.

Mark Calcavecchia was close to severing his left forefinger when trying to remove the labels from a new pair of trousers with a pair of scissors. Someone present advised Calc to get out the superglue – an old army trick, apparently – and he headed straight to the course. A 65 won him the 1998 Honda Classic by three strokes.

Superglue might not have done for the Italian opera singer who was practising a few arias as he waited to tee off at the Naples Country Club. Accidentally, we must presume, one of his partners, practising a few last-minute chips, shanked a ball into the singer's open mouth, chipping a tooth in the process.

Finally, there was the day at Wentworth when a 'snake in the grass' put David Feherty in hospital. We were playing a practice round for the 1992 Volvo PGA Championship against the well-established pairing of Richard Boxall and Derrick Cooper. We were three up after 11 holes, with me first to hit on the 12th.

That was when I found this tiny little snake. I pinned it under my 2-iron and called the lads to come over and have a look at this thing thrashing about under my club. On closer inspection Feherty, the fount of all knowledge, declared it an adder, proclaiming it to be the 'only poisonous snake in the British Isles'. Then he grabbed my club, slid his right hand down the shaft and tried to flick away the little serpent. But it wriggled up the shaft and nipped him on the end of his index finger.

'You've just been bitten by the only poisonous snake in the British Isles,' I said.

Feherty's version of what happened next is slightly different from mine but funnier. So, on the basis that facts should never interfere with a good story, I will let him complete the tale.

'I tell Sam I'm going in, and he says, "Like hell you are; we're two hundred pounds up." So I play on, and within a couple of holes my finger is swollen like a hot dog. I suggest again that maybe I'd better head in, but we'd won another hole by then. We were clubbing these guys like a couple of seals, so I knew there was no way Sam was letting me off the hook. He takes a look at my finger and says, "Don't be a girl's blouse – you're finishing." So I do, playing the last hole basically one-handed, because I was stiff and numb from the elbow down.

'We win three hundred pounds and collect the cash. I check in at the medical trailer. I tell the doctor I've been bitten by a snake, and he looks at me like I'm crazy.

'"How long ago?" he asks. About two hours, I said. The next thing, we've got blue flashing lights and sirens and I'm in a hospital bed with my arm locked in the Hitler-on-the-balcony position.'

The medic reckoned that the centrifugal force swinging a golf club kept the poison away from his brain, which would in any case have been difficult to locate. He was pumped full of cortisone and spent the night in hospital.

I was always more concerned about the welfare of the snake.

Ian Woosnam

Sam on Ian: 'Have I ever forgiven Woosie from posting a course record 62 in the final round of the 1990 German Masters to deny me a bonus pool for my third-round record 64? Of course I have. Woosie is a genuinely nice bloke with a great talent and a ruthless streak that took him to the world number one spot in 1991, the year of his brilliant Masters victory. Not only is he the best swinger and striker of the ball I have ever seen, he's a great laugh. Woosie's Woosie. He was the boxer from the Welsh border who started his professional career eating beans in a camper van and ended up flying around the world in his own jet. But he never let the money and the glory turn his head or lift his feet off the ground. My God, we have shared a few good times together and managed to get ourselves into – and out of – many a scrape.

Woosie won twenty-nine times on the European Tour, played in eight Ryder Cup teams and captained Europe to victory in 2006. There has probably never been a better long-iron player, especially the 1-iron, which has pretty much disappeared from the professional's bag.

A measure of the man is that every year he returns to the Masters he takes along a few friends from the old days for what they always say is the week of a lifetime.'

It happened at the hotel in Portmarnock, in Dublin, but it could have been in Spain or frankly anywhere because it happened more than once. I was fast asleep and then was awakened by a terrible banging on the door. The clock said 3 a.m. I recognised the distinctive tones of a Scotsman, a certain Samuel Torrance. I really did not need to hear the voice. When someone knocks on your hotel door in the middle of the night five will get you ten that it is the 'hairy one from Largs'.

I answered the door to be greeted by a figure as naked as the day he was born. Another ten would have got you twenty that he would be in the scud. If you knew Sam or had heard about his sleepwalking – or whatever he called it – you could have guessed the story.

'I got up for a pee, went through the wrong door and ended up out here,' he said. Or something to that effect. There was no need for an explanation.

This was Ireland during the Irish Open, so we could hear music from the party down below. The revelry never stopped that week. There was no temptation to join in. I had a tournament to win. Actually, I did win that week. Sam reckoned it was one of my great victories because, as he likes to retell with typical exaggeration, he 'carried me to bed every night'. I will admit only that the Irish Open can be a bit of an assault course.

My task, as ever that night, was to ring reception and arrange for someone to open Sam's door. There are countless night porters around the world who could say, 'I once let a naked Sam Torrance back into his room.'

Sam would not want me to tell you about the boiled egg, but I will. We were staying at the Sheraton Hotel in Kowloon overlooking the Victoria harbour and out to Hong Kong. You get a tremendous view from the restaurant, with its huge glass windows down one side of the building. We were sitting right next to the window.

Sam likes a boiled egg for breakfast. But he likes a boiled egg just right, not too hard and not too soft and certainly not with any uncooked gooey clear stuff.

The waiter was given the precise order. The eggs arrived. They were too hard and Sam sent them back. The next lot arrived. They were far too soft and again Sam sent them back. Ten minutes passed. More eggs were brought to the table. Too hard. They tried again. Too soft. And that was the final shell as far as Mr Torrance was concerned. He crushed the egg in his hand, sending runny gunge over me and the gleaming glass window.

Sam stood up in utter disgust and walked out with the parting shot aimed at me. 'That's what you call egg on your face.' I could not stop laughing at the sight of smashed egg slowly dribbling down the window.

You can put up with such outbursts. Sam is the most loyal friend who would always look out for you. I remember when he got me out of a huge disco in Acapulco when I took the most irrational – some might think rational – hatred towards Mr T of *The A-Team* fame. Now, Mr T is a genuinely tough, scary man, as he would have to have been to act, as he did, as a highly paid bodyguard for the likes of Muhammad Ali, Steve McQueen, Michael Jackson and Diana Ross. Apparently, stupidly, I thought that I could take him.

We're into our fifties now – heavens, Sam is sixty in 2013 – and our hell-raising days are long gone. A couple of beers and a glass of wine with dinner is how we relax after a round of Seniors golf. I view the European Seniors Tour as an opportunity to play golf with your buddies ten to fifteen times a year, with the added bonus of a chance to be competitive and win a few bob.

We all want to make a bit of money, but that is not really what keeps us going. It is our job, of course, but we love the game and we thrive on the competitive buzz. You are not going to tell me that the likes of Hale Irwin, with all his millions, is doing it for the money. Irwin, who was sixty-seven in 2012, just loves the competition and he loves golf. That's exactly the same for the vast majority of us.

I look back on my career and I think I was fortunate to win a major championship. By this, I don't mean either that I was lucky to do so or that I was not good enough to do so. I just mean that you can be a great player and not win one; like Colin

Montgomerie and – at least at the time of writing – Lee West-wood.

I got mine and it is still a huge thrill for me to return to Augusta each year as a former champion. Actually, I played well enough in 2012 to make the cut. But I just did not putt well enough. I rarely do these days. I had a four-putt and several three-putts that week at Augusta.

I find myself chopping back and forth between the long putter and a traditional-length club. Sam always used to say to me that if I committed to the long one I would have kept winning on the main Tour longer than I did. He would have had me start with it long before I did just after the millennium.

I tried it a few times previously but his broomhandle did not tuck under my chin – it went over my head! I am just a wee guy.

We have had some great times off the course over the years. He thrashes me at snooker as a scratch man to my 8 handicap, if we were handicapping. But I am a match for him on the dartboard.

I don't know about his dad, though. Bob can still throw the arrows. I remember the night before a party to celebrate my victory as captain of the 2006 European Ryder Cup team we had a great session playing darts in my local pub. Bob and Beefy, aka my good friend Ian Botham, against me and Sam. They took care of us pretty well.

Just as Sam took care of me when I was all for inviting Mr T outside. That would have been a big mistake.

Chapter Four

The Greatest Sporting Contest in the World

The Ryder Cup has dominated my career.

I cried at the end of my first match on my debut in 1981; I cried when holing the 'putt that won the Ryder Cup' in 1985; and I cried when captaining Europe to victory in 2002.

Tears of frustration, tears of emotion, tears of joy – I have shed them all during my eight appearances as a player, my one time as a vice-captain and when in charge. I feel myself welling up just writing the words 'Ryder Cup'.

I believe it to be the greatest sporting contest in the world, three days of intense head-to-head, *mano a mano*, passionate rivalry that can inspire lifetime friendship and camaraderie. It has generated controversy, acts of great sportsmanship and moments of thoughtless excess and any number of tales, some humorous and some touching.

Think funny, think one of my best friends, David Feherty. The master of the one-liner, this Northern Ireland-professional-turned-American-golf-broadcasting sensation has been cracking jokes and cracking people up for just about all of his fifty-three years.

When we both made the Ryder Cup team in 1991 for what became the so-called War on the Shore, it was pretty much taken for granted that captain Bernard Gallacher would put us together. We sat out the morning foursomes and emerged as the first pair in the afternoon fourballs against that golfing gunslinger Lanny Wadkins and Mark O'Meara.

To say Feherty was nervous is something of an understatement. His first putt from 15 feet did not so much threaten the hole as run away from it as the ball rolled 3 feet short and 4 feet wide. It was basically a duff. So jittery was he that I felt I had to say something of a consoling and encouraging nature, one friend to another.

'If you don't get your act together, I'm leaving you, joining them and you can play all three of us, you useless bastard!' I said. I wonder what the mind gurus that now litter our game would have made of that.

David was later to wax amusingly on what proved to be his only Ryder Cup experience. 'Kiawah Island was so difficult it was possible to drop a shot between the locker room and the first tee,' he told *Golf* magazine. 'The greens were harder to hit than Oscar de la Hoya's nose.'

Mainly due to my partner's good play we reduced a three-hole deficit to one by the short 17th, which I birdied by hitting a 4-iron stone dead. But O'Meara managed to match my two. That guaranteed the Americans at least a halved match. But David was faced with a 10-foot birdie putt on the final green to gain Europe a half point. For the first time in the entire day he asked me to read the line.

'Left edge,' I said positively. 'Just knock it in.' And he did.

Feherty's version was slightly more theatrical. 'I had read the greens like a Russian newspaper all day, so I asked Sam to aim me,' he said. 'Somehow I made a controlled spasm and the ball rolled into the centre of the cup. The crowd roared; I almost fainted.'

I remember speaking to David about the Ryder Cup. I likened it to having children. People who do not have kids cannot really relate to those who have. In the same way, you cannot really understand what a Ryder Cup is about unless you are lucky enough to take part in one.

Jose Maria Olazabal, the 2012 captain, understood. I remember kneeling beside him behind the last green at Kiawah when Bernhard Langer and Hale Irwin were approaching the dramatic conclusion to the match. Langer was to play.

'Come on, San,' he said. Like Seve Ballesteros and the rest of the Spaniards, Olly experienced difficulty pronouncing the letter 'm'. 'Come on, San, watch de ball, watch de ball, you can make it move, watch de ball.' He really believed our willpower could move the ball in the right direction. You never thought anyone could surpass Seve for passion but Olazabal came close. He is a fantastic man, a wonderful team player with a great head on his shoulders.

My first Ryder Cup was at Walton Heath in 1981, against the strongest team the United States ever assembled. At the time nine of their twelve players had already accumulated thirty-six major championship victories. Ben Crenshaw and Tom Kite went on to win majors leaving only Bruce Lietzke without one of the big four. And he was plenty good enough. Tom Watson, Bill Rogers and Larry Nelson arrived at Walton Heath having won the Masters, the Open and the USPGA respectively that year.

I made my first outing in the afternoon fourball with Howard Clark, who was to become my best and favourite Ryder Cup partner over the years. We still call each other 'partner' when meeting or telephoning each other. We were supposed to assume the role of cannon fodder to the American duo of Johnny Miller and Tom Kite. We had other ideas.

I remember eagling the 14th to square the match. And I had a 12-foot birdie putt on the final green to gain an unexpected point. I cried in frustration as the ball horseshoed out. That miss broke my heart. But our better ball of 65 proved we could handle the pressure.

The following day – my partnership with Howard surprisingly broken up – I teamed up with Nick Faldo. We were thrashed 7 and 5 by the combination of Lee Trevino and Jerry Pate. It was an extraordinary performance. Pate never hit a shot without Trevino telling him exactly what to do. Pate followed the instructions to the letter every time. As Trevino quipped, 'Jerry had everything . . . from the neck down. With my brains and his swing we were unbeatable. I told him what clubs to play and even gave him the line of the putts.'

I drew Trevino in the singles. We had known each other for years. 'Sammy, I am going to beat the moustache off you,' Trevino said, when we bumped into each other on the putting green at Selsdon Park Hotel, the base for both teams.

Well, Supermex whipped me 5 and 3, in about two hours and I shaved off my moustache for the official dinner that Sunday night at Walton Heath. Trevino never played another Ryder

Cup. I like to think that I saw him off! I saw off a few, in fact. Tom Watson never played another Ryder Cup after beating me 3 and 1 in 1989 and ditto Lanny Wadkins after halving his singles with me in 1993. No staying power these guys!

Europe should have won in 1983. Tony Jacklin had assumed the captaincy and the match at West Palm Beach marked the first collective appearance of the 'famous five', the five great European players who, as it happened, were born within eleven months of each other in five different countries: Seve Ballesteros from Spain, Nick Faldo from England, Bernhard Langer from Germany, Sandy Lyle from Scotland and Ian Woosnam from Wales. All would be major winners and, together, all contributed to changing the course of Ryder Cup history.

We should have won in 1983, but we returned home knowing we would win next time.

The 1985 Ryder Cup at The Belfry changed my life.

Not much more needs to be said about my holing the putt that won the Ryder Cup. It could have been Howard Clark had he not missed a 4-footer on the 17th moments before I sank mine on the 18th. Without any disrespect to Andy North, it helped my cause that I had been drawn against one of the weaker members of the American team. While Manuel Pinero stood up in the team room with his famous 'I want Wadkins' – and he got him – I was very happy to be drawn against North in the singles. When he drove into the water at the 18th I was virtually home and dry. Andy is now a distinguished golf broadcaster with ESPN and every time we meet we exchange warm smiles and hellos. In a sense he played his part in changing my life.

If 1985 was special, 1987 was more so. Europe became the first Ryder Cup team from this side of the Atlantic to win on

American soil. I proposed to Suzanne on Concorde on the trip over at perhaps the height of our passionate relationship. At least that is how it appeared, with the *Daily Mail* printing a cartoon showing Suzanne draped round me as I tried to putt. Tony Jacklin came out with his famous line, 'Sam, I'm resting you tomorrow morning – you're playing!'

My singles match against Larry Mize also proved influential in my career. For in my moment of victory, my first attack of the yips can be traced. I required two putts from just 15 feet below the hole to gain a crucial point. I settled over my putt and felt my hands shaking uncontrollably. I did not know when I eventually hit the ball if it would come up 6 feet short or 20 feet past. As it happened, it finished pretty much stone dead. But that is where the twitch began and my subsequent struggles on the greens only disappeared when I adopted the broomhandle putter the following winter. That is how Ryder Cup pressure can affect you. Ask Mark Calcavecchia, ask Eamonn Darcy, ask Craig Stadler, ask anyone.

Fred Couples, a dear friend, put it pretty well. 'The first time I played in the Ryder Cup I couldn't breathe,' he said.

Pressure, though, can also inspire moments of greatness. Ask Christy O'Connor Jnr, whose 2-iron to the 18th at The Belfry in 1989 pretty much ensured that Europe would retain the trophy. Of course, it was desperately disappointing for us that we lost the last four matches on the course to allow the Americans to salvage a 14–14 draw.

Christy played a blinder and not just on the course. Top singer Chris de Burgh may have been top of the bill at the gala dinner, but Christy was persuaded to do a turn. He stole the show with a tear-jerking performance.

There are two tales from that match that demonstrate the intensity with which Seve approached the Ryder Cup. He hated America in this context. 'I know they think they are the last Coca-Cola in the desert,' he wrote in a letter to the team and me ahead of the 2002 match.

Gordon Brand Jnr was my partner for the first-day fourball against Curtis Strange and Paul Azinger, two future Ryder Cup captains. It came down to the last, where my good friend and fellow Scot was confronted with an extremely difficult 65-yard bunker shot. They say the long bunker shot is the most difficult in golf.

Seve had already finished his match. 'San, San,' he said to me, 'tell Gordon to use a pitching wedge. It is too far for a sand wedge. Tell Gordon, tell Gordon.' He was beside himself.

That was a no-no. You cannot tell a fellow pro how to play a shot in those circumstances. There was only one thing for it. 'Fuck off, Seve,' I said. 'You tell him if you want to.'

Fortunately he did not, though it was a different matter when it came to his captaincy, when he tried to play everyone's shots. Gordon manufactured a fabulous recovery and holed the putt for a point.

If Seve was anxious then, he was apoplectic at the drop Paul Azinger was given having driven into the water at the final hole of a fiery top singles match. That allowed the American somehow to clear the water in front of the green with his third. That just never happens. Seve went bananas in the team room afterwards.

The aforementioned 1991 match has been well documented, what with Seve and Azinger at it again and poor Calcavecchia throwing away the final four holes to allow Colin Montgomerie a half point.

And finally there was Europe's strong man, Bernhard Langer, bravely fighting back against Hale Irwin and missing a 6-foot putt on the last that would have tied the contest. I say bravely, but I never did understand why he aimed to the side of two spike marks when they were directly on his line. What is the point of not aiming on the proper line? Better surely to hit the ball on the correct line and hope that the spike marks do not affect the ball.

No one is saying it was easy. I remember Michael Bonallack, the then R&A secretary, described it as 'the biggest pressure putt in the history of golf'.

The toe infection that ruined my 1993 Ryder Cup, forcing me to withdraw from the singles, made me all the more determined that it would not be my last. I would be forty-two by 1995. It turned out to be a good year, a very good year, my best in that but for a terrific inward nine at Valderrama in the final counting event by Monty I would have won the Order of Merit.

Somehow, in successive fourball then foursomes matches straddling Friday and Saturday, my partner Costantino Rocca and I lost 6 and 5 and then won by exactly the same margin against the pairings of Jeff Maggert and Loren Roberts, and Maggert and Davis Love III.

Love is a decent sort. But his wife Robyn is a hoot. I remember her at a World Cup cocktail party in a heavily pregnant condition, seemingly well on the way to giving birth. This puzzled Jane James, Mark's wife, who studied the bump and made what seemed a reasonable observation. 'I did not think they would let you travel in that state,' Jane said.

'They do when it is your own plane, sweetie,' Robyn replied.

The biggest disappointment that week was when Bernard Gallacher picked the all-Scottish combination of Torrance and

Montgomerie to be his banker on the Saturday afternoon, and somehow we lost 4 and 2. I have no idea how. I doubt if either Brad Faxon or Fred Couples broke 79 with their own balls. But they dovetailed, or 'ham and egged it' as we say, in extraordinary fashion.

The par 5 13th rather summed it up. I stiffed it for a birdie whereupon Couples, short of the green in three, holed an outrageous chip for a half. The normally placid Couples even managed a jump in the air.

'Fuck you, Freddie,' I whispered to Couples on the next tee. That tickled him. In fact, he never stopped telling the story for hours, days and weeks afterwards. That I could say it and he could enjoy it demonstrated the strength of our relationship.

My defeat of Loren Roberts in the singles, a key point (aren't they all?) in Europe's victory, proved to be my last playing appearance. I found myself 'in the zone' that day; that rare occasion professional sportspeople sometimes experience when everything works and you feel you can do anything. On reflection it was a pretty nice way to bow out.

Bernard Gallacher

Sam on Bernard: 'We have known each other since golf began, or so it seems, and have become good friends. My memory is of a fiercely determined, highly competitive Scot who had already established himself as one of the best players in Europe by the time I headed south to seek fame and fortune. Bernard won two of his twenty-two tournament victories in his rookie year of 1969 on the way to becoming, at twenty, the then youngest ever Ryder Cup player.

For more than twenty years he combined his tournament career with the prestigious position of head professional at Wentworth, where he subsequently became captain. Not many pros manage that progression.

I got to know a lot more about Bernard when I played in three Ryder Cups under him, in 1991, 1993 and 1995. I was totally impressed, by everything really. The way he handled himself. Just a top man. So, we were all thrilled for him when he finally guided Europe to success in 1995.'

No one remembers the day I beat Jack Nicklaus in a Ryder Cup singles match. No one, that is, except my family and the people I have bored over the years. And Jack, possibly.

The year was 1977. The captain was Brian Huggett, that most emotional and patriotic of Welshmen. These were more formal times, when you dressed for dinner with blazer, collar and tie. The practice was for the captain to read out the singles pairings at the meal, the first you heard of the identity of your opponent the following day.

I remember Nick Faldo, playing his first Ryder Cup, drawing (and going on to beat) Tom Watson, who earlier that year had won his second Open in that unforgettable 'Duel in the Sun' with Jack at Turnberry. Barnsie [Brian Barnes] got Hale Irwin, Mark James came out against Raymond Floyd and Howard Clark was paired with tough-as-teak Lanny Wadkins.

The Greatest Sporting Contest in the World

The elephant in the room was a bear, a Golden Bear. Everyone was waiting to hear who had drawn Jack Nicklaus. It turned out to be yours truly.

'You lucky bugger' was the reaction from my teammates around the table. Only that's not what they were feeling. Each player, no matter what his form and bravado, was mighty pleased to avoid the greatest golfer that ever lived.

Pretty soon, I retired to my room, making a conscious effort to relax. It was not easy. I thought ahead to the next day and how I might help my situation. I decided that I would go to the 1st tee at the last minute. I wanted not so much to keep Jack waiting, as to reduce the amount of time I would have to spend in the cauldron in the presence of his aura.

Our tee time approached and I remained on the practice putting green as long as I dared. I was sure he must have been waiting as I ignored several calls to the tee. My caddie's anxiety grew.

Eventually, I headed for the tee. The opening hole at Royal Lytham, unusually for a championship venue, is a par 3, starting from an enclosed area behind trees and the professional shop. I got there to find no sign of Nicklaus. He was obviously not going to be outfoxed by that old trick.

But hey, maybe he, too, had endured a sleepless night. Maybe he was as anxious as me. Maybe, but not likely. All sorts of thoughts were racing through my mind.

Of course, he arrived to be greeted by a huge reception. We might have been the home team but Jack Nicklaus was Jack Nicklaus, a favourite of galleries no matter what country he played in.

I did not want to watch his swing, but at the last moment I turned round to see the moment of impact. He seemed to hit it a little heavy and sure enough the ball came up short. I hit a 2-iron to the back left of the green, leaving a long putt. Jack chipped to perhaps 4 feet. I putted down to a little over 2 feet, but was left with a tricky downhill slider, not what you wanted on the first green against Jack Nicklaus.

I knew Jack would hole his and did not fancy being left with mine for a half. But before my anxiety level rose further, Jack bent down to pick up my marker, conceding a par 3. What to do? Do I pick up his? Do I concede him his par for a half? I didn't move; I didn't say anything. I made him putt and he missed.

And do you know the first thing that came into my head? 'The worst I can get beaten is nine and seven,' I thought. That's positive thinking for you. But Jack Nicklaus could have that effect on people. You can feel so inadequate in his presence.

Jack found trouble at the 2nd hole, which I duly won. Two up. The same at the 3rd. Three up. I birdied the 4th to go 4 up. Four up after four holes. This was getting ridiculous, so much so that for a fleeting moment I thought about winning by the maximum of 10 and 8!

Inevitably, Jack pulled himself together and launched the expected fightback. He won both the 7th and 8th to halve the deficit. I had to battle hard – some commentators said 'heroically' – to fend him off. The margin was still two holes with four to play. But he birdied the 15th and the 16th to get back to all square.

I spotted Tony Jacklin and Tommy Horton heading in my direction. They were obviously coming to offer support. But somehow I imagined they were arriving just in time for the execution. I pictured them as a couple of bloodthirsty voyeurs waiting for the guillotine to drop. All sorts of things go through your mind at moments like that.

Sometimes the condemned can escape the blade. Although Jack was better positioned than me at the 17th, I holed a monster putt of 84 feet – I have since measured it – for a winning birdie. A fluke? Maybe, but as I always say, I was trying to get the ball into the hole.

My nerve held at the 18th as, in front of the famous old clubhouse, I sank a 4-foot putt for the match. I had beaten Jack Nicklaus. 'Sorry about that, Jack,' I said. 'But everyone wants to beat you, and I am no exception.'

Nicklaus replied, 'It's you Scots who keep beating me. I can't handle you guys.'

And that was a reference to why no one remembers the day I beat Jack. Two years previously at Laurel Valley, Pennsylvania, my old mate Brian Barnes dumped Nicklaus twice in one day thanks to a combination of Barnsie himself, of course, and Great Britain and Ireland captain Bernard Hunt.

After losing to Barnes in the morning – there were two series of singles on the final day at that time – American captain Arnold Palmer went to his opposite number to ask if the draw could be fixed so that Jack and Barnsie could be paired again in the afternoon. 'Jack wants the chance of revenge,' Arnie told Hunt.

Hunt agreed to the request. Instead of getting his own back, however, Jack lost for a second time.

Barnsie told Jack it was down to the porridge!

Ken Schofield

Sam on Ken: 'Ken, former executive director of the PGA European Tour, is a dear ally and friend, with whom I have spent many a late evening over a glass of wine discussing everything from Ryder Cup politics to St Johnstone, his football team. He has always been someone I can confide in and such is his wisdom that he was brought in to investigate a way forward for English cricket. He seems to have done a pretty good job, as he did for golf in Europe. For thrity years, Mr European Tour ruled with a Midas touch. There were seventeen tournaments with total prize money of less than half a million when he began in 1975, figures that had swollen to nearly 50 and 70-odd million pounds by the time he retired.'

My first of countless visits to the United States came in 1975 for a Ryder Cup, which in the days before the birth of the European Tour and the addition of European players to our team four years later, was very different from how it is now.

I was added to the administration team only four weeks or so before the match. John Jacobs and I had been receiving some 'flak' from the then PGA officials regarding our questioning of the lack of progress in the setting up of the fledgling Tour. We were impatient for change.

I remember being excited but uncertain as to how the week would unfold. What a wonderful surprise on arrival. The Great Britain and Ireland team, captained by Bernard Hunt, and the official party were met by our PGA of America counterparts and Arnold Palmer, non-playing captain of the mighty American team.

If not the best team ever put out by the United States, it must have been pretty damn close. Those dozen household names included seven US Open champions, three Open Championship winners, two Masters champions and two who had won the USPGA Championship. Only J. C. Snead and Bob Murphy had not won a major. By his own estimation, Jack Nicklaus was playing the best golf of his life. He had already won that year's Masters, the USPGA and the American events at Doral and Heritage.

Palmer had been appointed non-playing captain of the US team not least because of his personal association with the venue. He had been the touring professional at Laurel Valley, Ligonier, Pennsylvania, while his father, Deacon, had been club professional at a different course in the area. 'I have achieved many honours in golf,' Palmer said, 'but this one tops them all, especially since we are playing the matches at Laurel Valley which has been a second home to me.'

Palmer had failed to qualify as a player for the 1975 team. Ironically though, victories in the British PGA Championship and the Spanish Open that year would have given him enough points to get into the GB&I team!

Arnie addressed us at the airport, offering a welcome to what he described as his 'hometown'. He insisted that we were all welcome at his own home for a beer. He also passed on to our officials an invitation from Nicklaus to visit his beloved Muirfield Village, which was nearing completion. His own private plane and that of Palmer's, already an enthusiastic qualified pilot, would be put at our disposal. 'Wow,' as Butch Harmon likes to say in television commentary.

There I was, a young man, twenty-nine, a former bank manager in Dunblane, on my first visit to the States and attending my first Ryder Cup being invited to both Arnold Palmer's home and Jack Nicklaus's pride and joy . . . with private air travel thrown in. Together with Colin Snape, then secretary of the PGA, we decided it would be prudent to remain at Laurel Valley and support Captain Hunt and his team in the final preparations for the matches. That left our senior officials to fly to Muirfield Village – which of course they did!

We did not, however, miss taking up Arnold's invitation to visit him and his wife Winnie at their home for a beer. And beer it was. 'Welcome guys, come on in and have a beer,' the great man said as we arrived at his front door. 'Have a Rolling Rock. Say hi to Joe Tito, he will pour it for you.'

As president of Rolling Rock, no man was better qualified to dispense the beer. So pour it Joe Tito did. To sit in the court of golf's greatest modern name drinking beer was fairy-tale stuff for me.

Nearly thirty years later, on the occasion of the launch of the Golf Channel in Orlando, I had the opportunity of again sitting with Arnold and Winnie (before her sad passing), having been asked along with PGA Tour commissioner Tim Finchem to say a few words. I checked the story with Winnie and discovered that not only was Joe Tito alive and well, but that he was living at Arnold's place at Bay Hill. They remained close friends.

Palmer, the Golf Channel's honorary president, loved the story, as we harked back to how it used to be. That for me was the beginning of a love affair with American golf that has always endured and always will. My love affair with the Ryder Cup had yet to commence.

As to the match itself, GB&I were trounced 21–11, exactly the one-sided margin that had been made favourite by bookies before a ball was struck. I remember Michael McDonnell in the *Daily Mail* writing in his preview that 'not even Perry Mason could make a plausible case for the British chances.'

There were some high points for the visiting team, though. I had what might be considered a 'bird's eye view' of Brian Barnes beating Jack Nicklaus in singles for the second time in a day. As a forward observer in the match ahead between Norman Wood and Lee Trevino, I was able to look back at what Barnsie was doing to the greatest player in the world.

And almost forgotten alongside that momentous achievement was Wood's astounding 2 and 1 defeat of Trevino. Norman Wood, one-time Dunblane Club champion. Great days indeed.

Chapter Five

Madness in the Method

Arnold Palmer's much-missed late wife, Winnie, used to kiss his balls before every round.

Steady on, I am talking about his golf balls. Or was it his clubs? One or the other, perhaps both. It is likely that she did it for luck one day and he played well. Maybe it worked a second time, enough for a superstition to be born. Even the greatest feel as if they can do with some help along the way.

Jack Nicklaus, surely a golfer more in control of his own destiny than any other, always embarked on a competitive round with three coins in his pocket.

If anyone had asked me prior to this book about golfing superstitions, I would have replied instinctively that they were not for me. That I did not believe in such nonsense. That I did not have a single one.

And then, for the purposes of this chapter, I got to thinking. What about balls? Well, for as long as I care to remember I have played a Titleist 1, 2 or 3. I would use 4s in the pro-am because it did not really matter what I scored. I had another habit – call it a superstition, if you like – of starting with a number 1 and changing it to a 2 if I managed a birdie. Another birdie and I would tee up with a number 3. Yet another birdie would return me to number 1 and the sequence would begin again. Malcolm, my caddie, used to carry a lot of balls in those days!

Marking the ball, as with so many other professionals, also involved an element of superstition. My preferred method was to use two coins of the same denomination. That way it did not matter which one I pulled out of my pocket. Before that, I might use two different ones – for the purposes of illustration let's say a 10p and a 5p. Now, if I marked my ball with a 10p at the 1st and holed the putt and then on the 2nd put down the 5p before missing, it would have had to be the 10p for the rest of the round. Two 10ps would free me from that thought and any possible confusion. Clear?

OK, there is madness in my method.

But I am not alone. Paul Azinger would mark his ball with a US penny bearing the head of Abraham Lincoln pointing towards the hole; fellow American John Cook used only quarters showing pictures of states he had played well in; Tiger Woods will decide at the start of the round whether to mark his ball with a coin heads up or tails up. If he has to move that to the side to allow a playing partner a clear line, he will place the other face upwards. That reminds him to return his ball to the correct spot.

Jesper Parnevik, one of those crazy but lovable Swedes, would never mark his ball with the head of the coin facing up. But it was not as simple as that. He would start with four dimes and toss them into the air. Any landing tails up would stay; the others would be discarded. On one occasion in the BellSouth Classic, Parnevik's caddie Lance Ten Broeck threw four dimes into the air four times before a tail revealed itself. Player and caddie were going demented before a ball had been struck.

The marker remains a popular source of superstition. My good friend David James, who runs a tyre-refurbishment company in Woburn, gave me a set of marker coins fashioned from the Blarney Stone ahead of my Ryder Cup captaincy. Although I was very grateful, I decided not to pass them around the team – I did not want to bring luck into it. That's how confident I was of Europe winning in 2002.

But I did use one myself. I was pretty upset when I lost it at Woburn. Five weeks later at another tournament, by absolute chance I noticed that Thomas Levet marked his ball on the first green with the very distinctive coin. 'Where did you get that?' I asked.

'Oh, I found it coming off the 72nd green at Woburn,' the Frenchman explained. 'I used it in the play-off because I thought it might bring me luck. It did. I won.'

The lucky coin, the lucky charm, the lucky shirt – they all establish themselves in the routine of professional golfers. I am sure that the influence of Nike more than superstition led to Tiger Woods always wearing a red shirt for the final round of a championship or tournament. Equally, I am pretty certain he would now never dream of wearing anything other than red in case he upset the golfing gods.

Similarly, Phil Mickelson began using special high-numbered Titleist balls – numbers 5 to 8 – in order to aid identification. Long ago, though, that practice probably evolved into a superstition.

Ernie Els used to believe – maybe still does – that a golf ball has only one birdie in it. He would make a birdie then discard the ball. That's a load of balls, if you get my drift – Ernie has always been a birdie machine. Payne Stewart, on the other hand, would throw a ball away after a bogey, even at the opening hole. Seve Ballesteros never used a number 3 ball, he considered them unlucky. I know many a pro who will not use 4s because they correspond more to bogeys and pars than birdies. Speaking of Seve, he, too, believed in a 'lucky' final-round dress code – dark blue for the Open Championship and light blue for the Masters.

Another common preference among professional golfers is the use of white tees. This is not so much a superstition as just common sense. Coloured tees can leave a mark on your ball. For some, however, white became a no-no after what happened to Doug Sanders. He stepped on to the tee of the final hole of the 1970 Open Championship leading Nicklaus by one stroke. A man dashed out and handed him a white tee peg, saying, 'Tony Lema used this tee when he won the Open in 1964. Would you use it in his honour?'

Not wanting to offend the man and figuring the tee would make no difference, Sanders agreed. It became part of Open lore that he three-putted the hole, backing off a 39-inch putt for victory to wipe away an imagined impediment, and he lost a play-off the next day. For a while afterwards some pros would not dare use a white tee. Shigeki Maruyama never uses white tees as green is his colour; Colin Montgomerie avoids yellow and red tees as he associates them with the stakes indicating a water hazard. Tom Weiskopf, meanwhile, was by no means alone in using broken tees on par 3s.

Madness in the Method

Gary Wolstenholme, the distinguished amateur who has gone on to carve a successful career for himself as a professional on the European Seniors Tour, apparently ensured that he never removed more than one club from his golf bag at any one time. That's an odd one. Christina Kim, the larger-than-life ebullient female pro, is careful never to step on the grass line that separates fairway from green, in much the same way that tennis great Rafael Nadal almost falls over himself avoiding the white lines when changing ends. These seem to me the sporting equivalent of a child's fear that stepping on a line would result in you marrying a donkey, or whatever. Laura Davies, I am assured, had the habit of leaving a little pile of things on her bedside table before going to sleep at night, comprising white wooden tees, a pencil and for marking purposes a coin from whatever country she was playing in. Superstition or merely laying out things for the next day's round?

Fellow Scottish professional Norman Wood, one of my good friends, would keep his waterproofs on, once donned, no matter the weather between then and the end of the round. I have seen sweat pouring off him as he stepped off the 18th wearing waterproofs in blazing-hot sunshine.

Still today, after everything Tiger Woods has achieved, boy and man, he never takes his clubs on to the course without the tiger head cover embroidered with a good-luck message in Thai from his mother Kultida. I wonder, though, if Jerry Kelly still has the Filipino coin given to him by a spectator in 1993, his first Nationwide Tour event? If Billy Andrade has in his bag the chestnut presented to him by a then 99-year-old neighbour in Atlanta? If Sergio Garcia wears a horn from Naples around his neck? If 2012 Masters champion Bubba Watson uses a ball marker engraved with his name, a present from his wife Angie? If Charles Howell III wears a crucifix given to him by a stranger in Burger King before a high-school match in which he shot 64?

Personally, and despite my own little quirks, I rather like the comment from 2010 Open champion Stewart Cink. 'I like to avoid superstitions as all they do is bring me bad luck,' he said.

The most pervasive superstition in golf that has stood the test of time is the belief that whoever wins Wednesday's Par 3 Contest at the Masters has effectively shot himself in the foot for the main trophy.

Forty-plus years of history have shown that no player has pulled off the double. Raymond Floyd came close one year, but lost in a play-off in 1990 to Nick Faldo, a defeat that merely added strength to the legend. Players in line to win the preliminary competition have been known to abort their effort just to be on the right side of providence.

Tiger Woods withdrew from a three-way play-off in 2004 in the Par 3 Contest just in case.

Renton Laidlaw

Sam on Renton: 'Renton has been a dear friend since I turned professional forty years ago. He would champion me whether working for the Edinburgh *Evening News*, where he began; at Scottish Television in Glasgow; at Grampian TV in Aberdeen, where he anchored the evening news; or the London *Evening Standard*. He was BBC Radio's golf correspondent for fifteen years and fronted the Golf Channel when it moved into Europe. What a career! Little wonder that a friend of mine's son from Norway spotted a table in a restaurant which included the great Gary Player and Renton Laidlaw, and turned to his father to say, "Look, there's Renton Laidlaw!" I look back fondly to the early days of the European Tour and a time when legendary journalists like Renton, Peter Dobereiner (*Observer*) and Michael Williams (*Daily Telegraph*) would host fantastic dinners. They were great raconteurs who knew their wine. We knew nothing. They really looked after us.'

In the early days of his career – when things were very different – Sam and I would occasionally room together. Imagine a professional sportsman and a journalist sharing accommodation. Agents would choke on their percentage if it happened now.

We were the most unlikely of double acts. Sam, a gregarious fellow who enjoys a drink or two or three when not in training, a larger than life character, one of the lads; me, somewhat subdued, less street sharp at that time, someone who would boringly content myself with an orange juice at the bar before slipping away quietly ahead of the real action.

But we always got on well and still do. Maybe the fact that we were both Scottish cemented the bond. He always called me Mr Laidlaw (I was older) and he was always Sam. Sam to me, Sam to his fellow golfers, Sam to the public. He stuck up for me and I championed him.

I remember one Italian Open when Sam needed a good finish to win a place in Scotland's World Cup team. But shortly after handing in his card he was disqualified for apparently taking a wrong drop from a ditch at the last hole. The incident had been watched through binoculars from a vantage point high on the clubhouse roof by Arthur Crawley-Bovey, one of the European Tour's more illustrious referees and a well-known connoisseur of red wine.

There were tears. Emotions were running high. Sam was utterly distraught. Supported by players and press – he has always had a good relationship with the Fourth Estate – he immediately lodged an appeal, arguing that he had done nothing wrong. Uncertain about where he should drop the ball he had sought advice from an elderly Italian referee who had been driving down the hole in an electric buggy at the time. Although he spoke no Italian and the referee no English, they apparently understood each other. An amicable decision was reached.

There was a problem, though. The man driving the cart with the big referee sign on the front turned out not to be an official at all. The real referee had loaned the cart temporarily to an old friend for some advantageous spectating. He very much enjoyed meeting Sam and, utterly oblivious to the seriousness of the situation, had merely nodded politely in agreement with everything Sam said.

In the end, Crawley-Bovey, brought up in the days when he and his family toured Europe every summer by car and private train, a pillar of the old school, relented. The decision was revoked and Sam was reinstated, leaving him free to play for Scotland in the World Cup. Justice had been done. We journalists, who had already sent stories back to London about Torrance's unfortunate disqualification, got back on to our papers – not without difficulty because of the inadequate telephone system – to file a much happier report. Sam was smiling again, as he has done through-out most of his career. There's always been a bit of mischief about the big-hearted fellow from Largs.

Sam loved travelling the world playing golf, making friends and entertaining fans with his exciting style of play. He hated it when he had nowhere to go and play. Indeed, a story was put about that during the old four-months close season when there were no tournaments he would head off to the airport anyway. He would travel a few miles down the road to Prestwick Airport just to sit there and read a book. He felt at home in airports as most golfers with a global schedule do. If you didn't you would go mad.

Both Sam and I have always been enthusiastic supporters of Scottish football . . . before it fell into sad decline. There was a time when Scotland legitimately expected to qualify for the World Cup and the European Championships. Today, it is so different. The headline 'Gallant Scots Just Fail' is a standing dish to be served every couple of years at qualification time.

I recall one occasion in the Midlands when Sam and I were joined in our hotel bedroom by Ken Schofield, then chief execu-tive of the European Tour and a human encyclopaedia of sporting facts and figures, to watch a vital Scotland World Cup match. Sam, tired and emotional, lay on his bed sound asleep throughout the game except for one miraculous moment when he sat bolt upright, asked the score, watched the only goal of the game being scored and then fell back into a deep slumber. Sam always had good timing.

He has always been a notorious heckler of speakers at dinners, though he spared me. The problem was that Sam's ad-libs were invariably funnier than the speaker's well-worked-out prose. It could be both intimidating and humiliating for the man giving the speech . . . but the guests loved it.

In contrast, public speaking is not his forte and he lived in dread of the public speaking that was required of a Ryder Cup captain before and after the match at The Belfry in 2002. It is well known that he enlisted the help of Professor David Purdie, himself a brilliant after-dinner speaker. As an unofficial speaking coach, he suggested that Sam might stay relaxed by saying, if appropriate, 'thank you, Renton' before speaking at the opening and closing ceremonies or, failing that, just imagining those words.

It worked. He spoke brilliantly as if he were just chatting to me. But then, we have always had a wonderful friendship.

It is difficult – no impossible – to find anyone who does not admire the big-hearted Scot who teed up more times in European Tour events than any other player and who when called to captain the Ryder Cup team did a magnificent job.

Thank you, Sam.

Chapter Six

The Best 18 Holes in Golf

T he best anything list is obviously going to be highly subjective and, therefore, open to considerable debate. It also very much depends on the criteria adopted. For example, it would be easy to confuse best with favourite. I know because I was halfway through thinking about another list when realising it was veering from one to the other.

That was the list that set out to go from 1 to 18 in strict accordance with their number on the course. It began with the opening hole at the Old Course and after the 2nd at Augusta (because I eagled it twice) it gradually ran out of steam. Rather, I did. Life is too short to play holes in my head when I could be out at Sunningdale beating the pants off some mates.

So, I finally decided to come up with a collection of great holes that either I like a lot or mean something to me, or both – six par 5s, six par 4s and six par 3s, making the classic par 72.

The holes are in no particular order, though I have grouped the various pars together.

The 18th at The Belfry (par 4)

Where else could I begin, though, but at the closing hole at The Belfry, the scene of my greatest golfing triumphs as both Ryder Cup player and captain? That was where I holed the winning putt in 1985 and, seventeen years later, where Paul McGinley gave me victory as the captain. The crowds, the amphitheatre, the drive across water, the approach over the lake and the giant scoreboard provide a dramatic combination. Say what you like about the course – and some have – there is no better place to determine the outcome of a Ryder Cup.

The 18th at the Old Course, St Andrews (par 4)

Chosen for its history and location as much as anything else. Not only the home but the soul of golf. There can be no better view than the one from the 18th tee looking across the Swilcan Bridge and up to the double landmarks of the R&A Clubhouse and Hamilton Hall against the backdrop of the spires and towers rising up from the old grey toon. I get goosebumps just thinking about it. On a personal note, I defeated Mark McNulty on that green to clinch the Dunhill Cup for Scotland.

The 18th at Carnoustie (par 4)

A magnificent hole that for this and future generations will be remembered as the place Jean Van de Velde came so spectacularly to grief in 1999, giving Paul Lawrie the opportunity to win the Open Championship. The meandering Barry Burn is in play at three places – for the drive right, the drive left and in front of the green to catch the short approach. I double-bogeyed this hole in 1969 to lose the Scottish Boys Strokeplay Championship.

The 11th at the New Course, Sunningdale (par 4)

I had to choose something from Sunningdale, my second home (Suzanne says my first), and I have opted for the 11th on the New Course, one of architect Harold Colt's finest. Stroke index 1, the hole doglegs quite sharply from right to left. Just a gorgeous hole.

The 10th at The Belfry (par 4)

The classic risk and reward hole which, thanks to the Ryder Cup and television, has reached iconic status in the golfing world. Drivable, of course, at around 300 yards, but only a perfect fade will take the ball between the trees on the right and the water on the left. A plaque commemorates Seve Ballesteros hitting the green (the first one to do so) in 1978 in a Hennessy Cup match against Nick Faldo.

The 17th at the Old Course, St Andrews (par 4)

Another icon, and in certain conditions probably the most difficult hole in golf. Drive over a replica of the railway sheds, aiming for whatever letter on the sign recommended by your caddie, and then face an approach that must avoid the magnetic Road Bunker and, er, the road. But the Road Hole is more than that.

The 13th at Augusta National (par 5)

A sweeping dogleg from right to left with a tributary of Rae's Creek on the port side and pine trees to starboard. The second shot, over water to a three-tiered green, will always be played with the ball above your feet. This marks the end of Amen Corner and is a birdie (or even eagle) chance despite the potential for disaster. Who can ever tire of watching the unbelievable 6-iron shot that Phil Mickelson hit round a tree a few yards in front of him over the water on to the green, a few yards short of the flag?

The 15th at Augusta National (par 5)

You can't have one without the other. The other famous 5 on the back nine, which plays under par but can produce big numbers. Gene Sarazen famously holed a 235-yard 4-wood for an albatross two in 1935 while, in 1986, Seve Ballesteros found the water with a 4-iron allowing Jack Nicklaus to win his sixth Masters.

The 17th at Muirfield (par 5)

What drama has been witnessed at a hole where trouble lurks, but which can also offer a birdie opportunity. The penultimate hole of the 1972 Open, this was where Lee Trevino chipped in for a par 5 and Tony Jacklin three-putted for a bogey – a blow from which he never really recovered.

The 9th at Gary Player Country Club (par 5)

The signature hole at probably the best championship course in South Africa. Another classic risk and reward, which plays as a three-shotter for the handicap golfer but is set up for pro events to encourage second shots to the island green. A lovely hole.

The 6th at Carnoustie (par 5)

Renamed Hogan's Alley fifty years after his victory in the 1953 Open. A hole for the brave – not the faint-hearted since the best line from the tee is between bunkers and the out-of-bounds fence. Jocky's Burn bites in from the right so care must be taken with the second shot.

The 17th at Royal Birkdale (par 5)

I still regard this as a great hole despite the controversial change to the green for the Open Championship in 2008.

You have to be accurate from the tee, avoiding sand dunes on both sides of the fairway and two nasty bunkers on the right.

The 12th at Augusta National (par 3)

The pond, the narrowness of the putting surface, the swirling winds, the diagonal green that means the further you aim right the further you have to carry the ball, the pressure. The Masters. Enough said. The most famous par 3 in golf.

The 8th at Royal Troon (par 3)

Aka the Postage Stamp. Just 120-odd yards long, a mere flick, but the green is long and narrow and surrounded by deep bunkers with vertical faces. When playing it at the Senior Open, I shanked my ball on to the 7th fairway and was faced with the hardest shot in golf – the one after a shank!

The 5th at Loch Lomond (par 3)

An absolutely stunning location as you play towards the edge of the loch with the hills in the background. Beautiful bunkering and a green with enough pin locations to make a four-club difference in the tee shot.

The 17th at TPC Sawgrass (par 3)

Next to the 12th at Augusta, this is probably the most photographed short hole in golf and is always a favourite with the television audience. Will the player go in the water or will the player find the sanctuary of the island green located in the middle of a lagoon? You need balls to play what paradoxically is essentially an easy shot.

The 17th at Kiawah Island (par 3)

The green is a small target to the eye, protected short and right by water and on the left by two huge waste bunkers. Guaranteed to get the bum twitching. I hit a 4-iron stiff there on the way to a halved match with my mucker David Feherty against Lanny Wadkins and Mark O'Meara on the first day of the 1991 Ryder Cup.

The 18th at Saint-Nom-La-Breteche (par 3)

Set beautifully in front of the most spectacular clubhouse you could imagine, an 18th-century French chateau about 15 miles west of Paris. I remembering losing the Lancome Trophy to Colin Montgomerie on the 72nd hole in 1995 when he upped and down for par. His tee shot would have careered out of bounds but for plugging in the mud!

Arnold Palmer

Sam on Arnold: 'I will never forget the first time I saw Arnold Palmer. It was at Muirfield in 1972, my first Open Championship. Jack Nicklaus had by then assumed the mantle of best player in the world but Palmer remained The King. He still is.

Arnie, with his "army" already in attendance, walked on to the practice putting green swathed in cashmere, bronzed and, it seemed, looking like an Adonis, like a god, certainly in golfing terms. I have never felt so intimidated in my life. You could almost see the aura surrounding his frame.

Palmer, of course, merited particular affection in Britain for having come over to our great championship at a time when many of his fellow Americans had forsaken the event. He played the role of Pied Piper with such swashbuckling effect that all but the most narrow-minded of his countrymen have followed for the past half a century.

His record of seven majors (four Masters, two Opens and one US Open) would have been more complete had he managed a USPGA success. But sixty-two victories on the PGA Tour represent a prodigious return for his talents. More than anything, though, it was the way he played. He would hitch up those trousers and go for every shot as if safety was a street never to be entered. Speaking of streets, there are thirteen throughout the USA named after him!

So loved is he in his native land that politicians used to beat a path to his door to talk about the possibility of him becoming governor, even president.

I am very proud to say that Arnold has written to me regularly throughout my career and when I used to bump into him during my commentary days at the Masters we always shared a warm hello.'

In 1965, just four years after Bay Hill Club and Lodge had been founded, the owners rounded up Jack Nicklaus, singer–golfer Don Cherry, local star professional Dave Ragan and me to help show it off to the general public, raising charitable dollars in the process.

That one day sold me on Bay Hill, and would have even if I hadn't won the exhibition handily by shooting a 6-under-par 66. How well I remember telling my wife, Winnie, 'Babe, I've just played the best course in Florida and I want to own it.'

Although the attraction of its solitude among the orange trees and pristine lakes soon gave way to the massive growth of the area, with the unexpected arrival of Disney and other attractions, I have never regretted one bit my subsequent acquisition and development of Bay Hill and everything that has gone with it.

I especially cherish the involvement my family and I have had in the establishment and growth of the Arnold Palmer Medical Center and its widely acclaimed focus on healthcare for women and children, mothers and babies in the Central Florida area.

I had been intrigued from the start by the Orlando area, which was one of my college team's stops during the annual tour to Florida. My college days at Wake Forest reaped many benefits for me in my future life, not least sharpening my game for the professional career that followed. In an unexpected and indirect way, Wake Forest also led me to my present winter home and club in Orlando, where I have enjoyed so many wonderful moments over the last forty-five years.

I was delighted when the opportunity came to move the existing PGA Tour tournament in Orlando from Rio Pinar to Bay Hill in 1979 and develop it into one of the top-ranking events on the schedule. Our field annually is one of the strongest of the season outside of the major and world championships.

Our televised tournament gives golf fans around the world the opportunity to see the game's elite tackle the 17th hole, a challenging, water-guarded, 221-yard par 3. It is a real beauty of a hole. I could almost fill a book with stories about incidents that have happened there, some involving me, others not.

Back in 1987, in the days when a million dollars really was a lot of money in golf, Don Pooley holed his 4-iron tee shot at the 17th in our tournament and split a pre-designated Hertz prize with my hospital in Orlando. An amazing $500,000 for the generous Pooley and the same for the hospital. That was unprecedented at the time.

Seven years later, Fuzzy Zoeller was headed for his second victory at Bay Hill when he hit a tee shot that strayed right; it struck on the head not just any spectator but, as it happened, his best friend who was on the far side of the water, and it bounced back into the drink. Double-bogey, tie for second place.

Davis Love III, the US Ryder Cup captain for 2012, normally

a soft-spoken, mild-mannered man, created quite a splash, literally, in the second round of the 1999 tournament. Upset with a buried lie in the front bunker and no happier with the subsequent recovery shot that finished 45 feet past the hole, Davis slammed his sand wedge into the turf above the sand, inadvertently breaking a sprinkler head. The fountain of water quickly flooded the bunker.

He made that monster putt for par and tied for the lead, saying after the round, 'I'd better win this week or Arnold won't invite me back.'

In fact, he finished third behind winner Tim Herron, and Tom Lehman, the loser in the play-off. As a joke, I sent Davis a mock bill for repairs and most certainly invited him back every year thereafter.

Just a few years ago, Englishman Greg Owen was within a tap-in par putt on the 17th of his first win on the PGA Tour. Calamity struck. Owen shockingly three-putted to wipe out his two-stroke lead and bogeyed the last hole to lose the tournament to Rod Pampling by a stroke.

As for myself, who knows how many times I have played that hole. Hundreds of times for sure. Two incidents stick in my mind.

Spiro Agnew loved golf and became somewhat notorious for errant shots that accidentally struck spectators during pro-ams. Even when President Richard Nixon's vice president, Agnew played quite a bit and was at Bay Hill several times with me. In 1973, we decided to do a taped TV show, shooting around the country at 'my favourite 18 holes'. The idea was that I would play the holes with a different professional, celebrity or prominent citizen.

We did Bay Hill's 17th with Vice President Agnew, but before the show was to air he resigned from office when engulfed by a political scandal. Since there was still time, the decision was made to reshoot that segment using somebody else, particularly since I was at Bay Hill at the time.

'Why not my father?' I suggested. The idea was immediately accepted, I talked Pap into doing it and the result proved to be great television. With the cameras rolling and no mulligans allowed, Pap, who was sixty-nine at the time, hit a nice 3-wood on to the green about 40 feet from the cup. I put my 2-iron about 8 feet from the hole.

So, doesn't Pap knock in that birdie putt and force me to bear down pretty hard to make mine, which I did. Great theatre.

I've made 19 holes-in-one in my lifetime – and one mulligan ace. That happened one day years ago when I was playing a casual, bet-filled round with some of my member friends at the club. At the 17th tee, I disagreed on club selection with my caddie, Tomcat. He said 3-iron, I thought I needed a 2-iron, but went ahead with the 3. The shot came up short and landed in the water.

I grabbed my 2-iron, teed up another ball and knocked it into the hole. I turned to Tomcat and said: 'I told you it was a 2-iron.' Undaunted, he fired back, 'No, suh, Mr Palmer. You hit that one fat.'

Although my competitive playing days are behind me, I still get a kick out of playing with the golfing regulars off and on in the daily shoot-outs there and with my gang in Latrobe, Pennsylvania in the summer months, even though my game is not what it used to be.

It's still wonderful just being out there in the fresh air enjoying the great game of golf.

Chapter Seven

That Putt's Slightly Straight, Sir

The most famous caddie of all time was surely Jack Nicklaus! OK, he was not a regular Tour 'rake-rat', but on one of the few occasions he carried someone else's bag in a tournament he was nearly chucked out for breaching the dress code. In 1997 Nicklaus turned up to caddie for his son Gary at the PGA Tour qualifier in West Palm Beach, Florida, bare-legged and wearing shorts. This was a clear infraction of the rules regarding dress and he was told as much.

Jack quickly slipped on some rainwear while his wife Barbara was summoned to bring a pair of trousers. For the record, Gary shot 78 and failed to advance to the next stage of the qualifying process. It is not known how many pounds Jack lost wearing waterproof trousers in the baking Florida sunshine.

Talking of inappropriate waterproofs, I remember an occasion at Loch Lomond involving one of the Sunningdale Tilston twins. I am not sure if it was Gary, who carried Robert Rock's

bag to victory over Tiger Woods in the Abu Dhabi Championship in 2012, or Guy, who has been working for Simon Dyson
on the Tour. Sorry. No matter, I spotted one of them removing
his trousers and wearing just waterproofs on a miserable wet
but warm day.

'That's for me,' I thought in Billy Connolly mode. 'That's the
very game.'

I whipped off my trousers and put on waterproofs directly
over my underpants. Within a few holes, though, the rain
stopped, the sun came out and I spent a most uncomfortable
four hours sweltering on the bonnie, bonnie, 'sweatie' banks of
Loch Lomond.

It's a tough life as a caddie, but not nearly as tough as it used
to be. Mostly, the money is much better, as are the conditions,
with the result that the desperados of years gone by have been
replaced by a group of real professionals. The weather-beaten,
hard-drinking conmen and convicts of generations past have
given way to a group of full-timers who are expected to be psy-
chologists, weather forecasters, nutritionists, shoulders to cry on
and all-round magicians. Only the nicknames remain.

Long gone are the characters like Mad Mac, who caddied for
1951 Open champion Max Faulkner, the father-in-law of Brian
Barnes. Mad Mac was a true eccentric. He wore a raincoat but no
shirt and read the line of putts with binoculars without any
lenses. 'That putt's slightly straight, sir,' he would say to Faulkner.

What colourful nicknames they had. Indeed, a professional
could spend ten years with someone he knew only by his nickname.

Cemetery, an Augusta National caddie who carried President
Eisenhower's bag, was thought to have earned his nickname by

waking up one morning on a slab in a morgue. He was said to have a heartbeat so faint that it defied detection by even the most sophisticated stethoscope.

These were the days of Ferocious Frank, Staggering Haggerty, Penitentiary Larry, One-Armed Mikey, and so on. There was nothing very complicated or subtle in how these caddies earned their names. Ferocious, staggering, penitentiary and one-armed – you do not have to be a crossword freak to work those out.

The fashion among my generation, and subsequent ones, was for a bit of wordplay. Seagull, for example, was so called because he was always shitting on everyone; Cornflake looked like a serial (cereal) killer; and Crunchy was a Scottish caddie who headbutted the aforementioned Cornflake, as in Crunchy – Nut – Cornflake. That nickname was the brainchild of David Howell, one of the sharpest pros on the range. The Brain, in caddie logic, apparently did not have much of one.

There have been caddie jokes and caddie stories since time immemorial, or at least since the Marquis of Montrose was recorded as having paid four shillings to 'the boy who carried my clubs'. That seems an extraordinary amount for those days, probably worth more than the winner's cheque Walter Hagen gave to sixteen-year-old Ernest Hargreaves after their Open Championship victory at Muirfield in 1929. The lucky Hargreaves, from Yorkshire, went on to caddie for The Haig, as Hagen was known, at the Ryder Cup at Moortown before becoming his valet and butler.

I doubt if Malcolm Mason, my caddie for the most successful twelve years of my career, or any of the other guys on Tour, would have fancied caddying for Hagen even allowing for all those major championship successes. Prior to the 14-club limit being introduced, Hagen played with a golf set consisting of twenty irons, resulting in his bag weighing in at around 40 pounds.

Caddie jokes, probably conceived by the fraternity itself, often portray players as useless and caddies as masters of the quick-witted one-liner, which in fairness they can be. It is not hard to imagine the hapless golfer and his caustic caddie.

Golfer: I think I am going to drown myself in the lake.
Caddie: Do you think you can keep your head down that long?

Golfer: You've got to be the worst caddie in the world.
Caddie: I don't think so, sir. That would be too much of a coincidence.

Golfer: Do you think I can get there with a 5-iron?
Caddie: Eventually.

Some of the classic stories, which include the same dry humour, veer towards the apocryphal. I am not sure, for example, of the veracity of the tale involving Lee Trevino and his overweight caddie, Herman Mitchell.

'What do you think?' Trevino is supposed to have asked of his retainer as they studied an important putt.

'Keep it low,' Mitchell apparently replied after some thought.

The same question was asked by Tommy Bolt of a caddie called Hagan, who had the reputation of knowing Riviera Country Club better than any others of his profession.

'What do you think?'

'A 6-iron,' Hagan suggested.

'No, it's a 5-iron,' Bolt declared.

'No, it's a 6 and when you hit it, just hit it firm and don't press,' the caddie insisted.

'You're crazy,' Bolt concluded.

Bolt proceeded to hit the 5-iron 20 yards over the green. The explosion was almost predictable as he broke the 5-iron over his knee. Hagan, who was holding the 6-iron in his hand, allegedly snapped that club over his knee, dropped Bolt's bag and walked away. I would love that story to be true.

Could the St Andrews' tale involving a group of wealthy Arab businessmen in their traditional headwear be anything other than a piece of fiction? At the completion of the round at the Old Course, it is told and retold, one of the visitors handed his elderly Scottish caddie a generous tip. 'Thanks very much, Your Excellency,' the caddie is supposed to have said, 'and I hope your head feels better soon.'

My old friend David Feherty tells a wonderful story about his caddie Stuttering Stanley during a tournament in South Africa that I know to be true. This was in the days when each professional would have his own bag of practice balls that his caddie would field at various distances down the range. Stuttering Stanley always sub-contracted this potentially dangerous task to a friend in the gallery and paid him accordingly.

The course, in Cape Town I think, had a railway line running down the side of the practice ground. It so happened this day that the guy helping Stanley was getting married in the afternoon and had already changed into his best suit. Suddenly, he fell down, leading Feherty to the reasonable assumption that he had struck the unfortunate man. He got up quickly but began staggering all over the place as he made his way towards Feherty and the rest of the golfers on the range. He was still 50 yards away when everyone became aware of a horrific stink.

It transpired that the groom had been hit, but not by a golf ball. A steward in a passing train had emptied the contents of the shit bucket through the window and, deliberately or not, covered the replacement caddie head to foot in the most foul-smelling human excrement.

The caddie breed is such that the more extraordinary the story the more likely it is to be true. The late great Henry Cotton used to tell a particularly macabre tale about a caddie of his called Louis. Apparently Louis, an athletic sort who loved to cycle, thought little of pedalling as much as 70 miles when Cotton travelled for a game of golf. He would leave in the early hours of the morning to time his arrival with that of Cotton in his little sports car.

He never failed to turn up, except on one notorious occasion. The explanation lay in his being preoccupied, if you can call it that, with axing his widowed mother to death following a row over money and his girlfriend. Louis was sentenced to life imprisonment.

Golfers did not come more arrogant than the Wolverhampton-born Archie Compston, who is reckoned to have been Britain's first 'celebrity' professional golfer. Compston, who enjoyed a singles victory over Gene Sarazen in 1929 in the second of his three Ryder Cup appearances, had the previous year thrashed Walter Hagen, no less, by the astonishing margin of 18 and 17. That's not as dramatic as it sounds, though only marginally less so. It was a special 72-hole challenge match, not a two-round contest. Compston employed three caddies, one to carry his bag, one for his sweater, raincoat and umbrella and a third to look after his smoking paraphernalia.

How ridiculous. Hang on a minute, Malcolm could tell you that he kept my tobacco wrapped up so carefully in his pocket that it once survived being submerged in a lake.

Malcolm was a member of the Esher crowd who would gather in the Albert Arms of a winter afternoon to play darts. The regulars included Rod Stewart, who stayed in a flat above the pub, and Jimmy White. And Sam Torrance. The Albert Arms was the reason my wife, Suzanne, would not buy a house in Esher. But I told her there would be a pub wherever we lived!

Jimmy White was exactly what it said on the tin, easily the most brilliant snooker player never to have won the World Championship. This particular Rod Stewart, however, had never sung 'Maggie May', not in a recording studio at least, nor slept with Britt Ekland. Maybe in his dreams. Andy Bladen was his real name, but everyone in golf knew him as Rod Stewart on account of the hair and an appearance he definitely cultivated. Many a time he would be asked for his autograph.

This was the era when caddies such as Peter Coleman and Dave Musgrove on this side of the Atlantic began to introduce a new level of professionalism with their yardage wheels, their careful measuring and plotting, ending up with yardage books. For all that, they remained great believers in the old three-step guide for good caddying – show up, keep up and shut up. Pretty much all the pro golfers had by then stopped using the 'eyeball' technique to decide on club selection and did their own yardage books. That changed with Coleman, Musgrove and co.

Coleman began working with Tommy Horton in 1974. He has since caddied for Nancy Lopez, Greg Norman, Seve Ballesteros,

Colin Montgomerie and Gordon Brand Jnr at various times in his career. That's a pretty impressive collection of clients! It was his association with Langer, though, which was most successful and enduring.

Musgrove began at almost the same time caddying for WB, 'Wild Bill' Murray from Dundee. Although Dave was to 'win' a major with Lee Janzen, it was his relationship with Sandy Lyle that lasted longest and brought most success.

Both men caddied for Seve Ballesteros, who could be one of the hardest taskmasters. 'I felt I'd served my sentence,' Dave said after parting company with the Spanish wizard. Everyone loved and was in awe of Seve, but it is fair to say that caddies could find it hard going.

No one was more admiring of Ballesteros the golfer than Billy Foster, who loves to tell how Seve could hit shots that no one else could even imagine. Yet it was Billy who gave Seve one of the biggest bollockings from caddie to golfer following a classic outburst from Seve.

The story goes that Seve needed to play a provisional drive because he had hit his first tee shot into the rubbish. He could not find a tee in his pocket and looked over to his caddie. Billy put his hand in the bag, pulled out a few and handed them to his boss. 'Why you give me three tees?' Seve asked with the irrationality of the angry. 'There are only two holes to go. You think I am going to hit another provisional ball?'

Well, Billy, who is never afraid to speak his mind when necessary, tore into him.

Foster is probably the finest caddie who ever worked for me. Malcolm gets mad when I say that. Billy caddied for me only once when I won the 1993 Heineken Open in Barcelona, an event curtailed to 54 holes because of bad weather. With Malcolm on his honeymoon, the agreement was that both caddies would share the percentage commission should I win. Billy, who is the only caddie I have ever allowed to read my putts, has since become acknowledged as the best caddie in the world.

I used to gravitate towards the caddies after a round. You were guaranteed to find someone with whom to have a pint and a good laugh. They knew the best jokes and the hottest gossip. I'm afraid that toilet humour prevailed. One time the caddies came up with seventeen different golfers who, shall we say, had pretty serious 'accidents' on the course. The more serious of the two possibilities. No names.

Sometimes it got really serious. Poor Harry Toan, a caddie from Northern Ireland, took a ferry to Jersey, leaving his car parked by the terminal at Southampton, or wherever. After he was gone a few days, the police became suspicious of the Ulster number plates and blew up the car. It did not do much for his golf clubs.

Yorkie Bill, who always smoked a big cigar under a mop of curly hair, and Jungle Jim boarded a train from Leeds to York for the Car Care International tournament with just the one ticket. 'What are we going to do? We have only one ticket between us,' Jungle Jim asks.

'Just stick with me, I'll look after you,' Yorkie Bill replies.

Yorkie, spotting a woman going into the toilet in the next carriage, knocks on the door and says 'Ticket please'. He persuades the woman to shove her ticket under the door. Job done.

Rocket Rodney, aka Rodders, Feherty's old caddie, once lost a complete day, as David recalls.

'In Italy, we shot even par 72 in the first round. Rodders went out with Olazabal Dave – Jose Maria's caddie as the name suggests – and both had a real skinful. They did not get back to their room until 4 a.m. Rodney said Olazabal Dave snored so badly he had to pull the curtains twice out of his nose.

'Rodders fell asleep in the back seat of the caddie bus on the way to the course. The other caddies filed off and forgot about him. Two hours later the bus returned to the hotel to pick up the afternoon caddies. He woke up thinking he had been caddying for the day and went to bed.

'He woke up at 8 p.m. and went down to what he thought was breakfast. Only it was dinner time. The caddies were all there wondering where he had been all day. The conversation went something like this: "I was caddying like you lot." "No, you didn't even turn up for work." "But we shot 72." "No, Rodders, that was yesterday."'

That was how Rocket Rodney lost a day. We have all lost days at one time or another.

Dave Musgrove

Sam on Dave: 'Mus is one of the all-time great caddies who, with Bernhard Langer's faithful retainer Pete Coleman, professionalised, if not revolutionised, the job of caddie. "Show up, keep up and shut up" was the typically laconic way he characterised his trade, a pretty

sound philosophy even if it seems much more complicated these days. Mus "won" four major championships
with three different players – the Open Championship
with Seve Ballesteros in 1979, the Open again with
Sandy Lyle in 1985, the Masters with Sandy in 1988 and
ten years later the US Open with Lee Janzen.'

In the 1970s there were not many caddies who travelled
around Europe, never mind all over the world as they do now.

Pete Coleman, Bernard Langer's man for much of his career,
and perhaps the first caddie to own a Porsche, was one of the
trailblazers. I was another. But when we went to Sweden, to take
one example, most of the 'caddies' came from the ranks of the
local junior golfers. They were not caddies so much as trolley
pullers.

One of their number was a young girl called Fanny Sunesson from Karlshamn in the far south of the country. She was
maybe fourteen at the time and a decent amateur player. But
she wanted to be a caddie. Little did we know then – though
we might have guessed from her determination – that this
little Swedish teenager would become the most famous female
caddie and, more than that, the most recognised of all caddies, male or female.

Pretty soon she turned up on the European Tour caddying for
Jose Rivero, who had made his Ryder Cup debut in that momentous defeat of the United States at The Belfry in 1985.

Rivero and Fanny won the French Open together in 1987, a
success that pretty much secured his place in the team for that
year's Ryder Cup at Muirfield Village in Ohio, the so-called
'course that Jack built'. (Jack was Jack Nicklaus, of course.) 'I will

take you to the Ryder Cup,' Rivero promised Fanny who, natu-rally enough, was thrilled at the prospect.

Four years earlier, a few of us had approached captain Tony Jacklin to request some sort of guaranteed aeroplane seat home so that we could get back in time to work at the next tourna-ment the following week. Jimmy Cousins, who had worked for Jacko in the past, was a member of the deputation. We might have been looking for a bit more but we never made any demands.

Jacklin came back to us with free tickets, and so began the practice of caddies being treated as part of the team. The ticket was from London to Miami; the USGA came up with some of the cost of getting us to and from Columbus, with the European players also chipping in . . . probably reluctantly. Professional golfers can be a mean bunch.

By 1987 caddies were allocated seats on the official plane and received free accommodation as well as clothing and assorted goodies.

Suddenly and disgracefully, Rivero changed his mind. Instead of taking Fanny, he brought along his brother, for pretty much a holiday. He was no caddie.

The European Tour caddies were incensed and we told Rivero so when a few of us cornered him in the locker room at Muir-field during the Open Championship. Somewhat taken aback, Rivero promised to make it up to Fanny later in the year by having her on his bag at the World Cup in Kapalua, Hawaii. The Spaniard did not deliver and unwisely asked us for yardages prior to practice on the beautiful island of Maui. 'If Fanny was here you'd have all your yardages,' I replied firmly. 'You are not getting ours.'

That Putt's Slightly Straight, Sir

In switching from Rivero to Howard Clark, Fanny achieved the equivalent of going from sand into water! Caddying for Clark was no picnic, as Malcolm Mason and, to be fair, the player himself suggest elsewhere in this book. He made it difficult for her to enjoy her first Ryder Cup in 1989 by which time her fellow caddies were urging her to find a new bag.

About the same time, Nick Faldo, who had added a Masters' title to his growing CV that year, was being promoted heavily in Japan. A new image was required. Out went Andy Prodger and in came Fanny. The rest is history that can be summed up in the fact that together Faldo and Fanny won two Opens and two Masters' titles in the space of eight years.

Speaking of Kapalua, I was caddying for Sandy Lyle when he and Sam represented Scotland in the 1987 World Cup. They lost out in a play-off to Wales, represented by Ian Woosnam and David Llewellyn. Everyone was delighted for Lu-Lu for whom, despite a couple of European Tour victories, this was his finest hour.

Really, though, Sandy and Sam should have walked it. Sandy had already won the Kapalua International in 1984 and knew the complexities of the difficult grainy greens with borrows that were difficult to read. Sandy suggested that he read Sam's putts in practice, a policy that served them well with a thumping victory in the pro-am.

For some reason, standing on the 1st tee on the first round, Sam told Sandy that he was uncomfortable having his putts lined up by someone else. It was just not what he had been used to. Fair enough.

But I think they lost the World Cup that year because of that decision on the 1st hole. They were easily the strongest team that year.

Malcolm Mason

Sam on Malcolm: 'My longest-serving caddie who was with me for twelve great years. We got together – as Malcolm relates below – after he sacked Howard Clark. I had known Malcolm, of course, for years. I liked a drink after a round and I would often gravitate towards the caddies for a gargle and a joke-telling session. Malcolm was one of the Esher mob who would gather during winter afternoons in the Albert Arms for a few beers and a game of darts. With his flowing long hair he looked like a rock star. I don't know if he can sing, but he was a very good and very loyal caddie. I hope he is enjoying his retirement.'

My twelve years as Sam's caddie were never dull. Like most of us he had his grumpy moments, but he was great to work for and even better when sinking a few pints together in the clubhouse after a round, no matter what he scored. There was nothing he liked better than trading jokes over a few beers.

We had our laughs on the course as well. Never more so than on one occasion in the Lancome Trophy at Saint-Nom-La-Breteche, that lovely French course about 15 miles west of Paris. We were playing with Nick Faldo, who had the legend that is Fanny Sunesson on his bag, and Swedish player Patrik Sjoland, accompanied by his wife.

That Putt's Slightly Straight, Sir

It all began with Sam driving into the right rough at the 5th hole. From there he got a flier that caused his ball to land in the greenside water hazard. Sam needed to drop under a penalty of one stroke on a mound steep enough to propel any ball into the water. So, as is normal practice, I positioned myself at the bottom of the mound, just outside the line of the hazard, to collect the ball, preventing it from rolling into the drink. The only trouble was that the bank was not only severe but slippy. I lost my footing and slid in dramatic slow motion into the water. Despite trying to stop myself by digging my fingers into the bank, I slid deeper and deeper into the pond.

The level of the water rose past my waist to my chest and still I had not reached the bottom of the man-made hazard. Shock gave way to panic at the thought of having to try to swim to safety.

Of course, by that time Sam was pissing himself laughing. Patrik and his missus were in stitches. Even Faldo, who never paid much attention to his playing partners, managed a chuckle.

Sam can still remember the look in my eyes as I appeared to be going under. 'He looked terrified,' Sam always says when retelling the story.

Anyway, amid all the hilarity, it suddenly dawned on Sam that I was going to need help getting out. Then it occurred to him that he could easily follow me into the murky depths.

You could always rely on Fanny in a crisis. Fanny positioned herself at the top of the bank, holding Sam's hand as he gingerly reached out to me. Fanny is not only as good a caddie as any man, better in fact, but she also possesses a lot more strength than most. Eventually this soaking-wet creature from the black lagoon made it to dry land. 'Look, it's the Man from Atlantis,' Sam said.

But Sam still had to drop the ball, meaning that I was required to assume the same position on the bank. So I took up my precarious stance and successfully caught the ball that Sam carefully placed on the correct spot.

So what happened next? Well, Sam only went and holed his chip shot to save par. Then Faldo sank a monster putt from the lower level of the two-tiered green for birdie.

I was soaked to the skin and still had 13 holes of the round remaining. (Fortunately, it was a hot day and I dried out fairly quickly.) It was several holes, though, before the others stopped sniggering at this figure splashing about the French countryside on a hot summer's day.

Sam had been a worried man but not, it transpired, about the safety of his faithful retainer. 'Is my tobacco all right?' he asked me anxiously. 'Are my baccy and cigarette papers still dry?'

Part of my job was to look after Sam's stash so he could drag on a roll-up from time to time. Sam knew that I kept it in a trouser pocket. Fortunately, everything was well wrapped and bone dry.

Of course, word quickly spread. And the names started. To this day, Thomas Bjorn calls me Splash.

That was 1998. I remember the year because the incident happened a few months before my fiftieth birthday. One of the features of my party at the local cricket club was a video (played on a loop) of a big ugly mermaid emerging from the water. My wife had liaised with an official on the Tour to get a copy of the video. Not everything was captured for posterity. With the cameraman just setting up at the time he missed me falling in. But he was sharp enough to snatch me coming out.

That Putt's Slightly Straight, Sir

Prior to joining Sam in 1988, I had caddied for two years for dear old Howard Clark. Howard was, shall we say, a hard taskmaster. Nothing was ever right, not the caddies, not their yardages. He blamed every bad shot on someone or something else. That was just his way. He was a great guy when not playing.

One day I snapped. He was doing my head in. I had had a right morning with him. I was thinking of quitting at the turn and leaving him to get someone else for the back nine. But I was sent up the 10th fairway and could not get near the clubhouse. We did quite well actually and finished under par.

But I hadn't changed my mind. I went to the locker room, grabbed my waterproofs and my yardage wheel – we did all our own yardages in those days – and was about to leave when Howard walked in. He always came to say sorry at the end of the round. As I said, he was a lovely guy, just a nightmare on the course. 'I'm going. I've had enough,' I told him.

'What do you mean you've had enough?'

'That's it.'

'Wait, you have got to find someone else for me for the next round.'

'Howard, I do not know anyone who would want to caddie for you.'

'What about my yardages? I need all the yardages.'

'No point giving you mine because they are obviously all wrong.'

I started with Sam in Dubai the following week.

Chapter Eight

The Greats

For a long time I held the view that there was never anyone better before Ben Hogan; then never anyone better before Jack Nicklaus; and then never anyone better before Tiger Woods. I might have to review that in the light of the Woods situation, depending on the rest of his career. But even if he does nothing from now on he would still remain in my top three greats.

One level down from those I would place Bobby Jones, Sam Snead and Byron Nelson, while a third stratum of all-time greats would comprise Lee Trevino, Seve Ballesteros and Tom Watson.

That should generate a whole lot of disagreement.

What about Walter Hagen, Gary Player and Arnold Palmer, I hear you ask? They are great players, I would reply. What about Henry Cotton, Greg Norman and Phil Mickelson? Great players. And there are others. But I would not change my three groups of three.

Ben Hogan was my father's hero and my father taught me. He has been my only teacher. So, growing up and growing old it has been a question of Hogan did this and Hogan did that. Hogan, Hogan, Hogan. That was fine with me.

I never met him and I never saw him play. I never laid eyes on him. But I know what he achieved and I know the circumstances. And when Dad said that he was the hardest worker and greatest practiser golf has ever seen, that is good enough for me. I have a picture of Hogan in my study flanked by my father, Bob, and my mother, June. Hogan has written a message to me that begins 'To S . . .', well it starts with an S. It looks like it was going to be 'Sandy'. It is not 'Sam'!

Hogan could freeze a geyser with his icy stare. He tolerated neither fools nor stupid questions. He was a hard man who feared a confrontation with no one. I love the conversation he was supposed to have had with Arnold Palmer at the start of Ryder Cup week in 1967 at the Champions Golf Club in Houston, Texas.

'Hey Ben, what's this about playing the small [British] ball?' Palmer asked.

'That's what you agreed before you decided to come,' Hogan replied.

'I don't play the small ball.'

'Who says you are playing, Palmer?'

The USA slaughtered GB&I 23½–8½, with Palmer taking a maximum five points out of five.

Hogan was the most precise of golfers. Every time he received a consignment of new balls he would use a magnifying glass to inspect every one. He would toss the odd one away on the basis that some of the dimples had too much paint on them.

Hogan won nine major championships between 1946 and 1953, the year of his victory in the only Open Championship he contested. He had been leading money winner in America in both 1940 and 1941 before spending three years in the US Army Air Corps.

No one – except perhaps Vijay Singh – has practised more than Ben Hogan. 'For every day I miss practising it takes me two days to get back to where I was,' he would say. 'I had to, my swing was so bad. But I also loved it.'

Retirement, when it came, meant precisely that. He never showed one iota of interest in Senior golf, in making public appearances or in doing interviews. He became pretty much a recluse. Asked in later life how he wanted to be remembered, he replied, 'First as a gentleman and then as a golfer.'

Back to Dad. He would always tell me that when Jack Nicklaus said 'go', the ball really went. The Golden Bear boasted a prodigious long game, a deliberate putting stroke that worked when it mattered most and the keenest of golfing brains. He virtually invented course management.

He was the man, as far as I was concerned. As a boy I noticed that Nicklaus did not ground his club at address. I thought that had to be right, so I did not ground my club. I never have.

He was my hero. I have a photograph somewhere in my memorabilia of Nicklaus on the practice range at the 1972 Open Championship. There I am in the middle of a throng of enthusiastic golf fans as the great man hit shots with one of those clubs covered in brown casing. I don't know what came over me. Without warning I shouted out, 'Is that a hickory shaft?' How dumb. My face went red. Thank God Nicklaus did not know I was a player about to compete in my first Open. Mind you, the fact that I was dressed in golf gear and carrying a club might have given it away!

Much later, when we knew each other pretty well, I said to him, 'The biggest compliment I can give you is that in all of the 400 majors I have won in my dreams you were runner-up.' He liked that. But it was true. Jack was always the man I beat.

In reality, of course, he managed eighteen majors to my none – four US Opens, three Open Championships, five USPGA titles and six Masters, the first when just twenty-two and the last that unbelievable 1986 triumph at the age of forty-six.

I was drawn with Nicklaus in two Opens when he was in his pomp. But don't ask me how I played. All I can remember is that I could hardly breathe, so overawed was I in his presence.

Then there was our unscheduled meeting in 1983 when Nicklaus captained the US Ryder Cup team. The European Team had been invited to the West Palm Beach Yacht Club, a short drive from the European team hotel. I noticed Fuzzy Zoeller giving directions to someone and, like in a film, ordered our driver to 'follow that car'. Ian Woosnam just giggled and, like me, paid no attention to where we were going.

Fifteen minutes later we arrived at a magnificent property to see Calvin Peete emerge from the car in front. We thought nothing of it. We made it to the door before the Americans and I rang the bell.

Nicklaus, looking somewhat bemused it has to be said, answered the door. 'Is this the yacht club?' I asked rather limply.

'No, this is my home,' the great man replied. 'But come in.'

Nicklaus poured us a drink and pointed out of the window to the yacht club on the other side of the lake. We had gatecrashed an American team meeting.

The Greats

I don't really know Tiger Woods. We shake hands at Ryder Cups and say hello if our paths cross. In golfing terms, though, what is there to know other than his phenomenal achievements and what he can do with a ball? The word genius gets bandied about too liberally – but Tiger Woods is a genius. And he will remain that even if, after all, he does not manage to overtake Jack's record number of major championship victories. At the time of writing he is stuck on fourteen, four behind. But I fully expect him to add to that in the years to come.

At his magisterial best, I defy any golfer of any ability to watch Woods – whether live in competition, on the practice ground or on the television – without open-mouthed wonder. No one is more athletic and no one can match his pretty much complete repertoire of shots.

I had the opportunity to play with Woods once and, stupidly, I bottled out. I was on the practice putting green at Augusta when Woods and his then caddie, Stevie Williams, walked past heading from the 9th green to the 10th tee.

'Do you want to join us for nine holes?' Stevie shouted across at me.

I panicked. 'No, that's all right, thank you, I'm fine,' I stuttered. I could have been in the form of my life but I did not think I was up to it. Crazy.

That may have been the same Masters when I walked into the locker room and there sat Tiger eating the biggest steak you have ever seen. It was 11 a.m.

Some of you will know that in my younger days in Scotland I was known as Slammin' Sammy Torrance. The name, which did not really travel south with me, is where the similarity with Slammin' Sammy Snead begins and ends. My father may have idolised Ben Hogan, but he thought Snead possessed the better – indeed best – swing. The rhythm, the power, the grace, the athleticism. Lee Trevino called him 'America's greatest athlete', which sounds like a bit of an exaggeration.

Snead possessed remarkable suppleness, however, which he demonstrated casually when bending over to take his ball out of the hole without bending his knees. Try it. He could also high-kick the top of doors well into his seventies.

While not exactly an eccentric, Snead could lay claim to some personal idiosyncrasies: his straw hats with different-coloured bands into which he would tuck a $100 bill; the dollar bills he folded into tiny squares and used to tip waiters or porters; golf balls with the figure 0 that Wilson made for him and him alone.

Snead was a country boy from Virginia who in his early days mistrusted cheques. He once asked Bing Crosby no less for cash when winning the singer's tournament. His passion for hunting and fishing took him to Africa occasionally and it was on one of those safari trips that he was press-ganged into playing a tournament in Nairobi. He won, of course – one of 165 professional victories worldwide, including seven majors – and was presented with a first prize of three leopard skins.

Snead, of course, was before my time. But I played Senior golf with his nephew Jesse, better known as J. C. Snead. We got on like a house on fire, cracking jokes and swapping stories. He was fascinating on the subject of Uncle Sam.

'Hey Sammy,' he suddenly says, 'I've got a black Labrador at home called Sam.'

'You are not going to believe this,' I countered, 'but I have a black Lab at home called J.C.'

The most astonishing element of the Bobby Jones story is that as an amateur throughout his career, who qualified in law and achieved honours at three different universities, he was not much more than a weekend golfer. He was a part-time player who won five US Amateurs, one British Amateur, four US Opens and three Open Championships, including his unique grand slam in 1930. It should be noted that as an amateur he was not allowed to play in the USPGA Championship and the Masters did not exist until he invented it!

Contemporary reports speak of him being a long hitter without a hint of trying to belt the ball. His backswing looked almost lazy. He got so keyed up during tournaments that he often was unable to eat anything and survived on whisky. He could lose as much as half a stone during four-round events. It seems that he was vulnerable to the stresses and strains of championship golf and retired at the age of twenty-eight.

I was standing on the 1st tee at the 1995 Ryder Cup, about to tee off, when I spotted Byron Nelson. I went over to him and asked if he would mind my having a picture taken with him. To hell with the time or the place – Nelson was a legend not just for his playing record, he was a golfer who appears on most lists of the greatest.

Nelson, who won five major titles, belonged to that select trio of golfers born within seven months of each other in 1912. Ben Hogan and Sam Snead were the other two. Nelson's annus mirabilis, indeed an annus mirabilis to set aside any other, was in 1945 when he won eighteen of the thirty-five PGA tournaments he entered, including a still unmatched eleven in a row. It is said that the fields were weak coming just after the end of World War II, but both Hogan and Snead were around and, in any case, you can only ever beat who is in front of you. And that is never easy.

My relationship with Lee Trevino goes back to 1972, the year he successfully defended the Open at Muirfield, when I was just eighteen. Jimmy Letters, the club manufacturer and a friend of my dad's (and now after all these years my club sponsor), fixed up a fourball at Dalmahoy, near Edinburgh, for me and Ewen Murray, now the lead Sky Sports golf commentator, with Trevino and Gary Player.

Lee and I were firm friends by 1985 when I holed the putt to win the Ryder Cup. 'I am glad it fell to you, Sammy,' Trevino, the US captain, said.

Trevino was much, much more than the master of the one-liner. He went from working as a five-year-old in the cotton fields of Texas to being a six-time major champion. He could move the ball in the air any way with any club from all distances with a variety of different shots. Speaking personally, he taught me the escape shot from a plugged lie in a bunker so well that I reckon I became just about the best in the business.

It's easier than it looks. You take the club back steeply and drop it down like an axe. But you don't have to hit the ball hard. It pops up in the air so gently and lands so softly that you can almost see the name of the ball in flight.

Tony Jacklin tells a story which illustrates perfectly the Mex's wisecracking ability. They met in the semi-final of the Piccadilly World Match Play Championship in 1972. A few months earlier at Muirfield Trevino had chipped in at the 71st hole to snatch a second Open title away from the English hero.

'I love you to death,' Jacklin said to his opponent on the 1st tee, 'but honestly I do not want to talk today. I just want to concentrate on my golf.'

'That's OK,' Trevino replied. 'I don't want you to talk either. I just want you to listen.'

Trevino, no doubt chattering non-stop as usual, played brilliantly in the morning to take a four-hole lead into lunch. Jacklin responded with a magnificent 63 in the afternoon yet still lost on the final green.

Just occasionally, very occasionally, you might get the better of Trevino. I had already lost a fourball and a foursome match to Lee on my Ryder Cup debut in 1981 when I was drawn to play him in the singles.

We bumped into each other in the hotel car park that morning. He was planning to go in a courtesy vehicle but I offered him a lift in my own car. We reached the end of the drive and instead of turning right for Walton Heath I swung left.

'Hey Sammy, where you going?' Trevino asked.

'Fuck you, Lee,' I replied. 'I'm going home. I'm out of here. Let's call it a half.'

Just for a second he was unsure. Then the arch wisecracker cracked up. I turned round. I wish I hadn't. He beat me 5 and 3 in the top match in about two hours. We were back in the clubhouse having a pint before Jack Nicklaus teed off in the 12th and last singles.

Years later on the Seniors Tour, as life sometimes dictates, we met in a hotel car park in Mexico. Trevino was waiting for a courtesy car.

'Hey, Lee, want a lift?' I asked.

Quick as a flash, he feigned horror. 'Hell, no, I remember what happened the last time I took a lift with you.'

Everyone has their own personal memories of people. When I think of Seve Ballesteros I think of him farting away like a trooper.

'Come on, Seve, that's disgusting,' I said, waving my hand in front of my face.

'I eat food, no flowers,' he replied, before breaking into that most infectious of smiles.

One of his earliest golfing victories came over Peter Thomson at Dalmahoy. The writing appeared to be on the wall when the young Spaniard sent his approach shot over the final green and behind a 10-foot-high mound. Thomson was already on the green in two. But Seve played a 'miraculous' recovery shot over the mound and straight into the hole to win the tournament.

'That was such an amazing shot that it could take you a million attempts to do it again,' an interviewer said to Seve during the subsequent press conference.

'Yes, but maybe only one,' he replied.

That was Seve. He believed he could do anything and often he did.

Who can forget the 3-wood he smote from a fairway bunker at the final hole of his singles match against Fuzzy Zoeller in the 1983 Ryder Cup? The distance (240 yards), the lip of the bunker, the equipment and the situation made it a shot of sheer genius, perhaps the best in the history of the event.

I saw him play a shot that intrigued me at the Irish Open at Royal Dublin in 1983. He was no more than 20 feet from the pin and maybe a yard off the green, needing to get down in two to win the tournament. The surface was as bare as a badger's arse. Every pro I know would have played the percentage shot and putted. Seve took a 9-iron and caressed the ball stone dead. The confidence, the nerve.

I was privileged to play seven Ryder Cup matches in the same team as Seve. I was lucky to watch this extraordinary man at work in his favourite environment. He loved the Open and the Masters, but he loved nothing more than beating Americans.

Seve disliked the country, many of their players, the food and the frequency with which announcers would call him Steve. He believed it to be a combination of ignorance and deliberate rudeness. Most of all, he hated how the American media labelled him 'the car park champion' after his great triumph in the 1979 Open at Royal Lytham. You drive the ball into one car park . . .

All these slights, perceived or otherwise, were repaid in full by his inspiring performances against the United States in Ryder Cup after Ryder Cup.

I will never forget the letter he wrote to the team and me in 2002 when I was captain. 'Dear Sam,' he wrote, '. . . I know they think they are the last Coca-Cola in the desert but you have a better team, a better captain, so go and get them.'

Although I did not always get on with Tom Watson, it would be very petty if I ignored him from a list of great players. He upset me at the official Ryder Cup dinner in 1993 when he wouldn't autograph my menu. He insisted that he had banned signature-seekers from the team table and did not want to make any exceptions. I was furious.

But my good friend David Feherty insists that Watson is a top man and that's good enough for me. He has certainly been a brilliant player with a brisk timeless swing and manner that has not changed throughout his career.

He has continued to play terrific golf into his late fifties and approaching his sixties. How astonishing it would have been had he, at the age of fifty-nine, managed to seal victory in the Open at Turnberry in 2009.

Everyone was willing him to win and I was no different. That would have brought him a record six Open victories and what would have been a ninth major.

Tony Jacklin

Sam on Tony: 'Tony was a big influence in my life in many ways. I remember near the start of my professional career in 1972 boarding a plane from London to Madrid. You had to walk through the club-class cabin to get to the back where the players usually gathered. Jacko was in club, of course. A few of the lads were trying to take the piss out of him as they passed. In my mind, however, that was where I wanted to be. Having won the Open Championship in 1969 and the US Open the following year, Tony was a hero to all young British golfers. Someone to follow and emulate. Later, he would transform the Ryder Cup as Europe's best ever captain. When it came to my turn he was a huge help and inspiration.'

During the early part of the week of the 1970 USPGA Championship in Tulsa, Oklahoma, Jackie Burke asked me if I would like to play a practice round with the legendary Ben Hogan. Burke had won the USPGA in 1956, the same year as he triumphed at Augusta. In fact, his Green Jacket hangs in the locker he shares with Tiger Woods, no less, as the gold nameplates on the wooden door indicate.

'Absolutely,' I replied enthusiastically. You didn't say 'no' to Mr Hogan. And you would not dream of missing the opportunity to play with one of golf's greats.

Hogan was then fifty-eight. Everyone in golf knows the story of how in February 1949 an overtaking Greyhound bus crashed head-on into his car; how he spent two months in hospital suffering from a double fracture of the pelvis, a broken ankle, a broken rib and a broken collarbone; how when back home, his legs bandaged from hip to ankle, he weighed just 95 pounds; how, despite being told that he might never walk again, let alone play golf, he returned to action in January 1950 to lose a play-off in the Los Angeles Open to Sam Snead.

How, limping and suffering from painful circulation problems, he memorably won the US Open that summer.

Scottish golf fans fell in love with the 'Wee Ice Mon', as they christened him, when he lifted the Claret Jug as Open champion at Carnoustie in 1953 at his first (and only) attempt. He had already won the Masters and US Open that year and was denied the chance of a unique (and impossible, as it transpired) grand slam because our Open clashed with the USPGA Championship.

Mr Hogan, as he always was, aka The Hawk, with those piercing eyes, high cheekbones and square jaw under that trademark white cap – always the white cap – captivated the Scottish galleries, which included, for one week only, a certain Frank Sinatra.

Sinatra, who bizarrely was playing to half-empty auditoriums at the Caird Hall, Dundee, watched daily as Hogan, still limping, put together improving rounds of 73, 71, 70 and 68 for a famous victory. He was said never to have missed a fairway that week.

Anyway, my practice round with Hogan, sorry Mr Hogan, was

arranged for 10 a.m. on the day before the start of the championship.

The invitation, via Burke, no doubt came because I was the reigning US Open champion. I had won the title – the first and still the only Englishman to do so since 1925 – at Hazeltine in Minneapolis. To say I felt at home there is an understatement – lots of the kind of blind shots you find on British links and 40 miles-per-hour winds that most of the field could not handle. I remember I shot 71 on that first stormy day, two strokes clear of the nearest challenger, while The Big Three of Arnold Palmer, Gary Player and Jack Nicklaus carded 79, 80 and 81 respectively.

The course had been the talk of the week. When asked how he found Hazeltine, Dave 'Mad Dog' Hill replied, 'I'm still looking for it.' He thought it would be improved by 'eighty acres of corn and a few cows'.

Lee Trevino, always good for a quip, commented, 'If anyone shoots 281 on this course, the Pope is a possum.'

Guess what my winning score was, possums?

The day dawned. I felt pretty excited at the prospect of playing with Hogan. I was on the putting green at about 9.30 a.m. when Terry Dill, the tall Texan who went on to become a lawyer and a politician, came up to me and asked, 'Hi, Tony, do ya'll have a game?'

'Yes thanks,' I replied.

'Do ya'll have four?' was his follow-up question.

'Let me check,' I said.

I went over to Hogan, who was also a Texan, on the other side of the putting green.

'Ben [it might have been "Mr Hogan"] do we have four?'

'Who's asking?' he responded somewhat gruffly.

'Terry Dill,' I responded.

'We're set,' Hogan said, before heading to the 1st tee. Burke and I followed and we teed off as a threesome. Dill was left on the putting green. I felt awful.

Five holes into the game, during which not a word was spoken about the incident, Hogan suddenly turned to me and said, 'He once came up to me before, you know.'

'What, where, who?' I stumbled.

'That Terry Dill.'

'Oh.'

'I was on the practice putting green. Do you know what he said to me? He said, "Mr Hogan, how do you prepare mentally for a major championship?" Do you know what I said to him?'

'No, what did you say?'

'Well, I said, the first rule I make is never talking to other people on the putting green.'

My how he laughed.

A game with Hogan and seeing him laugh. Now that did not happen every day.

Alastair Johnston

Sam on Alastair: 'A man I like and admire greatly apart from his football allegiance. I am a Celtic fan and Al is a blue-nose Rangers supporter through and through. In fact, the Glaswegian served as chairman of the club a few years ago. We tease each other mercilessly about

our football rivalry. Al has been associated with IMG
pretty much since he left Strathclyde University in the
late 1960s. He is now vice-chairman of the company in
the post-Mark McCormack era. But he is probably best
known for his long association with Arnold Palmer,
dating back nearly forty years. He is currently chief
operating officer of Arnold Palmer Enterprises. A
renowned authority on the game, he possesses one of
the most extensive golf-book collections in the world.'

I don't suppose many of you will know that the great Arnold
Palmer has an endearing habit of using the wrong word in the
wrong place. What is even more delightful about his occasional
lapses into the world of malapropism has been his refusal to
understand or acknowledge his error. He just does not get it.

Winnie, his dear departed wife, would correct his grammar
along the way, but she could do nothing about his infrequent
lurch into a decidedly dodgy choice of word.

I remember one memorable example, oh perhaps forty years
ago, when I spent some time with the wonderful couple at their
home in Latrobe. I had begun looking after his business interests
in the mid-1970s, a great time, when I might be jogging with
him at six o'clock in the morning or drinking beer with him at
ten o'clock in the evening.

'How long are you here for?' he would ask.

'Until you throw me out,' I would reply.

He liked that. All champions, no matter how grounded and
how humble, possess an ego and Arnie was no different from
many top-class sportspeople in demanding some undivided
attention. I was there to give him undivided attention. Of

course, we became great friends as well as colleagues and now I am chief operating officer of Arnold Palmer Enterprises.

Back to Latrobe. Winnie had brought out the cool drawer and the three of us were sitting down enjoying a few glasses of wine. We chewed the fat about many things, in golf and away from golf. That night we got to talking about Scotland, about 1960 when he came to St Andrews having already won the Masters and the US Open and how Kel Nagle foiled him from making the Centenary Open the third leg of his grand slam quest. That narrow failure remains one of his greatest regrets to this day.

He was reminiscing a little wistfully when suddenly he declared, 'I have got Scottish blood in me, of course.'

'No, you haven't,' I replied.

'Yes, I have,' he insisted.

There was no way this proud Scot was going to demur on that one. I knew my client.

'No, you have not. You come from the Balmers of Western Pennsylvania. You are German!'

'No, I'm Scottish,' he repeated. 'And I've known a lot of Scots before you.'

Whereupon, he proceeded to list the Scots he had met and known. He informed us that Latrobe Golf Club – where he first learned to play and which he now owns – had a Scottish professional in 1929, three years before his father, Deacon, took over the job. Ken Stewart was his name.

He was adamant. He was Scottish. Winnie laughed. I laughed. We all laughed. But Arnold would not give up on that one.

'Why do you think you are Scottish?' I asked.

'It's upstairs, I will show you,' he said. 'It's in my gynaecology!'

It was not even in his genealogy!

Arnold Palmer was idolised by Scottish golf fans, though, and he returned the sentiment with his love of Scottish golf courses. Nowhere matched St Andrews, where he became an honorary member of the R&A. Many's the time he would fly his own plane over to Scotland to take part in the Spring Medal.

His two Open Championship victories came at Royal Birkdale in 1961 and Royal Troon the following year.

The Open returned to Troon in 1973. I had just joined Mark McCormack's International Management Group. Arnold took a few of us out to watch a practice round. He was particularly keen to show us the plaque commemorating a particularly sensational shot that was regarded as significant in his victory.

'I can't remember where it was,' he said, hunting around the rough on the left of the 16th fairway. 'Where is it?'

'About 200 miles south of here!' someone replied.

The plaque lies in the rough on the 16th at Royal Birkdale, a reminder of the brilliant 6-iron recovery shot he hit from wet, thick grass in the most appalling weather.

I reckon that when you have won so many major championships, two Opens in successive years and hit countless swashbuckling attacking recovery shots in a glittering career you can be forgiven for a tiny memory slip.

Arnie's Army would forgive him just about anything.

Chapter Nine

Planes, Trains and . . . Caravans

Veteran golf broadcaster and journalist Renton Laidlaw tells a nice story about me loving travel so much I would spend some hours during the winter closed season in the terminal at Prestwick Airport near my Scottish home just to combat withdrawal symptoms. I'm not that sad.

It is true, however, that unlike many of my fellow professionals I enjoyed the actual travelling part of tournament golf. By land, air or sea, it did not matter to me, I relished the lot.

Setting out as a teenager I was terribly innocent and naive. I didn't know anything about life.

When I picked up my first sponsored car in York in 1972 and drove to London I was not sure if there were petrol stations in the centre of the city. So, I stopped at a motorway service station – and spent the next eight hours there. I had filled my petrol tank with diesel.

Life was such an adventure. My sponsor, wishing to make sure I was comfortable for my first tournament abroad, booked me into a lovely hotel that had just one drawback. It was a four and a half hour drive from the golf course.

I loved driving. I would drive up and down, like a whore's knickers, between Scotland and England. My first car was a VW, then I had a Fiat, then a Vauxhall from British Car Auctions. The first car I actually bought was a Ford Capri 3 litre, which went like stink. But I loved my Saab Turbo 99 with the starter button. If I shared with John O'Leary, as I often did, I insisted on doing the driving. I have never been a comfortable passenger.

David Chillas, the old Scottish pro with the blink-and-you-will-miss-it swing who has made a packet in the antique business, was the restaurant fixer, seeking out the best places to eat. Funny thing was that 99.9 per cent of the time he had prawn cocktail and fillet steak. My favourite was Chicken Maryland, but when I was an assistant at Sunningdale I ate at the local Chinese restaurant about 300 times in a year, always ordering chicken and sweetcorn soup and breaded chicken breast with chips. My tastes have since become more sophisticated.

That would also apply to Ian Woosnam, who in his early poverty-stricken days on the tour travelled by caravan, lived off chips and beans and on one occasion in France filled his practice-ball bag with apples. He ate so many in one day that he would have kept a hospital of doctors away had he not fallen ill from the unwashed fruit.

There was another fabled occasion involving Woosie. He and Joe Higgins drove from Scotland to Italy, would you believe, in a coughing and spluttering vehicle that eventually packed up in a street in Milan. At 5 a.m., Woosie hitched a lift on the handlebars of a passing cyclist to the nearest garage. A mechanic went to fix the broken car at a cost of 20,000 lira, i.e. ten quid.

The broadening of horizons served only to increase the sense of adventure. Having queued for visas, received our yellow fever and cholera jabs and begun our daily intake of malaria pills, we set off for Africa and the fabled Safari Tour. There we found oil and sand browns instead of greens, roadblocks, frequent power cuts and armed guards on the gates of the ex-pat homes where the players were often billeted. If the rebels did not get you, the dehydration would. But first you had to get where you were going. Never an easy task. I remember flying for twenty-four hours and being further away from my destination than I had been when I left London. That's what happens when you fly to Kenya via Zambia and Johannesburg.

One flight from Lagos to Yamoussoukro, which was supposed to take just over an hour, lasted nearly two days when you added in a night at an airport – the hotel beds were dirty and insect infested – and a long bus journey on uncharted roads at the other end. That was when there was a danger of us not getting home for Christmas. Nothing would have been worse than that.

We took in our stride – well almost – a tournament in Nigeria that coincided with a military coup. The practice was for the field to be split into three or four groups to play pro-ams at different courses prior to reuniting for the tournament itself. Three of the four pro-am venues were all within an hour's drive of Lagos, the capital. Chillas and I were among the unlucky ones who found ourselves upcountry in the middle of nowhere, with the airports closed and a 6 p.m. curfew in operation. Three of us, including a Swedish reporter, hired a taxi – a big Merc – for a trip that we were told would take two days. We planned ahead, booking a hotel we could reach prior to the curfew. We did not fancy being shot. However, we could not have planned for our driver brushing against a boy on his bike as we drove through a typical mud-hut village. Suddenly we were surrounded by locals brandishing spears.

I'm afraid my reaction was to laugh, as if we were in a road movie with Bob Hope and Bing Crosby. But the locals were clearly upset. And the smile was knocked off my face when I saw our terrified driver put his foot flat to the board and speed off as quickly as possible. By the time we arrived in Lagos the coup had been put down and normal service had been resumed. The first aircraft carrying golfers from our point of departure beat us by ten minutes. Our drive had been futile, but dramatic and crazy as this may sound, I really enjoyed the experience.

A party in the clubhouse or an early night was the choice that confronted me on arrival in Zambia. I was being met at the airport by the ex-pat couple that were putting me up for the week. I opted for the early night, of course. Actually, I did. So, they took me to their home while the husband loaded all the clubs in his car and headed to the course. The poor chap was held up at gunpoint. He never saw his car again and I never saw my clubs. But I did once see a dead man with an arrow through his back at the side of the road. I also saw spiders and snakes on the ceiling without a drop passing my lips. That's how fever can grab you.

The house-high termite mound and marching ants in the Copperbelt town of Ndola were no hallucination as Jack Newton discovered. He was forced to strip naked – any excuse – and jump into a lake to rid himself of the creatures.

Then there was the sight of President Kenneth Kaunda of Zambia personally serving guests with lunch after hosting an

Africa versus World match on his private 9-hole course at the State House.

The 1970s and 1980s in golf were pioneering days, and not just in Africa. I remember Renton Laidlaw regaling me with a story from Florence of how the press telephones had been installed in the women's showers. The echo was so bad that he stuck his head inside a cardboard box to create his own sound-proof studio.

You would think that by 1991 and in the good ole US of A, a simple journey between the course and the hotel would not cause too much of a problem. My great friend Queenie, almost never known as Michael King, discovered otherwise. He was trying to get back late one night from Kiawah Island during the Ryder Cup. He tells the story better than I do.

'We had taken several wrong turnings and ended up very much on the other – shall we say non-golfing – side of the tracks in deepest South Carolina. Here I am in a car with a pair of beautiful other halves, one blonde and the other brunette, and Peter Townsend, the former Ryder Cup player, fast asleep in the back. Dear old Peter, who only ever worried about where his next meal was coming from.

'It's 1 a.m. and I had been going round in circles for seemingly hours. I call into this petrol station and there are ladies of easy virtue hanging around and cut-throats of no virtue at all and I'm saying pathetically, in this terribly posh accent, "Hello, my name is Michael King from Sunningdale, I must go in and do what ladies do." Not a good move. Eventually, a state trooper's car comes behind me. I am definitely a good mark for someone. Rule number one in those circumstances is not to get out of the car. I get out of the car. I am staring at three guns.

"Hello, my name is Michael King from Sunningdale and I'm here for the Ryder Cup."

'He looks at the passengers and gives me a stare. "You're a bit out of touch here, boy," he says. The police car and the troopers, bless their black boots, guided us to our hotel. Peter wakes up, smiles and, oblivious to everything, asks what has been going on.

'I tell him with my usual measure of exaggeration that apart from his wife nearly being raped and the odd gun pointed in our direction, pretty much nothing.'

Des Smyth

Sam on Des: 'I love Smythie, or Desdemona as I sometimes call him. We have known each other since our early days on the Tour. And more recently we were nightly dining companions for the short period I played full time on the Champions Tour in America. I will never forget him telling me about the night his wife answered a middle-of-the-night phone call from their son, Greg.

"You've won the what?" he heard Vicky say, as she tried to wake up. "You've won what?" she repeated.

It turned out that Greg had won a cool €9.4 million on the Irish Lottery. As you do.

Des, from Drogheda where he still lives, won eight times on the European Tour and played in two Ryder Cups. He also has the distinction of having won pro tournaments in every decade since the 1970s.'

Planes, Trains and . . . Caravans

Back in the early 1970s when I turned professional we had to be very careful about money and it was by no means automatic that we would jump aboard an aeroplane for the journey to the next tournament. Business class was certainly out of the question.

In fact, at the start of my first full season on the Tour, 1974 to be precise, three of us decided to hire a car for a three-week, three-tournament 'swing', as it would now be called, on the Iberian Peninsula.

Big mistake.

It may have been Roddy Carr's idea. Roddy, whose subsequent career has included tournament promotion, golf-course design and even managing Seve Ballesteros, had played in the victorious 1971 Great Britain and Ireland Walker Cup team. Warren Humphreys, the third of the triumvirate, had been a member of that same team. I had enjoyed a less distinguished amateur career and was very much the new boy on Tour.

We had all entered the Portuguese Open (which Warren was to win in 1985) at Penina, the Spanish Open at La Manga and the Madrid Open in, er, Madrid.

Roddy hired the car from Joe Duffy, the well-known car-hire firm in Dublin. It was a Datsun 120Y, for the petrolheads among you. We christened it the Joe Duffy Express, though, in truth, the express element was a bit of a misnomer.

I was charged with picking the car up in Dublin, taking it on the ferry to Liverpool and driving down to pick up the other two in Twickenham. Roddy, son of the Irish golfing legend Joe Carr, was based in the south of England at that time, while Warren was a Surrey boy.

We set off, three suitcases in the boot and three sets of clubs on a roof rack, looking more like three mates on a boozy golfing holiday than three professionals heading on a business trip. We drove down through France and across the snow-covered Pyrenees on icy, narrow roads with sheer drops into the valleys below. I can tell you it was pretty hairy. But we were young, adventurous and full of a devil-may-care enthusiasm. We continued through Pamplona and on to Madrid where we stopped for the first time. By then we had been in the car for thirty exhausting (and smelly) hours.

Eventually, after God knows how many days, we arrived in Penina. We had kept costs down and we were ready to play. Or rather we were far from ready to play.

Move forward three weeks. Time to return home; time to take stock. Tournaments played: three; cuts made: zero; money won: zero; bouts of flu: three. Together, the three of us had not earned a penny. We drove home with nothing except experience, memories and one valuable lesson.

Always, always, prepare properly for tournament golf.

The three weeks were not entirely wasted, however. We had such a laugh and every time we have met over the last forty years we have had so much fun recalling our adventures.

Happily, my career progressed. In fact, like so many these days, I have enjoyed two careers, first as a regular pro and then as a Senior, the chance for the over-50s to make hay into the twilight of their competitive days.

One of my proudest moments came as Ian Woosnam's vice-captain in the successful 2006 Ryder Cup match in my native Ireland. Any delusions I might have entertained – and that was certainly not the case – about the role being a bit of a jolly vanished within minutes of the start of the first day. I knew I would be busy and I knew some difficult situations would arise.

First up was a mouthwatering tie between Colin Montgomerie and Padraig Harrington and the potentially crack American pairing of Tiger Woods and Jim Furyk. Tiger, you may recall, fired his opening tee shot into the lake on the left of the 1st fairway.

Woosie had asked me to go out with that first match. So there I was at the K Club, in my Ryder Cup gear, in my own official buggy, with the gallery singing 'Ole, ole, ole, ole' and Tiger's ball having already taken a bath in the nearby water. And there in the middle of the fairway stood Monty preparing to play his second shot. The same Monty who possesses the most sensitive antennae in golf.

My radio crackled into life. It was Woosie back on the 1st tee. I would need asterisks, exclamation marks and several ampersands to describe accurately and without offence what the captain said. Suffice to say that he wanted me to expedite the swift removal of an observer standing 30 yards directly behind Monty.

The trouble was that the offending spectator happened to be Sir Michael Smurfit, only the owner of the K Club, the man chiefly responsible for bringing the Ryder Cup to Ireland and someone accustomed to standing precisely where he wanted to. Actually, I need not have worried. Sir Michael, understanding the situation immediately, moved when asked and without complaint.

That week was memorable for so many things, including the emotional scenes surrounding Darren Clarke.

A personal memory for me – and something I could never imagine happening to a wee boy from Drogheda – was meeting two US presidents within the space of a few hundred yards and a few minutes. I was in my buggy at the side of the 6th when Bill Clinton jumped into the passenger seat for a wee rest. He was heading to behind the 7th green, so I offered him a lift. I was going there anyway. 'No thanks,' he said. 'It would not look right for me to be seen riding in a European team cart.'

When I arrived at the 7th green a few moments later, who should be there but George Bush. Introductions were made. Both men were perfectly charming.

Let me end with a Seve Ballesteros story. I was delighted to accede to Sam's request to contribute to this book, doubly so when he informed me that he was making a contribution to the Seve Ballesteros Foundation.

Seve played the greatest shot I ever saw. I can remember it as vividly now as when the Spaniard was strutting his genius stuff on the fairways and greens of the world. It happened during the third round of the European Open at Sunningdale. I was playing with Seve and another, I can't remember who. Sorry, whoever you are. Seve hit his approach through the 6th green on to a bank, leaving himself an 'impossible' third shot. The green falls steeply from back to front. There was considerable doubt that he would manage to keep the ball on the green.

He weighed up his options for a minute or two and then conjured up the most extraordinary shot I have ever seen. He took a huge divot, with the ball and the divot flying through the air together, landing a few inches on the green. Blow me but the ball popped out of the divot and rolled gently down to about a foot from the hole. No one else could have done that. No one else would have imagined such a shot.

We kneeled down and bowed to a true great.

Chapter Ten

The 19th Hole

Never mind the Ryder Cup or the major championships or the hundreds of professional tournaments around the world offering varying amounts of prize money, golf remains at its very heart a social game.

And since it is a social occasion it would not be unreasonable to have a drink. Golf even has a special hole for the purpose – the 19th! Also known as the 'dirty bar' or the 'spike bar', it is designed in its most basic form to accommodate players straight from the course who prefer to shower and change their shoes later.

OK, alcohol is not absolutely compulsory. You could sit there going over the round – the missed putts, the unlucky bounces and 'the best drive of your life' – drinking a John Panton or an Arnold Palmer. That's a ginger beer and lime, named after the old Scottish pro; or a half iced tea and half lemonade cocktail, named after the man himself. But there is nothing quite like a pint or two, or even more on occasion, after a game of golf. 'The pint and the punt are essential parts of Sam,' my friend David Feherty once said of me. And who am I to disagree with him?

Just occasionally, one drink turns into a session that can develop into a marathon binge. Let me tell you about one evening prior to the 1985 Ryder Cup, when I holed the winning putt.

The Tuesday prior to Ryder Cup week in 1985 saw the Tour roll up to Crans-sur-Sierre, an Alpine ski resort where the scenery is magnificent, the nightlife lively and the ball flies 10 per cent further than at sea level. A last chance to unwind, I thought, a view shared by others judging by the crowd that crammed into the George and Dragon that night.

One drink led to plenty more, which in turn led to me climbing on to the table, stripped to the waist, conducting the community singing. 'We're gonna fuck the Yanks, we're gonna fuck the Yanks, ee aye addio, we're gonna fuck the Yanks' we sang to the tune of that children's classic 'The Farmer's In His Den'.

As if on cue, in walked Tom Kite . . . and out walked Tom Kite. He had seen enough. His swift departure prompted a huge roar from the assembled gathering, which included a fair number of my Ryder Cup teammates. I punched the air and missed, hitting instead a whirligig fan, which took a chunk out of my hand. There was blood everywhere. I wrapped a towel around the wound and carried on, ignoring the fact that I might have done enough damage to threaten my participation in the forthcoming contest. All was well, as history shows.

Our victory in 1985, ending a barren period going back twenty-eight years, sparked off the party to end all parties, at least at that stage in Ryder Cup history. My good friend John O'Leary, a member of the European Tour board of directors, and I began a celebration that lasted the best part of four days, pretty much non-stop. Sunday night at The Belfry carried on until nearly dawn on Monday, culminating with everyone jumping into the swimming pool. A few hours' kip and we headed for London in a chauffeur-driven car, though only after a breakfast washed down by half a dozen bottles of champagne. We called in to see our friend Mike Kemble at his house in Woburn, a good reason to continue the revelry. That, too, lasted all night.

I first met Mike during a pro-am at Woburn thirty years ago when I spotted a well-endowed woman in the gallery. 'Look at the knockers on that,' I said. Of course, it was his wife. He is one of the so-called '12 Undesirables' who have been going to Spain for the same pro-am for the past fifteen years. Their wives got a bit fed up with this, so arranged to go for their own bit of fun the week before the tournament.

'It is a bit quiet,' Mike said to Alphonso, the barman.

'You should have been here last week,' Alphonso replied. 'There was a crowd of wild women here.'

Mike is the guy who found an entire Sunday dinner – meat, gravy, peas, potatoes, etc. in his golf bag. He is also the chap who was reading the newspapers in the kitchen one day when he saw the window cleaner laughing like crazy. Mike went up the stairs into his bedroom and found his golf clubs and caddie car on the bed with a sign on top that said 'You might as well sleep with them'.

On the Tuesday morning following our Ryder Cup victory I somehow got myself to Heathrow for a flight to Spain where I was playing in the Madrid Open at Puerto de Hierro. One of the best bits of a Ryder Cup victory is seeing all your mates who didn't make the team for the first time, feeling their enthusiasm and delight, and relating to them all the tales from the match. There was no way that Tuesday night was not going to be a big one!

A couple of hours sleep again and I managed to make my starting time for the pro-am on the Wednesday. Some drinks after the pro-am led to a few more and eventually another late night of merriment. By about 3 a.m. I could not physically get another drop of anything into my body.

The next day I teed off in the first round of the tournament and on the Friday I made the halfway cut. Outside of the Ryder Cup and a few tournament wins, that represented just about my greatest performance. To make the cut after four days on the sauce when I could barely stand up!

I am not the first professional golfer to step on to a course the worse for wear and I will not be the last.

It used to be said of American Jimmy Demaret, three times a Masters champion, that not only did he never practise, but he never slept. The surge in prize money and the awareness of physical fitness changed that sort of approach. As Fuzzy Zoeller remarked, 'The younger guys don't drink. They eat their bananas and drink their fruit juices, then go to bed. It's a miserable way to live.'

It used to be very different. I love the story from France concerning Christy O'Connor Snr, Himself as the Irish lovingly refer to him. He was partial to a glass or two, not so much a habit as a way of life which, I suppose, might have prevented him from winning more than he did.'Twas the World Cup, then known as the Canada Cup, at Saint-Nom-La-Breteche in 1963 and Christy woke up with a hangover of monumental proportions. Prior to teeing off he asked a favour of a London journalist.

'Can you bring me some coffee?' was the request.

The journalist rightly pointed out that it would not look good for Ireland's great champion to be seen staggering to the 1st tee carrying a jug of coffee.

'Fine then,' O'Connor pleaded. 'Can you fetch some coffee, some very black coffee, and head down the first to the 200-yard marker? From there march off sixty-five paces and wait in the woods for me.'

The writer agreed.

He acquired a pot of the black stuff – no, not that black stuff – and took up his position among the trees. He heard the crack of O'Connor's drive, the telltale sound of the ball penetrating the canopy of leaves and the thud as it landed within a few yards of where he was standing. Knowing the ability of O'Connor, the journalist was not too surprised. But he still judged it to be one of the greatest pressure shots he had ever seen.

If only I could have been as accurate finding the bathroom over the years as Christy was locating his pot of coffee. You see, I have this unfortunate history of waking up after a few, stumbling in the dark towards the toilet and finishing up out of bounds, in a cupboard or worse in a hotel corridor. There was, for example, the occasion when I was locked out of my room in Walt Disney World, Florida. O'Leary (again) and I were playing in a tournament there, though I found myself actually sharing one of those Polynesian Village rooms with Billy Longmuir. We had a few on the flight across and what with the jet lag we were sleeping it off in our beds during the afternoon. I got up for a pee and ended up in the corridor. The door had swung closed and no amount of banging on the door could stir Billy from his drink-induced nap. Fortunately, I was wearing swimming trunks as a result of going for a dip on our arrival. But I was in considerable discomfort. I looked up and down the corridor and spotted an alcove that I hoped would be a toilet. I made a dart in that direction only to discover an ice-making machine. However, by a room door there was a tray with a coffee pot and mugs on it. There was no alternative in my mind. I picked up the coffee pot and started to relieve myself when the door handle turned and the door began to open. I dropped the pot, ran out the fire-escape door, sped across the lawn and dived into the swimming pool where I hid to the utter puzzlement of the sunbathers.

O'Leary – there's a trend here – and I were staying in a hotel near Porthcawl in Wales during a tournament. We had enjoyed a good week, particularly John who was leading, if I recall, going into the final round. I was about 10th. So, we were on our best behaviour on the Saturday evening. The next day we were up bright and breezy but our good humour left us when we could not find the car keys. The car had been given to us for the week by a Sunningdale member. The trouble was that both sets of clubs were locked in the boot. There was no initial panic because we were both late starters and still had plenty of time. We had breakfast and paid the bill. Then we panicked. We were forced to take a crowbar to the boot to retrieve the clubs, which we threw into the back of a taxi. Not the best preparation when trying to win a tournament. Neither of us did.

I was walking towards the 9th green when I spotted the hotelier waving the missing car keys between his fingers.

'Where the fuck were they?' I asked.

The 19th Hole

It transpired that they had been found on a bathroom floor on the fourth floor. Our room was on the third floor. I must have slung on my jeans to go to the toilet and they had fallen out as I sat down. Just one of my wee wanders, I suppose. The strange thing was that we had a toilet in our room!

My nocturnal escapades did not always involve alcohol. One night I found myself, not for the first time, in a very hot hotel bedroom in Spain. I hate trying to sleep with the air conditioning on because of the draft on my neck. That night I could not sleep. So, I went on to the balcony, closed the sliding door and, not bothering to put any clothes on, sat down to smoke a cigarette. The view was stunning. Gradually, I began to feel the chill and headed back into my room. Except that the door was locked. Try as I might I could not get it open. I shouted and screamed and banged on the door but could not attract the attention of anyone. It was past midnight in a quiet area. I was stranded there for two hours, freezing my butt off. The thought occurred that I would have to smash the patio door with the chair. Fortunately, at about 3 a.m., I saw someone in the distance. It turned out to be well-known golf photographer Stephen Mundy, who raised the alarm. And, happily, he did not have his camera with him. The cold had got to me by then!

There was a time when I went on the wagon for twenty-two months. I had failed to make the Ryder Cup team in 1997, ending my streak of eight consecutive appearances. I was determined to win my place back in 1999. I lost 2 stone, maintained a strict training regime in the gym and got myself very fit. But I made little progress towards my objective and when I was forced to pull out of the Open at Carnoustie with a back injury I accepted the inevitable.

'I can't play in the Open, darling,' I said on the telephone to my wife, Suzanne. 'I'm not going to be in the Ryder Cup now. I know it. I won't be in the Open next year. Everything's gone, my career is over. I will be forty-six next month.' I was somewhat distressed.

'I think you should have a drink,' she said

'I think you are right,' I replied.

But I had my son, Daniel, with me. That night we sat on the rocks on the beach and had fish and chips. The next day we flew home.

I shared a bottle and a half of wine with Suzanne and a couple of cans of beer. That was enough after twenty-two months of abstinence. I was sozzled.

The word went out. Torrance was back on the booze. I was legless for weeks because of the number of drinks people wanted to buy me.

Michael King

Sam on Michael: 'Known to all his many friends in golf and beyond as Queenie. My best friend in life. We speak most days and play golf together most weeks. I first met him when I was a tousled-haired Scottish teenager working as an assistant at Sunningdale. Every day I would ask "young Mr King" if he had a game. He was my escape route out of the professional's shop and into money matches that would supplement my meagre income and stir my competitive juices.

Mr King became Queenie after the stock-market crash of 1974 forced him to shed his gentleman tag and turn professional. He had played for Great Britain and Ireland in the Walker Cup matches of 1969 and 1973 and would surely have turned out in 1971 had he not emerged from a flight back from an international amateur contest in New Zealand wearing a Qantas stewardess uniform. I am given to understand that it had been a flight of much merriment!

Queenie was a fine player, good enough to win the TPC at Moor Park and represent Europe in the Ryder Cup in 1979. Unfortunately, his career was cut short by ankylosing spondylitis, a debilitating arthritic disease. Just recently a new "wonder drug" has enabled him to return to the game he loves. He is always my partner. I never play against him, just as I have never played against John O'Leary and David Feherty. They just can't all be in the same fourball.'

The early days of a beautiful friendship could have been the final days of a beautiful friendship after one night in the Alpine resort of Crans-sur-Sierre. Sam and I had ensconced ourselves in a local bar prior to the start of the tournament and were playing cards. Gin rummy, if I remember correctly. What I do recall is that I was losing heavily, something like £500.

My only way back was to up the stakes. Sam agreed to my suggestion. I turned things around, won back what I had lost and began to make a few bob.

'Right, that'll do me,' I said. 'I'm off.'

This apparently breached the rules of gin-rummy etiquette. It was now up to the losing player to decide on the end of the contest. Sam was not amused. Actually, that does not do justice as a description of his anger.

Up went the table and over went the chairs in a reaction that had its origins in tribal behaviour found in the west of Scotland. I have to say that Sam had a point and he made it most forcibly. We were fine by the next day.

There was a postscript to that story. The following year's European Tour Book displayed a picture of two good friends, i.e. us, relaxing by playing cards during a tournament in Switzerland. Or so the caption suggested. We thought there should have been a 'What happened next?' aspect to the feature. The answer was bloody mayhem.

But that's not my story.

Both of us love Sunningdale Golf Club. I have been a member since my amateur days while Sam, who had been afforded courtesy as a pro, was invited to become an honorary member under the system of captain's prerogative. It was only natural that we would want to give something back to the club. So, the Sam Torrance Trophy is given to winners of the father and son tournament and the Michael King Trophy is awarded to the junior champion.

One year the club thought it a good idea to film the young Jonnies playing in the Junior Championship. Kids love seeing themselves in action. The idea was to show them all driving at the 1st, with the filming being done by the assistants from the professional shop.

There was a large crowd gathered in the clubhouse for the prize-giving – the young golfers themselves, proud fathers and mothers and other interested members. The atmosphere was one of excitement and expectancy. I stood at the back of the room, ready to present the trophies.

But first the video. The tape was inserted and the show began. And there on the screen was someone – a biggish fellow – giving a rather enthusiastic young lady a right seeing to.

What could a chap do but burst out laughing as shocked parents opened their mouths and young Jonnies opened their eyes to a piece of unscheduled sex education? The tape was removed. That was the longest walk of my life as I stepped forward from the back of the room to dish out the cups. I do not know if young Jonnie, now grown up, still bears the scars of that evening. But I do know the evening has never been spoken about since.

But that's not my story either.

The world had spun deliriously round to 2006. We are at the K Club outside Dublin for the first Ryder Cup to be staged in Ireland. Ian Woosnam, a good friend of us all, was European captain. There was no way Sam and I would dream of missing the occasion. To avoid putting pressure on those organising hotel rooms, we decided to accept a kind offer from Irish businessman Ben Dunne to stay in his magnificent house on the course. We would eat with the team and officials and, usually tired and very emotional, we would make our way back to Ben's house climbing – and occasionally falling over – a lovely trellis fence. That poor fence took some battering that week.

One night, fairly well lubricated, Sam tripped on the way to the front door and landed with the most perfect dive into a bush. It was the classic example of man falling into hedge. And sure enough the next morning the bush revealed the most perfect human imprint.

Out of Bounds

Later that morning I found myself where I should not have been, behind the 16th island green among a tiny handful of onlookers. I must have walked through security because there stood President George Bush.

'Have you met Queenie?' John Paramor, Europe's top referee asked Mr President.

We got talking. Specifically, we spoke about arthritis – his wife Barbara, like me, was a sufferer – and I told him how his country had saved me. How the Harvard Medical Center had come up with this really brilliant 'wonder drug' that improved my condition out of all recognition. It turned out that he had not heard of it and Barbara had not tried it. So I wrote down the details.

As we chatted, I asked him if he knew Sam Torrance. He did. Which is how I came to tell the president of the United States how I had pulled the former Ryder Cup captain out of one bush and then met another a few hours later. We had a good laugh. Sam was not laughing that evening when I told him the story of the two bushes.

A few weeks later I received a lovely letter from President Bush, written in pencil from his home in Maine, thanking me for the information on the new drug.

Meanwhile, I was still getting it in the neck from my best mate.

Brian Barnes

Sam on Brian: 'All anyone needs to know about the kind-hearted giant that is Brian Barnes is encapsulated in the following story. We had tied for first place in the 1975 Zambian Open and reached the first green of the play-off. Barnsie putted up to 9 inches, clearly concession distance. I bent down, picked up his ball and threw it to him. I went on to "win".

But this was a stroke play event and I should have allowed Barnsie to hole out. The officials wanted to give the tournament to Brian. He would have none of it. He absolutely insisted. "It's Sam's tournament. He beat me fair and square." As a huge friend of President Kenneth Kaunda, who he called "Dad", believe it or not, his word went in that part of the world.

Barnsie possessed a huge talent which might have brought him even greater honours than he achieved but for his liking for a tipple. As it was, he won nine European Tour events, including the national titles of France, Holland, Spain, Italy and Portugal, and played in six Ryder Cups. He will also always be "the man who beat Jack Nicklaus twice on the same day".

A lovely man and a true gent, I love him to death.'

The Tia Maria and milk was to blame.

Jamaican Cow, I think they called it. We had never heard of it, at least not unless preceded by the word 'that'. Sorry, not very pc. Anyway, that was the name of the cocktail that did for Sam on the eve of the 1976 World Cup. (Sam swears it was the previous day.)

Sam was making his debut. I had played the previous two years and was to make a fourth, and final, appearance in the event in 1977. Obviously, we were very proud to represent our country. But it was at a time when things were a little more relaxed than now. We were much more accessible to the fans, much more matey with the media, much more relaxed about being seen to enjoy ourselves. Players would frequently dine with reporters, sharing a few drinks without worrying about hacking, and I don't mean in the golfing sense.

Many were the functions at team events when we were required to sit with the punters. I invariably wore the kilt on such occasions, especially when representing Scotland. Sam preferred to wear trousers. Not everyone has my legs. I know, thank God.

But I convinced Sam to wear the kilt. And I arranged for the *Scottish Daily Express* to kit him out with the full works – kilt, dress jacket, waistcoat, garters and long woollen socks, not forgetting the skean-dhu. We probably could not get the dagger through Customs these days.

The event was staged at Mission Hills in Palm Springs. It was bloody hot which, as you will soon discover, is relevant to the story.

The gala dinner on the eve of the competition saw each country host a table made up of the two players and ten golf fans.

Each team was introduced as they took their seats. I suggested to Sam that we hang back till the end to make the grand entrance. The Yanks like nothing better than a couple of Scotsmen in their kilts. As we walked into the room, the band struck up 'Scotland the Brave'.

'The night drave on wi sangs and clatter,' to quote Sam's fellow Ayrshireman, Rabbie Burns. Everyone was having a great time. That was when the locals introduced us to what proved to be a potent combination – Tia Maria and milk. Never mind the land of milk and honey – for that night, at least, it was the land of milk and Tia Maria!

Then I did something out of character. I went to bed. At about 11 p.m., if I remember correctly. I'm a man, you may recall, who was known to enjoy a drink or two. I'm a man who has been known to mark his ball on the green with a beer can. (Official-dom did not like that.) I'm the man who liked to drop into the Clydesdale Mobile Bank during the Northern Open – an early-season Scottish tournament they sponsored for many years – for a heart starter at the beginning of my round. Just to ward off the cold, you understand.

Anyway, I was lying in bed watching the television when Sam staggered (Sam says marched) into the room looking and feeling slightly the worse for wear (Sam says he looked great and never felt better).

Kilt wearers will know that the removal of the tartan is not a difficult manoeuvre, provided you remember to untie the buck-les. Once undone, it is really just a case of stepping out of it. That night, Sam forgot to undo the buckles, he failed to let go of the kilt and, while attempting to walk from the garment, tripped up. He fell into the wardrobe with all the majesty of a sturdy

Scots pine crashing to the forest floor. And there he lay. Much laughter ensued.

Eventually, he got up and went to bed. But that was not the end of it. He lay on his side, leaning on his elbow, trying to talk to me. What was I watching? That sort of thing. But he was falling asleep and, as he did so, he slowly, ever so comically, fell out of bed on to the floor. Christ, I laughed. We both did.

We were both bright and breezy on the 1st tee the following morning. Well, that's a bit of an exaggeration. To be honest, Sam was looking a bit green about the quarter gills. I always remember Sam facing an 18-inch putt on the 1st green – the ball never touched the hole.

But we quickly got into our stride and were scoring quite well despite the oppressive heat. This was long before the time when medical advice would have insisted on us maintaining our fluid intake with a constant supply of bottled water. But I was thirsty and the sight of a concession stand at the side of the 13th fairway seemed like an oasis in the middle of the desert. And this proved no mirage.

I bought myself a beer and walked down the fairway on to the green with a bottle of the cold stuff in my hand. I like a beer, as you may know. I liked to wear shirts with big breast pockets in those days. So, I stuck the bottle into my pocket and holed a decent putt for a birdie two. I would have been fined had it happened now. In truth, I got into trouble on other occasions for quaffing the sponsor's product on the course.

Back to Palm Springs. I was walking from the 18th green at the end of the round when a guy asked me if I had liked the beer. Like millions around the world, he had seen my beer birdie on television.

The 19th Hole

'It was great,' I replied. 'Not too strong. Very thirst quenching in this heat.'

The stranger introduced himself as the West Coast manager for Coors, if I remember correctly. He asked me if I would like to have a few beers during the week. Guess what my reply was?

The next morning we turned up on the 1st tee to be met by two dolly birds and a buggy full of ice-cold beer. For the next three days, the buggy followed us around, breaking away only at the turn to replenish the stock. Before you become alarmed dear reader, we did not drink the lot ourselves. We gave most of them away to the fans who flocked to see us in increasing numbers as the word got around. By the end of the week we attracted the biggest gallery, bigger than the winners Spain (represented by a young Seve and Manuel Pinero) and bigger than the runners-up, the home American combination of Jerry Pate and Dave Stockton.

I felt like the Pied Piper of Palm Springs.

As I said, the European Tour would have come down heavily on me if I had behaved like that in the modern era. I remember well the first time I was fined, an occasion of considerable notoriety that has gone down in the annals of tournament golf.

It all happened at the French Open in 1968. I had just finished in a tie for sixth at the Open Championship at Carnoustie, including a ruinous third round 80. It was my practice always to take the week off after the Open in order to recharge the batteries and avoid the feeling of anticlimax. I invariably found it very difficult to raise any enthusiasm in such circumstances. But in 1968 there was pressure for me to play in France. So, I did. I was doing all right, I had hit a couple of really nice shots when I got to the par 3 8th at Saint Cloud. I struck a nice shot in there but underclubbed and landed in the bunker right in line with the flag. I splashed to about 4 feet from the hole, leaving a friendly right to left putt for par.

As soon as I hit the ball I knew I had not taken enough borrow. As the ball passed the cup I tried to drag it back and started playing hockey with the moving ball. No one was quite sure how many times I hit it and how many penalty shots I incurred for hitting the ball as it moved. But one of my playing partners, George Will, and I settled on a score of 15. That was more than enough for me. I picked the ball up and with a brief apology of 'Sorry, fellahs', I walked off the course.

The European Tour had not yet been formed. So, I was summoned to the Oval Cricket Ground by the PGA for the disciplinary meeting. It was no surprise that I was found guilty of bringing the game into disrepute.

I was fined the princely sum of, wait for it, £25.

Chapter Eleven

The Majors

T he Open Championship has a history that no other major championship can match and it is our very own. And I love it.

But there is no question that because the Masters returns every year to an Augusta National with which we have become so familiar thanks to television, it possesses a certain unique magic. A golfer needs only to think of Amen Corner, that trio of holes from the 11th to the 13th, to feel a special thrill. I played the Masters three times and, despite returning on several occasions as a BBC commentator, I remain in total awe of the place.

The first time in 1985 (Bernhard Langer's year) was, of course, very special. I went a week early with my caddie and good friend Brian Dunlop. We literally dumped our luggage in the hotel and headed straight to the course. The drive up the 330 yards of Magnolia Lane to the clubhouse was everything people say it is, almost a mystical experience.

I introduced myself to the professional who could not have been nicer. He showed me where everything was, told me there was no one on the course and urged me to go ahead and have fun. I went through the usual process, though with an extra awareness that comes of a determination to save the memory: into the locker room to change my shoes, out to the practice range to hit some balls, on to the putting green for a few putts and finally to the 1st tee. Out came the pro, to wish me well I presumed.

'Sorry Mr Torrance, you can't use your own caddie until next week,' he said. 'If you wait here a few minutes I will send one of our caddies round.'

The caddie arrived and I was ready to go. Or so I thought. Back came the ultra-polite club professional.

'I am very sorry again Mr Torrance, but your caddie is not allowed to walk round with you.'

Poor Brian, he is in Augusta all week and he can't get on to the course. As is often said about Augusta National – and there are some who dislike the famous club because of its rules, regulations and attitudes – they do things their own way.

There is a story that says much about the place and about the late Clifford Roberts, the Wall Street investment banker who, as co-founder and chairman of Augusta National, ruled the club in the manner of a benevolent despot.

Among his areas of control, which covered pretty much everything, Roberts had complete authority over membership. If he decided that you were no longer going to be a member, you were history. No discussion, no appeal.

When one of the select few members telephoned to arrange a visit and a stay in one of the cabins, he was put through to

Roberts who informed him that his membership had been cancelled.

'For what reason, Cliff?' the astonished man asked.

'Non-payment of your bill,' Roberts said abruptly.

'But I never received a bill,' the member protested.

'Precisely,' Roberts declared, before hanging up the phone.

I had reached the 11th of my first practice round and needed a 7-iron for my approach. (It was a lot shorter in those days!) The caddie got into a panic as he could not find it. It turned out that someone had been looking at my clubs, taken one out for closer inspection and returned it to the wrong bag. It was eventually returned to me.

When it finally came to Monday and Brian could join me, we had a great week. As to how I played, not bad at all, and my final position of joint 31st would have been even better if I had not played the downhill dogleg left par 5 2nd in 7 and 6 on the first two days. I should not complain since I eagled the same hole in both the third and fourth rounds!

You might want to know how I played the famous short 12th, which goes by the name of Golden Bell (all the holes are named after flowers indigenous to the area and that are found on the course). It is an extraordinary little golf hole that plays not much more than a 9-iron, yet its complexities are compounded by an ever-changing, swirling wind. The great Jack Nicklaus always aimed within the width of the front bunker, regardless of the pin position, and never hit the ball until the flags on the 11th and 12th were blowing in the same direction. His six Green Jackets would suggest he knew what he was doing.

I wish I had been there the following year when he won at the age of forty-six. More precisely, I wish I had been standing behind the tee at the short 16th when he struck his shot.

'Be the right club,' his son Jackie Jnr said, who was his caddie that memorable week.

'Don't worry, it is,' the great man said, bending down to pick up his tee and not even glancing at the ball's flight.

Bert Yancey, Tony Jacklin's great friend, certainly had the 16th taped. In 1967 and 1968, despite never challenging, he made eight consecutive birdie twos at the hole.

And as for how I played the12th: mostly pars, two birdies and once in the water in the first round in 1994. I finished in a tie for 33rd that year as Jose Maria Olazabal won the first of his two Masters titles. I was joint 39th in 1997 when Tiger Woods won his first Green Jacket by a margin of 12 strokes. And to think I turned down the chance of nine holes practice with him as much out of fear as anything else. I could have passed on my knowledge of the course to him!

Ike's Pond on the par 3 course. Ike's Tree at the 17th. The Eisenhower Cabin. President Dwight D. Eisenhower, Supreme Commander of Allied Forces during World War II, loved his golf and he loved Augusta. He installed a putting green on the White House lawn and was said to have been mainly responsible for doubling the number of people playing golf in America.

My first of twenty-seven consecutive appearances in the Open, the greatest championship in the world, was at Muirfield in 1972. I tied for 46th as Lee Trevino lifted his second Claret Jug in a row and, in the process, rather broke the heart of Tony Jacklin. My main memory that week was less what I did than what I saw up close to some of the greatest players the game has produced. I remember, for example, Arnold Palmer walking on to the putting green, swathed in cashmere, with the kind of deep suntan only acquired by the rich and successful. He looked like a bull. I had goosebumps the size of golf balls all over my arms.

By Carnoustie in 1975 I was ready to challenge rather than just gawp. I was on the fringe of contention prior to the final round, which I played, as it happened, with good friend and fellow Scot Brian Barnes. I recall hitting the 1st green and having an 18 footer for a birdie.

'Save it till it counts,' Barnsie rather mysteriously said.

I thought if it does not count now, it never will. I never got close that day but I did beat Brian.

In 1976 at Royal Birkdale I played the first two rounds with Jack Newton and Johnny Miller, who went on to win when at the height of his magical powers. No one ever hit the ball closer to the stick than Miller in his heyday. But my dad was not happy with either of them. I lost a ball at the 16th in the second round and was forced to trudge back to the tee to hit another. I can trudge for Scotland when it is not going well, though don't be misled by the head constantly down; that is not despondency, just me keeping a lookout for rabbit holes. You can easily go over on an ankle on a golf course.

Miller and Newton played their second shots to the green. Dad thought they should not have left me on my own and should have waited for my second drive. I never thought anything of it. I was in the Open playing with Miller and Newton. I was as happy as a pig in shit.

A lot happier than the R&A officials who certainly did not see the funny side of the Maurice Flitcroft Story.

Flitcroft, you may remember, was the crane driver from

Barrow-in-Furness who duped his way into Open qualifying at Formby in 1976 when claiming to be a professional. He had, in fact, only ever knocked balls around a local beach.

He carded a 121, triggering a frenzy among the British press. 'I have called about Maurice and the Open Championship,' one reporter stated, announcing himself to Flitcroft's mother.

'Oh my, yes,' she replied, 'has he won?'

To the embarrassment of officialdom, Flitcroft repeated the deception on two more occasions: he managed 9 holes and 63 strokes as Gerald Hoppy, a Swiss professional in 1984, and in 1990, disguised and purporting to be American Gene Pay-checki, he lasted a couple of holes of regional qualifying at Ormskirk GC in Lancashire before being escorted from the links.

Turnberry, 1977, the famous 'Duel in the Sun' between Tom Watson and Jack Nicklaus. It was a bad week for me, a bit of a blur really. My gran, my father's mother, had just died and the funeral was scheduled for the afternoon of the Thursday, the first day of the championship. I made a mistake in asking for a morning start time so I could attend the funeral. It was not the done thing. I teed off in the afternoon.

My personal memory of 1979 at Royal Lytham, Seve's first victory, was hitting my opening shot at the par 3 to 6 inches from the flag on the way to an 85, my worst Open score. You might think this is a strange thing to say, but I was not good enough for those types of courses.

I holed in one at the 16th in the final round in 1981 before finishing in a tie for fifth, my best ever placing. I thought at the time that if I could finish birdie, birdie at Royal St George's I might put some pressure on leader Bill Rogers who still had the back nine to play. The weather was pretty wild.

But I missed my birdie and double-bogeyed the final hole. I drove into the right rough, pulled my second left into the up slope of a greenside bunker and was faced with a difficult third to a pin on a shallow third tier with out of bounds a few yards away. It was a tough shot that I could have played conservatively to try to save par, but I played the pitch deliberately thin trying to hole it, a much harder shot. It went through the green and I took three more to get down from there.

My mate John O'Leary was impressed that I went for it. 'Don't ever lose that,' he said. I like to think I didn't.

I love St Andrews. It is strange; like so many I had no idea where I was going the first time I played the Old Course. But it gets better and better every time I have played it and I have played it countless times now.

I may have finished fifth at Sandwich in 1981 and ninth at St Andrews in 1984, but it was a return to the Old Course in 1995, John Daly's Open, that offered me what I remain convinced to this day amounted to my best opportunity in the championship.

That was my best year on Tour. I was playing brilliantly. I eventually had to give best to Colin Montgomerie in the Order of Merit but only after the race came down to the final hole of the final round in the final counting tournament.

I had by then forged a long and still-surviving relationship with the broomhandle putter that saved my career. But the longer putter tucked under my chin has never been much good in the wind. That final round it blew a fair bit. And my challenge was blown away when I three-putted three greens and, would you believe it, four-putted another in a crushing run between the 7th and 10th, the very stretch where it is essential to gain strokes. I finshed joint 11th.

My Open run ended in 1999 when a pulled stomach muscle forced me to withdraw before a ball was hit. I was not that bothered since I had already discovered in practice how Carnoustie had been ruined by a combination of ridiculously narrow fairways and inappropriate thick rough. My last Open was in 2000 when, sadly, I missed the halfway cut.

The rules governing world golf are very different now to the way they were during most of my career. I did not play in the USPGA Championship until 1991 – two decades after turning pro – and in the US Open until 1994. My 16th and 21st finishes in the US Open suggested what I might have achieved in that major. I loved the US Open and had the game for it. The courses were usually set up to punish bad shots and reward good ones. That has always seemed to me the right test.

John O'Leary

Sam on John: 'Jack or Johnno, as I called him, was just about my best friend on Tour back in the 1970s and 1980s. He labelled me "The Hairy One" for obvious reasons, though he switched to another nickname after my victory in the 1979 Colombian Open (when I beat the great Lee Trevino). I became Elsie after a picture of me appeared in a local newspaper above the caption "Elsie Torrante". I never did understand that.

O'Leary was Charlie Charm, a fine-looking man with

a twinkle in those piercing blue eyes. The more mature among you will remember that ridiculous pair of black and white trousers – one black leg and one white – a fashion faux pas that only he could have pulled off.

As a sparring partner of the mischievous Jack Newton, O'Leary would occasionally behave in a manner, shall we say, not entirely to the liking of officialdom. Like so many of us, however, he transferred successfully to the dark side as a long-standing and valued member of the European Tour board of directors.

Johnno's greatest triumph on the golf course came at Portmarnock in 1982 when securing the Irish Open title. He remained the last Irishman to win his own Open until Padraig Harrington's victory in 2007.

We shared a room on Tour for ten years, in the days when prize money did not allow the extravagance of individual hotel bedrooms. He may have been a charmer but he was a horrific snorer. It was imperative to get to sleep first or there was no chance. That said, I had a cunning plan involving the bedside table that would usually separate our two single beds. When he was asleep and growling away, I pulled out the drawer, slammed it hard and then pretended to be asleep. He would wake up not knowing where he was or what was happening. That was my chance to get to sleep before him.'

As Sumrie Fourball champions, a now defunct modest little title we won at Queen's Park, Bournemouth in 1974, Jack Newton and I thought we could take on the world.

Actually, that's a bit of an exaggeration. But Newt the Beaut, as the typically bold Australian was known in the press, feared no one on (or off) a golf course and when he saw Jack Nicklaus and Tom Weiskopf setting off on a practice round together the week before the 1975 Open Championship at Carnoustie he just could not resist the temptation.

'Hey, Jack, are you up for a game?' Newton called out as we caught up with the two American golfing giants on the 2nd hole.

Nicklaus had won thirteen major championships at that stage of his career, including that year's Masters. Weiskopf, who had lifted the Claret Jug in 1973, strangely his only major success, was pretty much at his peak. He had been runner-up to Nicklaus at Augusta three months earlier.

Nicklaus and Weiskopf were in the habit of coming over to Britain the week prior to the Open and getting in a few practice rounds. I later discovered that Nicklaus would rarely keep a score on these occasions, preferring to concentrate on how he was going to tackle the course when the real action started. That would explain why he politely declined our challenge. Well, Newton's challenge really.

But the stubborn Aussie was in playful mood. A gallery of a couple of hundred had gathered as word spread that Nicklaus was in town. The Scots love their golf and those who could – and those who really shouldn't have – made their way to the links.

Newton made sure the spectators heard as, speaking in stage whispers, he started badgering our American cousins. 'You're supposed to be the two best players in the world but you're afraid to play us,' he joked, if memory serves me correctly.

Although Nicklaus and Weiskopf had every reason to be pissed off, they retained their decorum. Newton, meanwhile, birdied the 3rd (our first hole as a quartet) and rolled in a 30 footer for another birdie at the 4th.

Newton picked his ball out of the hole, looked over at Nicklaus and said, 'Do you want a press?'

A 'press', for readers not familiar with the special betting terms in golf, is a second bet which begins during the course of a round, joining and running concurrently with the original bet. Newton was offering Nicklaus a press before a match had even been agreed.

Nicklaus, who was facing a much closer birdie opportunity, fixed Newton with those penetrating blue eyes and gave him the kind of look that Tony Soprano reserved for the eventually dismembered Ralphie Cifaretto.

'Jack,' Nicklaus declared, 'we're not two down yet.' And with that he nailed a 10-foot putt for a matching birdie. The game was on. We decided to play $10 (always dollars) automatic one-downs, the sort of friendly wager that would be played of a Sunday morning at clubs around the world.

Weiskopf later told us that Nicklaus took him aside on the 5th tee and, almost shaking with anger, said, 'Tom, I want you to try like you have never tried in your life. We are going to bury these guys.' He had never seen Nicklaus as intense in a bounce game as he was that day.

To continue the *Sopranos* metaphor, they took us apart, limb by limb. The golf they produced was unbelievable. I have never, ever, ever seen anything like it. Nicklaus and Weiskopf, who were to win two out of two when paired together in the Ryder Cup, produced twelve birdies and an eagle, including a hole-in-one, over the next 14 holes. We were massacred.

It was Weiskopf who aced the difficult par 3 8th, though you would never have known it by the polite applause that greeted the shot. With Nicklaus already on the green, Weiskopf aimed straight at the pin, which was mostly hidden behind some mounds. When we reached the green there were only three balls visible. We began to search, to no avail until Nicklaus checked the hole and found Weiskopf's ball nestling in the cup.

Everyone was dumbfounded, not because of the hole-in-one but because no one in the gallery thought to mention it.

'Can you believe it?' Nicklaus said to Weiskopf. 'You made a hole-in-one and nobody said anything.'

Weiskopf later told the story – perhaps as an embellishment, though knowing the Scots perhaps not – about how Jack (Nicklaus, that is) walked over to these two old natives perched on their shooting sticks.

'Were you there when Tom hit his shot?' Jack asked them.

'Aye, Jack,' one of them replied.

'Did you realise it went in the hole?'

'Aye, Jack,' came the reply from the same guy. 'But this is only a practice round, isn't it?'

Never was I so thrilled to lose a fourball. The experience was worth a lot more than the $90 I had to hand over as my share of the bet. Or rather, I didn't hand over.

We were delving into our wallets when Nicklaus suggested we buy lunch instead. We agreed readily, knowing that another hour or so in the company of the great man would merely add to the experience, something to tell the grandchildren. Off we trotted across the road to the old Bruce Hotel, where the best players and the officials stayed during a Carnoustie Open.

Nicklaus was in great form. We hung on his every word. Personally, I was so glad that Newton had been such a pain in the ass, goading The Golden Bear into making us eat humble pie.

Nicklaus did not even eat that much. His lunch consisted of an ice cream. Nothing more. I can't remember the flavour.

Chapter Twelve

Groundhogs, Fire Hoses and Electricity Cables

The best practical jokes take planning. And the best practical jokers are prepared to go that little bit further.

It was not enough, for example, for the late, much-missed Payne Stewart to exchange his keys for David Feherty's. Nor was it sufficient for Stewart to let himself into the Ulsterman's room and let loose a groundhog. He somehow managed to get the groundhog to don a pair of Feherty's underpants.

That's what you call a practical joke.

Mark Roe, the Tour's most tumultuous prankster in my day, believes less in an eye for an eye and more in a full set of dentures for a tooth. There was the notorious occasion when Russell Claydon, ironically known in Europe as Tinkerbell, got more than he bargained for and probably more than he deserved.

'I was sitting beside Tinkerbell on the short flight to Holland for the Dutch Open,' Roe recalls. 'We usually sat together because we played a lot of Scrabble on aeroplanes. I was reading – and very much enjoying – Michael Crichton's *Jurassic Park*. I remember going to the toilet at one point.

'Anyway, we arrived at the hotel at Hilversum late on Monday night and I settled down to finish the book. I read a few pages and turned over to discover the last chapter was missing. It had been ripped out. I knew immediately who was to blame. It had to be Claydon, that 20-stone pile of irritation. I was not happy.

'I was not at all happy. Swift retribution was called for but it did not need to be a knee-jerk reaction. I knew his room along the corridor and I knew that because it was Tuesday he would be getting up at 8 a.m. for breakfast.

'I set my alarm for 7 a.m. and camped out in the corridor outside his room beside one of those huge fire hoses. The kind with the 2-inch gauge attached to the wall, not a little fire extinguisher as I have subsequently read in various reports of the incident. I sat and waited.'

Players were apparently walking past, nodding at Roey, perhaps saying 'Good morning' but not batting an eyelid. It was Roey on manoeuvres. They would know something was up. They would know it was about to kick off.

Roe again. 'I waited for the door to open and I let Claydon have it. I could not believe the force with which the water came out. It knocked him across the room, soaked his clothes and his suitcase, flooded the entire room and even dripped down to the floor below. There was mayhem. Randy Fox, the travel guy, had a lot of explaining and apologising to do to prevent the management from throwing us out. Claydon took it in good part. He could give it and he could take it.'

He had to. He may have dished some out over the years but he was also a regular victim. One time the terrible twins, Roe and Robert Lee, dismantled the big man's bed and reassembled it, I think, on the balcony.

All you heard was Claydon shouting, 'Where's my fucking bed?' He liked his bed.

Even more of my generation was David Jagger, a master of the practical joke. He could plant a carefully calculated rumour and watch it grow into mayhem. Once, playing at La Manga in southern Spain, we were all really pissed off that there was no flight home that night. Everyone is always desperate to get home as soon as any tournament finishes.

Worse still, the first available flight was not until Monday afternoon, a disaster for family men who valued their days at home during a long season of pretty constant travel. The buzz went around that a jumbo jet was coming in from Florida and would depart for London at 4 a.m. Great news. By 2.30 a.m. it seemed that the whole hotel had assembled in the foyer, packed and eager to board non-existent buses for a fictitious aeroplane. Everyone except Jagger, that is. Guess who had started the false rumour?

The same Jagger, who perhaps a little bizarrely won the Nigerian Open three times, was also responsible for an evening of chaos at the Calatrava Hotel in Madrid. I stayed there for twenty years or so and thoroughly enjoyed the comfortable informality of the place. We would help ourselves to our room keys, which hung on a board behind reception.

This proved too much of a temptation to the Yorkshireman. Jagger removed all forty keys, jumbled them up and returned them all to the wrong hooks. It took ages to get everyone into their right rooms.

Out of Bounds

As much as I admire Colin Montgomerie, I liked to wind him up on occasion. He was a good target. Although possessing a lively sense of humour, his exploding tendencies made him ripe for torment. I remember at one of those ten-man shoot-outs in Sweden, Malcolm Mason, my caddie, got hold of a credit-card thing that made the noise of a mobile phone. This was too good an opportunity to miss. The crowds were huge as ten players were reduced to one, with players dropping out as the exhibition progressed. Every time Monty reached the top of his swing I pressed the button on the device in my pocket. He was going crackers trying to identify which spectator was using a phone. He never did find the culprit.

Monty was also the victim of Phil Mickelson, whom I had never thought of as being a prankster, but this story from Arnold Palmer's event at the beginning of the 2000s suggests a high mischief level. Phil apparently arrived at Bay Hill having read an interview with his friend Colin. Colin had complained about poor tee times and lesser-known playing partners, and that his start times were nearly always either too early or too late and this, he thought, contributed to why he had never won a PGA Tour event. Phil acquired some headed PGA Tour stationery and wrote an official-sounding letter reminding Montgomerie that PGA Tour policy was to pair winners with fellow winners in the first two rounds, generally not at extreme tee times, and if Monty wanted to remedy the situation he should try winning a Tour event. The phoney letter was placed in the Scotsman's locker to be read the following morning.

Mickelson made sure he was around to see the reaction. He watched with delight as Monty muttered and spluttered his indignation, aiming the brunt of his verbals at caddie Alastair McLean, as he was the nearest person around.

Eventually, Phil gave himself up. I would have loved to have been there to witness the explosion, then the laughter.

I also like the story involving Justin Leonard, who despite a dry sense of humour is not the most obvious practical joker. But the word is he pulled off a beauty during the 2009 Presidents Cup match in San Francisco. Leonard had apparently missed a short putt amid some controversy and was absolutely steaming. No one spoke to him; no one dared go near him. Leonard knew this and he anticipated a very uncomfortable atmosphere in the team room when he eventually walked in.

So, he hatched a quick plan in which he enlisted the help of Fluff Cowan, Jim Furyk's caddie. He asked Fluff to line up on the bar five shot glasses filled with cold tea or water. And at the end a cold beer.

In walked Leonard to the expected silence. Nobody knew what to say. Leonard marched to the bar and started knocking back the shots. He was deadpan about it, slamming each glass down with great drama like the meanest, hard-drinking cowboy in a western movie.

Leonard has never been a drinker. The occasional beer, perhaps. His teammates sat speechless as he drank the lot, including the beer. No one was more surprised than his open-mouthed wife Amanda who, like everyone else in the room, was completely taken in by the stunt. Leonard wanted to show everyone he was ready to return to the fray.

The aforementioned Roe and Lee were not to everyone's taste, but you have got to admire their deviousness and ingenuity. We were at a tournament on the island of Albarella, just south of

Venice, which did not allow any motor vehicles. So, most of the lads rented bicycles. As you can imagine there was much hilarity with handlebars being turned around, saddles being removed and chains tampered with. The lovely John Bland, being one of the most senior guys on Tour, got himself a tricycle. The younger crew found this hilarious. Daily, Blandie would speed back from the course to the hotel, a route that right at the end involved negotiating a gap between two concrete bollards. It was a tight fit.

I don't know how they did it, but Roe and Lee narrowed the gap and positioned themselves in the hotel to see what happened. Blandie came scooting round the corner as usual and caught the back wheels of his tricycle on the bollards. There are those who witnessed the crash who swear that Bland shouted the names of Roe and Lee as he went flying through the air. Fortunately, he was not injured.

Revenge, they say, is a dish best served cold. But, as Jack Newton demonstrated, it can also be served with the finest port. His great mate Ian Stanley, known in his native Australia as the Clown Prince of Golf, was sipping from his post-dinner drink when he noticed something staring at him from the bottom of his glass.

Newton, who lost his arm and the sight in one eye in a terrible accident, had surreptitiously dropped his glass eye into Stanley's port.

Stanley fell off his chair while everyone else fell about laughing.

Mark Roe

Sam on Mark: 'A total prankster, one of the mad men of the Tour, Mark used to be nicknamed Thrush. As crazy as his behaviour sometimes was, Roey has always been immensely likeable. I have played dozens of very enjoyable rounds with him.

I have to say he has never targeted me with one of his elaborate practical jokes just as I have never tried to do him "in cold blood". There is just too much mutual respect between the two of us. Both of us recognise it would be too dangerous, the revenge might be too much.

Mark won three times on the European Tour, twice in France and once in Spain, but became known to a much wider audience when disqualified for a scorecard error in the 2003 Open Championship. Mark behaved with such dignity when it was discovered that he and Jesper Parnevik had not swapped cards before the start of the round. But the punishment was thought to be so severe that the R&A subsequently changed the rule.

Since retiring Mark has become an integral part of the Sky Sports commentating team as well as a highly respected (and highly rewarded) coach of the short game.'

W e used to say, 'If you are in the game, you are always in the game, the game never ends.'

The game had very little to do with golf. The game was played by bored – some would say boring – like-minded pranksters who in the days up to the start of a tournament would try to 'do someone in cold blood' as they say, and test each other's tolerance to the limit. The usual suspects included my old mate Robert Lee, Russell Claydon and me. Barry Lane and Gordon Brand Jnr were also fully paid-up jokers.

When I aimed a fire hose at Claydon and flooded his hotel room in Holland, for example, I was merely getting him back for something he did to me. If you dish it out, you have to be able to take it. Rule number one. The only rule, really.

Of course, what we now in our more mature years consider over-the-top irresponsible behaviour would sometimes impinge on others. The worst of several food-throwing incidents involved an innocent French family, a poodle and some pretty messy spaghetti bolognese.

We liked to eat well and always sought out the best restaurants in the area. Lee was there, as was Claydon and, if my dodgy memory serves me well, Mark Davis, a two-time winner on the European Tour from Essex whose career was curtailed through injury.

Claydon ordered the Dover sole, I went for a bowl of pasta. His fish looked beautiful. I have no idea why, but no sooner had the waiter deposited his plate on the table than he picked up the piece of lemon and squeezed it in my eye. Now that hurts. That hurts a lot. I was in agony. When I could focus again, I picked up my steaming bowl of pasta and threw the whole lot over his face. With deep regret, I have to confess there was considerable collateral damage.

A very elegant woman was sitting at the next table with, presumably, her two teenage daughters and the family poodle. And, of course, she had to be wearing a white trouser suit. I am afraid to say the white suit took a hit. The woman was quite rightly furious. Her teenage daughters thought it a hoot and laughed hysterically. The dog, meanwhile, tucked into one of the best dinners of his life. He lapped up every morsel. This one took a good deal of sorting out. Apologising profusely, we bought the family dinner and covered the cost of the dry-cleaning bill.

It looked as if my reckless antics were going to cost me more money on a visit to Glasgow for the Scottish Open. Haggs Castle was a very decent venue that suffered a little from having the practice range on some rugby pitches adjacent to the clubhouse. There were floodlights down the side, maybe 150 yards away and 50 feet in the air. By the time Lee arrived I had found my range, worked out the best trajectory and was shaping swinging hook shots in the direction of my target.

'What odds will you give me on taking out one of those floodlights first shot?' I asked Robert.

'No way, any odds you like,' he replied.

I put a ball down and with a 4-iron hit this perfect bendy shot that smashed into a floodlight and sent shattered glass in all directions.

'That's unbelievable,' an open-mouthed Robert said.

'What odds if I do it again with a second ball?'

'Don't be so silly.'

I took another ball and hit exactly the same shot into the casing where the glass had been broken.

'That's outrageous,' my giggling friend remarked.

The following week I arrived at the French Open to find an

envelope in my pigeonhole. Inside was a letter on headed Glasgow City Council notepaper saying that I was responsible for deliberately smashing a floodlight and that I was required to send a cheque for £300 to the local authority. I went ballistic. I was muttering away about how I could be charged when a practice range was located beside floodlights. I was about to storm into the Tour office when Robert smiled and told me to hold on a minute. I knew immediately. He had arranged the whole thing.

By the way, despite his recollection suggesting otherwise, Robert was very much to blame for the notorious television cable incident at Lake Como. I did not start it. I was in my bed asleep because of an early tee-off time the following day. He came back at about midnight and insisted on putting the television on. I turned it off. He turned it on. I turned it off again. You get the drift. I did, however, take a pair of scissors to live electric cable and I did end up rummaging about outside trying to find the piece of cable that I had thrown out of the window.

We obviously had a thing about electricity. Robert and I removed all the fuses from everything electrical in Barry Lane's room ensuring that nothing worked. Later that day we saw the hotel handyman in the corridor. He'd removed the ceiling panels and was pulling away at the wiring as he sought to discover the problem.

Barry was also involved in a bit of tit for tat that was fairly typical of what went on. He had thrown the gauntlet down when he tore off the ear of my beloved Garfield driver cover and put on a piece of sticking plaster. It was a present from my girlfriend. I was enraged, so I sneaked into his room and went through his entire wardrobe for the week cutting out the gussets of his underwear and chopping off the toes of his socks. He took it fine.

Robert, whose memory is about as selective as mine, is right about one thing. I did not have the best record with cars. My dad was a car dealer and for a while I was a car basher. I wrote off so many that when I phoned home from a tournament my mum would say 'It's not the car again', before enquiring about my score.

There was an Austin 1800, a great car, which I drove through a wall at the golf club when demonstrating handbrake turns in the ice. I wrote off an Austin Princess on the narrow coastal road between Sandwich and Deal. I am sure the national speed limit of 60 miles per hour applied but 60 was too fast for the hump-backed bend that I missed. The car flew through the air and on impact the engine came through the bonnet. I think Robert and Martin Thompson were in the car at the time.

My first buy was a black Ford Escort XR3i, which went like stink. I loved that car. I was at Robert's house one day with the car when he started mucking about with a scooter doing wheelies and the like. He lost control and flew across the bonnet, taking a huge gouge out of the bodywork. He thought it was funny. I was horrified.

'Roey, so sorry, I'll get it fixed in a couple of weeks unless of course you write off the car in the interim,' he said.

I had a bit of an accident on the Sheffield bypass the following week. I telephoned Robert. 'Do you want to know the good news or the good news?' I asked.

'You've written it off!' he exclaimed.

The game never ends.

Robert Lee

Sam on Robert: 'Robert Lee, now a respected golf presenter with Sky Sports, could "go low", as they say in golf when describing a player with the capacity to put together terrific rounds. He shot 61 twice at Monte Carlo in 1985 and in Portugal two years later. On both occasions he carded 27 for nine holes. Rab, as I call him, won twice on the Tour, in Cannes in 1985 and Portugal in 1987. In his playing days he was one of the inveterate pranksters, with his great friend Mark Roe and Russell Claydon being the other members of a terrible trio. Now, as he sits in a Sky studio, a Mars bar would not melt in his mouth! My father taught Rab for a while.'

Before I tell you a story involving my old mate and fellow Sky Sports commentator Mark Roe, Chubby Chandler the prominent golf and cricket manager, a pair of scissors, an electric cable and a wet bathroom floor, let me tell you about a football match between sides captained by Seve Ballesteros and Bernhard Langer.

The year was 1984, the venue was El Saler in Valencia, one of the very best courses in Europe, and we were playing in the Spanish Open. Sunday saw Langer produce one of the greatest rounds in his career, one that still maintains a prominent position in the annals of European golf. Starting the day 7 strokes behind leader Howard Clark, Langer carded a 10 under par 62 in tough conditions to win by 2.

The brilliant German is no Franz Beckenbauer, however, as we discovered not long after the prize-giving ceremony.

With no flights home out of Valencia that evening, a football match had been organised between a Spanish side skippered by Ballesteros (who else?) and a Rest of Europe team led by Langer. Although just a bit of fun, the word spread and 2,000 spectators turned up.

It is at this stage that I must mention Philip Parkin. Parkin, some readers may not know, was a brilliant but eccentric young golfer whose career was curtailed by eye trouble. His victory in the Amateur Championship in 1984 earned him a spot in the 1985 US Masters, after which he turned professional. No one was surprised when he was named Sir Henry Cotton Rookie of the Year.

Parkie, in particular his big hitting, caused a bit of a stir at Augusta, to say the least. Jack Nicklaus, Arnold Palmer and Ray Floyd, a threesome not easily impressed, watched open-mouthed as the Welshman fired balls over the fence at the end of the practice range. Maybe there was a bet on, but they urged Parkie to try from a point as near the bleachers as possible. Still he cleared the fence.

Parkie, who now does some television commentary, possessed amazing spring in his body. I have seen him throw a golf ball on to a green from a distance of 140 yards. He would have made an amazing baseball pitcher!

He was also very fast. So quick, in fact, that you might imagine he would have caused considerable trouble to a makeshift Spanish defence, to the left-back in particular.

There was a problem. Parkie could not cross the ball while moving at speed, indeed while moving at all. He had to stop himself – no easy task – turn 90 degrees and only then could he attempt a cross. Let's just say there was little threat from that area.

Langer assumed the role of midfield general, except that he was more of a midfield sergeant. While clearly boasting a Mercedes engine that drove him up and down the pitch for the duration of the game, he was somewhat lacking in skill and creativity.

What can one say about Seve? We could be charitable and say that football was not his game. Or we could simply say he was useless. As you might expect, however, Seve insisted on taking every free kick and every corner. It was his bat and ball, so to speak.

The match finished 2-2, after which four of us picked up a startled, increasingly infuriated Ballesteros and ran towards the pool with the intention of depositing him in the water. You should have seen him wriggle. It was all we could do to keep a hold of him. Worried that we might slip or trip at the edge, injuring a golfing genius, we decided in those few seconds to jump in with him without letting go. He was incandescent.

He was also a pro, bless his memory. Seve emerged from the pool, clocked the cameras and flashed that million-dollar smile.

Moving not so swiftly on to the Italian Open at Lake Como. I was sharing a room, as usual, with Mark Roe who – you might not guess from that upright figure of respectability on Sky Sports – used to be quite mad. An eccentric, a practical joker, game for a laugh, others can describe him how they wish. I prefer 'barking'.

Groundhogs, Fire Hoses and Electricity Cables

Late one night, with both of us in bed, like Eric and Ernie only in singles, I was speaking to my missus on the phone. The television was on and Mark was holding the remote control. He increased the volume. I spoke louder. He increased the volume another notch. I spoke louder still. The volume went higher and I could not hear either myself or the wife. Of course, he ignored my pleas to turn down the sound. Eventually, I gave up.

The time came for him to phone home. I had the remote. That was the cue for me to turn up the volume. Mark would have been unable to contemplate the equity in his receiving a taste of his own poison.

Suddenly, he jumped out of bed, bollock naked, grabbed a pair of scissors and cut through the cable connecting the television to the electricity. He was illuminated in a shower of sparks and gave the appearance of being surrounded by a halo. I thought he was a goner. But he was fine. The scissors weren't so good. They were buckled and soldered to the cable.

The cable was also a goner as he picked it up and flung it out of the window in the general direction of Lake Como, shouting, 'That'll fix you.'

Roey had also fused all the lights in the hotel. I pointed out that had he not been so hasty I could have fixed the problem the following day without anyone knowing any better. Whereupon, he disappeared outside and spent fifteen minutes in the dark clambering around the vegetation before returning with the broken lead.

The next day we bumped into Chubby who was staying at the same hotel. He revealed how he had got back to his room late, slightly the worse for wear, and headed for the toilet for a much-needed pee. All of a sudden the light went out and unable to see anything in the pitch black he made quite a splash, in a manner of speaking.

I am pretty sure that it was also at Lake Como where the aforementioned Parkin nearly got himself lynched.

Parkie had gone to bed at 7.30 p.m., as was his wont. Come midnight, he was still not asleep as outside a throng of Napoli football fans were going ballistic. I think there had been a big match against Milan.

At 12.05 a.m. – the timing is important – Parkie filled a bucket of water and poured it on the blue and white bedecked hordes below. Only he was spotted doing it.

At midnight the electric doors had been closed. That, and a stubborn night concierge, kept the sodden baying fans from exacting whatever revenge they had in mind.

Chapter Thirteen

Getting Lucky

Professional golfers have been known to decide in advance to split any prizes for holes-in-one. Sometimes the proposition is put and accepted, on occasion declined.

Ronan Rafferty was my opponent in the 1984 Hennessy Cognac Cup third and fourth place play-off between Scotland and Ireland. An £8,000 car was available for a hole-in-one at the 120-yard 4th.

'Do you want to split, Sam?' Rafferty, who had the honour, asked as he walked on to the tee.

'No, that's all right, go ahead,' I replied.

Rafferty had taken a couple of practice swings and was addressing the ball when I changed my mind. 'Sorry,' I interrupted, 'but I will share, if that's OK.'

The Irishman, only marginally miffed that I interrupted his routine, agreed and proceeded to hole his tee shot! I am not sure he was that thrilled. As it happened, I very nearly holed mine for a half.

Holes-in-one are like sex – you remember your first and your most recent and the rest are a bit of a blur. My first ace came at the 5th at Routenburn in my hometown of Largs. I remember it well because it was reported in the local newspaper under the headline 'Eleven year old son of Routenburn pro gets hole in one'. Snappy, eh?

That might have caused a problem at the local Stevenson Institute where I went straight from school every winter's day to play snooker. You had to be fourteen to get in. But Mary Beck, the 4-foot tyrant who ruled the hall with a cue of steel, liked me and continued to welcome my custom.

My latest competitive hole-in-one came at Slaley Hall in a Senior event. I have had one since in a friendly fourball at Sunningdale. Those of you out there still trying for your first hole-in-one will probably be horrified to know that I have no idea of my tally. I would guess about twenty.

I note that Jack Nicklaus, Gary Player, Arnold Palmer and Tiger Woods all boast around the twenty mark, give or take a few. Sam Snead made thirty-seven holes-in-one in his career, including one with every club in his bag except a putter. He even holed-in-one with a 3-iron using only his left hand.

Walter Hagen, however, a winner of eleven major championships, had only one in his life – curiously with a 1-iron and using a ball bearing the number one!

My favourite hole-in-one came during the 1981 Open Championship at Royal St George's. There are few greater thrills than achieving an ace in front of packed stands in your own Open. It happened in the final round at the 16th, the same short hole that cruelly denied Thomas Bjorn his moment of major glory twenty-two years later. The pin was in the same final-day position near the cavernous bunker on the right.

When I saw my ball disappear into the hole I dropped my 7-iron to the ground and ran to grab playing partner Lee Trevino. I put my arms around him and lifted him into the air.

'Watch my back, Sammy,' Mex screamed, fearing further damage to his chronic back problem.

Trevino, as it happens, is something of a hole-in-one specialist if the measurement is by reward rather than frequency. Forget the car worth eight grand. Chicken feed.

Trevino holed-in-one in 1987 at the annual Skins Game at PGA West. Playing with Jack Nicklaus, Arnold Palmer and Fuzzy Zoeller, Trevino aced the 167-yard 17th, a hole known as Alcatraz because of its island green, to pick up $175,000. They were playing $35,000 dollars a skin and there were four carry-overs by the time they reached that hole. Throw in a couple of cars and you can understand why his caddie Herman Mitchell, a 22-stone character, grabbed him and said, 'Thank you, Santa Claus.'

Trevino dwarfed that haul in 2001 when winning what is claimed to be the most amount of money for a single shot. His hole-in-one at the Par-3 Shootout at Treetops Resort in Michigan earned him a mind-blowing $1.09 million, half a million of which he donated to the St Jude's Children's Research Hospital in Memphis.

All manner of studies and field tests have been undertaken over the years in an attempt to determine the odds against someone achieving a hole-in-one. Once in New York, 1,409 players with holes-in-one behind them were gathered together. Each golfer was allowed a total of five shots at selected par 3s in the city, giving an aggregate of 7,045 shots. No one holed-in-one.

As further proof of the requirement of a measure of luck, there was no hole-in-one when an American pro by the name of Harry Gonder stood for more than 16 hours, hitting 1,817 balls at a 160-yard hole. He had two official witnesses and caddies to tee and retrieve the balls and count the strokes. His 1,756th shot struck the hole but stopped an inch away. This was his nearest effort.

Results of studies vary but by averaging some of the figures I have seen it would appear that 3000-1 covers the approximate odds against a professional golfer making a hole-in-one. About 67 million-1 for two in a round.

Multiply that again – by how many I have no idea – for the extraordinary scenario of someone holing-in-one at consecutive holes. That is what John Hudson did in the 1971 Martini International Tournament at Royal Norwich Golf Club. He used a 4-iron for the 195-yard 11th and a driver for the downhill 311-yard par 4 12th. John finished ninth in the event and received a cheque for £160.

Holes-in-one are as old as golf itself. The earliest recorded was in 1868 at the Open Championship when Young Tom Morris aced the 145-yard 8th hole at Prestwick. The first televised hole-in-one came in 1967 at the Dunlop Masters at Royal St George's. I can remember the *Grandstand* football scores being interrupted to show Tony Jacklin at the 16th (my hole) in good old black and white. Lionel Platts had the distinction of recording the Open's first televised hole-in-one at Royal Birkdale's 4th in 1971. I have the vague recollection of a ball bouncing on the back of a bunker and rolling 20 yards across the green into the hole.

Arguably the most famous hole-in-one, captured live on television, involved one of the greats of golf. Gene Sarazen, one of only five golfers to have won all four majors, made one last trip to take part in the Open Championship at the age of seventy-one. He played at Royal Troon in 1973.

Troon can be a monster of a course. But its most famous hole is the diminutive 8th, just 126 yards long and known throughout the world because of its small green surrounded by bunkers as the Postage Stamp. Sarazen missed the halfway cut, of course, but not before playing the Postage Stamp twice without using his putter.

Sarazen, accompanied by Irishman Fred Daly and Englishman Max Faulkner, Open champions all, choked down on a wee 5-iron into a slight breeze. The ball landed on line, hopped a couple of times and jumped into the hole. The crowd went potty.

The next day, encouraged noisily by spectators to repeat the feat, Sarazen dumped his tee shot into the sand before amazingly holing his bunker shot for a birdie two. A newspaper captured his feat beautifully with the headline 'Sarazen Licks Postage Stamp'.

Sarazen was not alone in holing-in-one at the Postage Stamp that week. Amateur David Russell (DJ, as he was known after turning pro) did likewise, with the result that the youngest golfer in the field emulated the oldest.

The Ryder Cup has produced six holes-in-one over the years. I witnessed one first hand. Costantino Rocca and I had been hammered 6 and 5 by Jeff Maggert and Loren Roberts in the afternoon fourballs on the first day of the 1995 match at Oak Hill Country Club, Rochester, New York. We returned the next morning to thrash Maggert and Davis Love III by the same margin in the foursomes. We were already 3 up boarding the 6th tee.

Tino asked me about the wind. He wanted to hit a 6-iron but I persuaded him to go with a half 5-iron. The ball started 2 or 3 metres to the right of the flag and drew nicely into the target. He is such an emotional man – so am I – that I might have expected his reaction. He gave me the bear hug of all bear hugs. I thought my balls were going to come out of my ears.

But I have never seen Tino since without a wee cuddle. The bonding from Ryder Cups lasts forever.

Contrast that with the incident at Augusta's famous 12th hole at the 1947 Masters. Butch Harmon loves to tell how his father Claude holed-in-one at that focal point of Amen Corner while playing with no less a great than Ben Hogan. Hogan himself managed a birdie two.

'You know, Claude,' he said to his playing partner, 'that's the first time I have birdied that hole in six years. What did you have?'

With anyone else other than Hogan you would swear the tale was a tall one.

There's cock and there's bull. But I am kind of tickled by the fact that the North Korean Ministry of Information claimed that their beloved dictator Kim Jong-il managed eleven holes-in-one during his first round of golf!

A fast learner, eh?

Howard Clark

Sam on Howard: 'The best Ryder Cup partner I ever had. I will never forget the impromptu jig we danced on the 15th green at The Belfry in 1985 when Howard rolled in a sweeping right to left 60-foot putt, which

was made all the longer and more difficult by having to negotiate three tiers. That proved the key moment in a 2 and 1 defeat of Tom Kite and Andy North. Ever since then we have called each other "partner". Howard, who won twelve European tournaments during his career, finished inside the top 30 of the Order of Merit for fourteen years in a row between 1976 and 1989. You would never know from his placid manner on Sky Sports that he could be a tortured player in his playing days, one of those who gave the impression of wearing his spikes inside his shoes. And what about those yellow trousers!'

It was never easy being Howard Clark's caddie. There were many occasions when my caddie could do nothing right, at least in the eyes of someone who tended to blame others for his own mistakes. I have to admit I was pretty hard on them, almost as hard as I was on myself.

My best ever caddie was Lawrence Heraty, a Chicagoan who came with a good reputation having worked for the likes of Greg Norman, Tom Watson and Bob Shearer. Boasting a full name – a first name and a second – was fairly unusual at a time when many a caddie went merely by their nickname. For tax reasons, you understand – they did not want to pay any.

I remember one Epsom-based character called Yorkie Bill, who liked to keep me updated on his mail.

'Hey Clarkie,' he would shout from a seat in front of the club-house, 'look what Maggie sent me.' Maggie, of course, was Prime Minister Margaret Thatcher who, as far as I am aware, did not personally send Yorkie Bill his weekly giro.

Anyway, Lawrence teamed up with me at the start of the 1978 season. Our first three weeks together saw me win the Portuguese and Madrid Opens and in between finish runner-up in the Spanish Open to Brian Barnes. That little run earned me around £23,000, if memory serves me correctly. And Lawrence received his percentage. We were working well.

Later that year – though it might have been 1979 – we were at the Jersey Open. I was either leading or very close going into the final round. Now, Jersey is a small place where everyone pretty much knows everyone else. There is a good social scene, especially during the week of the Jersey Open. Lawrence, as I later discovered, received an invitation to an all-white party, which was not as nasty as it sounds. The guests attending the Saturday-night shindig were expected to wear all white, not the easiest of dress codes for a caddie struggling with washing facilities on the road. A dirty-white party would have been better for the guys.

I was blissfully unaware of any of this come the morning of the final round. I reached the course at about 10 a.m. for a 12-ish tee time. I was in the last group. Lawrence was nowhere to be found. I asked around but no one had seen him. I decided to head off to the practice range, which was about 3 miles from the course. A minibus was provided for the journey.

We were still using our own practice balls, still sending our caddie down the range to collect them. Without Lawrence, I could not risk going through the clubs and trying to retrieve them from the different distances. That would have been too dangerous. So, I stuck to one club, hardly the best preparation for someone trying to win a tournament.

Half an hour from tee-off, by which time I had moved to the practice putting green, there was still no sign of the missing caddie. I asked around. No one had seen him, either that day or the previous evening.

Ten minutes to go, with Tony Jacklin and Queenie (Michael King) about to tee off, I asked if anyone else was interested in carrying my bag. Just then I saw Lawrence poking his head through an archway. Sheepishly, looking like shit, bleary eyed and beery breathed, he approached me.

'What do you want to do?' he asked.

I told him that he should take the bag, make a start and, after negotiating the first few tricky holes, he could tell me where he had been. I hit my approach into a greenside bunker at the opening hole but made a nice up and down to save par. I birdied the 2nd, parred the 3rd and hit a nice drive at the 4th.

'Right, what happened?' I asked as we walked down the 4th fairway.

He told me about the party and the problem he had had finding something all white to wear. He found a solution, of sorts.

'I had nothing remotely suitable so I ripped a white sheet from the bed in my digs and wrapped it round myself like a toga. And off I went,' he explained. 'I wasn't there long when a young lady came up to me and asked what I had under my toga. I asked her if she would like to find out. She said "Yes" and suggested we could talk about it over a gin and tonic. The next thing I knew it was 11.45 in the morning.'

He swore blind he could not remember if he had had a good night or not.

I did not win the tournament – Brian Huggett did – but understandably I did not sack Lawrence. He was too good a caddie. Apart from that aberration – and you could say it was understandable – he never put a foot wrong. Eventually, Lawrence returned to the States and the last I heard he was caddie master at La Costa Resort in California.

As for Sam, he will always be 'partner' to me. That's what we have called each other since our Ryder Cup playing days. We played together in five teams and were paired five times in four-balls and foursomes.

I remember our first foursomes together at The Belfry in 1985. Sam wanted to play the odd holes and our practice was geared to that, with plenty of time devoted to rehearsing the likely shots I would face at the various holes. I was happy to take a lead from the more senior man.

Walking to the 1st tee, he turned to me and said, 'By the way, do you mind taking the first drive?'

Sam, one of the most fearsome match-play golfers when a bet is involved, was a bag of nerves. The Ryder Cup can do that to you. It can do that to anyone.

Chapter Fourteen

Club Chuckers and
Temper Tantrums

Y ou only have to be aware of the fuss that is made every time Tiger Woods slams a club into the ground to appreciate how temper tantrums have largely disappeared from golf. 'A bad example to the young' is the familiar refrain, and fair enough. Television cameras miss very little these days. The same can be said of the rest of the media, who just love a bit of controversy. They are never happier than when lecturing people on bad behaviour.

Of course, losing your cool – whether throwing a club or throwing a fit – is rarely good for your game. John McEnroe might have raised the level of his performance after throwing a wobbly, ruining the concentration of his opponent in the process, but that kind of behaviour does not really work on a golf course.

I did have a temper when I was young but woe betide me if my father ever saw me throw a club or anything like that. I have broken a club on the ground as a professional. A temper can show how much it means, but it is about controlling it and turning that into adrenalin and aggression. That's the key, as Monty would say.

If I sound somewhat sanctimonious on the subject, don't worry. I love the old stories about club throwing as much as anyone, not least because of the humour involved. You can frown at the behaviour but also laugh at the antics.

No chapter on temper could be written without mention of the fabled Tommy Bolt, Terrible Tempered Tommy or 'Thunder' Bolt as the press christened him. Despite being a sweet swinger and a player good enough to win the US Open in 1958, Bolt seemed destined to be notorious for his bad behaviour rather than famous for his achievements. Still, he was good enough to be elected to the World Golf Hall of Fame in 2002.

'Throw it, throw it,' galleries would shout at Bolt.

'They want to see me blow my top – and I'm sorry to say I've obliged them,' Bolt said with apparent regret in his voice.

Clubhouses still reverberate to the sound of Tommy Bolt stories, at least among the more venerable members. But they are rarely not worth the retelling and I make no apology for including here some of the more memorable ones.

Bolt's own favourite has been told so often and in so many different forms, but the horse's mouth (and memory) is probably most reliable, so below is the version he gave in his acceptance speech when becoming a Hall of Famer.

'I was playing in the Bing Crosby Pro-Am at Pebble Beach,' he recalled. 'I had about a 135 yards left for my approach to the 16th green. "It's either a 3-iron or a 3-wood," my caddie said, adding without pause for breath and in the most deadpan fashion, "those are the only clubs you have left."'

My own favourite occurred at the Masters or the Los Angeles Open, depending on which of the numerous accounts you wish to believe. Bolt was obviously in one of his moods when he firmly ordered his caddie, Snake, not to speak to him during the round. Not a word, no exceptions. He made that crystal clear.

Snake obliged, knowing only too well that to risk disobedience was to risk the sack. Coming down the stretch, Bolt found himself blocked by a tree.

'What do you think about a 5-iron?' he asked Snake.

The caddie never said a word, determined to follow the previous instruction to the letter. Bolt struck a beautiful recovery shot before turning proudly to his caddie and saying, 'Now what do you think of that?

Answer came there none.

'You may answer,' Bolt declared.

'That wasn't your ball, Mr Bolt,' Snake replied, as he threw the bag over his shoulder and marched away.

Throwing clubs was Bolt's principal modus operandi. Drivers disappeared into a canal in Miami and into a pond at Cherry Hills during the 1960 US Open. 'Always throw your clubs ahead of you, that way you can't waste any energy going back to pick them up,' was a stock piece of advice that he reputedly gave to the young, fiery Arnold Palmer.

There was more, including 'Never break your driver and putter in the same round.'

The putter assumed the role of frequent victim. One day after missing another short one, he tossed down his putter and looked menacingly to the heavens. 'So it's me again, Lord,' he shouted. 'Why don't you just come down here and we'll play? And bring that kid of yours. I'll play your better ball.'

Experience produced one observation. 'Here's an irony for you,' he once said. 'The driver goes the shortest distance when thrown; the putter flies the furthest.'

But Bolt's transgressions were by no means restricted to chucking clubs. So often did he fall foul of authority that he created a special fund from his winnings to pay for fines.

Walking out of tournaments never went down well with officialdom, as I once discovered when I withdrew during an event in India. I started well enough in the second round to lead the tournament, before just picking up my ball and leaving. I was not proud of myself. I just couldn't take it any more. I had never seen poverty like it, people washing themselves in the open sewers that passed for streets.

Bolt walked out on the Philadelphia Classic in 1962. He had apparently curved his tee shot out over a water hazard and brought it back to about 10 feet from the hole. A brilliant shot, one that has now become the trademark of Masters champion Bubba Watson. But not a murmur came from the gallery. That proved too much for Bolt, who turned to his caddie and said, 'If that is not good enough, go pick up my ball.' Bolt departed the course and the tournament.

Tony Jacklin tells a tale about Bolt at a tournament in San Diego, California. A bad start to his round had already increased his temper temperature when he hooked his tee shot over a cliff at the 5th. Player and caddie disappeared over the edge and down the steps to look for his ball. Jacklin waited and waited and waited for him to reappear. No sign.

'He never came back up again,' Jacklin said. 'I didn't see him till the following week. I asked him if he ever did find his ball.'

The reply was instant. 'No, but I found the Eastern Airlines ticket counter,' Bolt said.

As I said at the beginning of this chapter, the good old-fashioned tantrum has pretty much vanished. But I have witnessed a few boil-overs through the years, some on the spur of the moment, as the term suggests, and others more calculated. I remember playing the first two rounds at Royal Birkdale with Mark Calcavecchia (a great bloke, by the way) who, having missed the halfway cut, summoned the scoreboard carrier. He proceeded to give him all of his irons, one by one, from No. 2 to a lob wedge. The man has style.

So, too, had the late Max Faulkner, the 1951 Open champion. I think it was after an Open at St Andrews that he threw his clubs, again one by one, out of the window of a train as it crossed the Forth Bridge.

I am not certain but I think it was English professional David Lynn who told me about the occasion that one of his playing partners 'lost it'. The unnamed player reacted to three-putting by walking off the green and starting to kick a golf bag. He kicked it three times and all the while Lynn was waiting to tackle a tricky 5 footer.

'Have you finished?' Lynn eventually asked.

'Just one more,' he replied, before aiming another size 11 at his target.

'You know that's my bag,' Lynn said with commendable calm.

Roberto Bernardini was a lovely player, but a horrible putter, who featured in several World Cups around the end of the 1960s and into the 1970s. He also played twice in the US Masters, 1969 and 1970. I remember the Italian walking off a green and heading for a tree, which he started to headbutt shouting *porco* this and *porco* that. In Italian *porco* means pig. He played on as if nothing had happened.

Golf can get to you that way. It happens. Tiger gets hot. Sergio Garcia used to get very hot. You might have seen Sven Struver break a club over his knee or Henrik Stenson toss a wedge into the drink. You might have laughed at the antics of Hennie Otto when six-putting from 12 feet in a Japanese tournament. The same Otto took a long time to live down his performance at the 2001 South African Masters when breaking all fourteen of his clubs in the car park then depositing them in a river on the drive home.

Jose Maria Olazabal broke a bone in his right hand when punching the wall of his hotel room at a WGC event in La Costa, California. Who knows what John Daly has smashed in his wildest days? (And I am not talking about his waywardness from the tee.)

I still remember the live television coverage of the volcano that used to be – maybe still is – Pat Perez. Perez looked to be heading for an inaugural victory on the US Tour when he managed to explode and implode at the same time in the 2002 Bing Crosby Pro-Am at Pebble Beach. His eruption began at the 14th in the final round when he fired a 3-wood second shot out of bounds. If there is a verb 'to tomahawk' – even if there isn't – that is what he did to the turf with that club. The same 3-wood was involved in a final-hole collapse almost on a par with what befell Jean Van de Velde at Carnoustie in 1999. Perez had regained the lead walking on to the 18th tee, only to knock his drive out of bounds on the right, albeit by only 18 inches. He positively stomped back to the tee, reloaded, found the fairway and, needing a miracle, blasted a fourth shot with his 3-wood into Monterey Bay. His reaction was in its own way magnificent in its splendour as he slashed the club repeatedly on the ground like a machete trying to clear a path on the forest floor.

Television also captured known hothead Woody Austin leaving a 30-foot putt a good 8 feet short and proceeding to bang his putter against his skull four or five times and with sufficient force to bend the shaft, maybe even his head. John Huston, another with a short fuse, hooked two balls into a lake at the Honda Classic in Fort Lauderdale. Not wanting to risk a third in the water he overcorrected, sending his ball into the right rough. That was it for Huston, who spun round and threw his driver into the lake. The story goes that the sight of the graphite club bobbing about irritated the player so much that he waded in after it. What he did not know – indeed could not have known – was the existence of a step. Suddenly he disappeared under the water. Paul Azinger looked around a few moments later to see a hat on the surface of the lake and no playing partner. Huston emerged and had to play the remaining holes soaking wet. That earned him his nickname Swamp Thing.

Colin Montgomerie has never been a club thrower. But with his 20/20 vision he can spot the slightest movement, no matter how far away. And with his perfect hearing, no sound escapes detection. And boy, can he get mad. I remember once in Italy there was a man following our match, not an official but he had some involvement in the event. This guy was particularly noticeable because of a big bushy moustache. The worse Monty played, the more irritated he became by the man and his moustache.

'Who's he, what's he doing?' Monty asked. 'What's he doing inside the ropes?'

We were on an elevated tee above a narrow road. There were cars going backwards and forwards tooting their horns. It was pretty noisy. Inevitably, Monty hit a poor drive.

'So sorry, Mr Montgomerie, so sorry about the cars and the horns,' the moustache said.

'It's not them, it's you,' Monty replied. 'Who are you? What are doing here? Go away. Go.'

Fulton Allem, a dangerous man to have a drink with, used to declare, 'I can't handle mediocrity.' It appears his caddie took the same view judging by one tale that both Nick Price and Vijay Singh like to relate.

'Give me something to break,' an angry Allem said to Bullet, his trusty caddie.

'Why don't you break par?' Bullet replied quick as a flash.

The exchange was overheard by playing partners Price and Singh, who laughed so much that both experienced trouble hitting their tee shots on the next tee.

Cary Middlecoff also suffered from a short fuse. Once when following one bad shot with another and another in the US Open at Oakmont, he glared at his ball lying in a greenside bunker and in a moment of clarity decided he didn't have to put up with this. The 10th green was located right beside the Pennsylvania Turnpike, which sliced through the course. He suddenly turned in the opposite direction to the green, drew back his wedge and slammed the ball towards the traffic. Without a word he climbed from the sand and set off for the clubhouse.

Finally, a word on 'Lefty' Stackhouse. After driving his sixth ball in a row into a lake in Texas he threw his club into the hazard. The rest of his clubs and his bag followed. That brought laughter from his caddie. Big mistake. Lefty picked up the caddie and tossed him into the lake. And just to complete the tantrum he threw himself in. Now that's what you call a tantrum.

Sir Ian Botham

Sam on Ian: 'What can be said about Beefy, or should that be Sir Beefy? A great man. I never cease to be impressed by how one of the biggest legends in any sport can remain such a nice and friendly guy. England's greatest ever all-rounder, with fourteen centuries and 383 wickets in Test cricket, Botham loves his golf almost as much as he loves his fishing, and that's saying something. Many's a time we have played 19 holes together – with Beefy the 19th is compulsory – either in a pro-am or just a bounce match, usually with his great mate Ian Woosnam. He played 102 Tests for England, most memorably the home Ashes series of 1981. As if his cricket exploits and expert commentary were not remarkable enough, his charity walks have raised millions of pounds for Leukaemia Research. No sportsman was more deserving of his knighthood.'

Sam has been a good mate for many years and we have played many a round together, often with Ian Woosnam, my best friend in golf, pro-ams, bounce games, all manner of occasions. I knew that if I invited him along to support my fund-raising walking for Leukaemia Research he would be there like a shot.

You would never put him down as a walker, though. You just have to spot that classic trudge, head bowed on the course no matter how he was doing, to know that Sam views walking as a necessary evil between golf shots and not to be attempted at any other time. Exercise his brain or his right arm or his tonsils, but that's as far as it goes.

He turned up at one of our Land's End walks. There he was standing on the start line rolling one of his legendary cigarettes – the ones he half smokes and sticks behind his ear – looking quite the athlete. Not. Pretty soon he fell a hundred yards or so behind and not much longer after that he was nowhere to be seen.

'Where's Sam?' I asked of the people around me.

'Where's Sam?' I wondered, as I took a rare glance around. Anyone who has been on my walks knows that from the moment I start to the moment I finish I look straight down at the ground and press on. It is the only way to endure the pain.

Of course, I have to stop both to take on fuel and empty waste, as it were. We have a support vehicle that roughly every 4 miles overtakes us and stops up ahead and serves as a feeding station so people can load up with ice cream or chocolate or chips or whatever. I'll never forget seeing the mobile pass with Sam sitting in the back window, feet up, another rollie in his mouth, making a few friendly gestures in my direction.

Sam has always been one of the lads. More than that, though, he opened the door. The same with Woosie. They showed that golf need not be an elitist sport, that it can be available to everyone and that it does not matter who you are or where you come from, you can climb the ladder to the very top. You don't get a loftier position than captaincy of a Ryder Cup team.

Mind you, I like to think that I played my part in Sam 'retaining' his captaincy.

We were at Augusta for the Masters. It was the first time Sam, Woosie and I had got together since Sam had been officially appointed captain for the 2001 – it turned out to be 2002 – match. A few beers were called for. Instead, we downed a few very strange-looking pink things that they seem to drink in Georgia. No time for that nonsense. Anyway, we then moved to the clubhouse. Or at least we tried to. But we were told it was members only and, without fuss, the very essence of politeness, we left the building.

That was when a problem arose.

Sam tripped over a kerb and went flying into a rhododendron bush. Not just any rhododendron bush. A rhododendron bush just outside the Augusta National clubhouse at the top of Magnolia Lane. A rhododendron bush just outside Augusta National clubhouse at the top of Magnolia Lane during Masters week. The eyes and the ears of the world were watching. More specifically, the eyes and ears of the press were watching, or at least they would have been in a second or two had something not been done.

It would have been some story if the recently appointed Ryder Cup captain had been spotted lying in a bush outside the Augusta National clubhouse, not drunk by any means, but not exactly stone-cold sober either. I swung into action. I threw Sam over my shoulder, fireman-lift-style, flagged down a passing courtesy car and manhandled him into the back of the vehicle.

Crisis averted. We got away with it.

It is fair to say that when Sam and I get together we like to have a few. I remember one very hot day at Forest of Arden when we stopped at the turn for a refreshing chilled pint of Guinness. One became two, two became three and we may have stopped at about five each. We let group after group through until we were bringing up the rear.

That may have been the same day that I took a quirky old putter much loved by Robin Smith, the England Test batsman, and lobbed it into the lake in front of the 18th green. He was not amused.

Great times. I always have a great day when in the company of Sam, especially on the golf course, when you can expect a battery of jokes and stories told in that unmistakable voice. 'Lang may yer lum reek,' as they say in the land of golf and fishing.

PS from Sam: 'Sir Ian Terence Botham is also a lying bastard! While it is perfectly true that I would have been spotted smoking a roll-up on the start line of the walk, his recollections of the rest of the day are a bit of a wide. I had got myself pretty fit ahead of the 23-mile walk by jogging on a running machine. Just 100 yards into the walk, my back went. But one of the physiotherapists took me into the support vehicle and gave me a bit of a pounding. I then proceeded to walk 19 of the 23 miles – in no small way sustained by Beefy's notorious "fruit" drink, made up of seven parts tequila to three

parts orange, before grinding to a halt. Only then did I climb aboard the bus, light a fag and raise my glass to him as we sped past.

At least that is how I remember what became a somewhat hazy day.'

Chapter Fifteen

(Not So) Simple Simon

What can you say about Simon Hobday, this son of Mafikeng (and two vets) who did not turn pro until the age of twenty-eight and who, despite a glorious swing and a fine talent, became famous for his antics rather than his golf? An emblem of a bygone era, he never took himself or the game too seriously before or after an explosion in prize money that changed behaviour and attitudes.

It was not that we did not care in the old days. There was just a bit more gay abandon. You could keep your card more easily and you could make money more easily. But the European Tour got stronger and the players got better. For some, the possibility of Ryder Cup selection entered considerations. Everyone had to tighten up their game and sharpen up their act. Inevitably, as golf became more professional, the Tour became less sociable.

Yet, there have always been characters in golf and there always will be. Golf, you see, tends to send those who play it a trifle bonkers.

Hobday never won a major championship, though he did win a Seniors major. He won only twice on the European Tour, six times on the South African Tour. Yet he remains a legend within golf, a man who has spawned so many stories that they could fill an entire book, let alone this one chapter.

Bernhard Langer tells a lovely story about the very early days of his professional career when young players shared rooms in order to save money on hotel expenses.

Hobday was a legend for the German, even if Langer, a very different sort of character, had not yet turned into the intense and serious individual he was to become.

'I was playing the Dutch Open and had already checked into the hotel when Simon swept in,' Langer recalls.

'A quick "hi" and with bag still in hand he asked his first question. "Do we have a bath tub?"

'Yes, we have a shower and a bath tub, I replied. He then went straight into the bathroom, put the plug in the bath and filled it up with water. He reappeared, picked up his suitcase and returned to the bathroom. I watched as he emptied the entire contents of his case, without any exception, straight into the water.

'Then he took a bar of soap and threw that into the water as well. A few minutes later he went over to his golf bag, grabbed the 1-iron and used it to stir up the contents. I had to consciously close my gaping mouth.

'Simon saw my astonishment and told me with a grin, "Bernhard, this is my laundry for the week."'

This was typical Hobday, who in Switzerland once went all sophisticated and hung his wet washing on his balcony rail to dry. The wind blew it all off on to the dirt below. Once retrieved, his mucky wardrobe was dumped into his suitcase ready for another bath. Mind you, I can think of no finer use for a 1-iron!

Langer, who I have always called affectionately either Fritz or Herman the German, is, of course, one of modern golf's elite. Two Masters victories despite dreadful intermittent problems with the putting yips. You cannot say better than that. One of the hardest workers in the game whose steely resolve is matched only by his unswerving faith. His Christianity is well known, but his love for a game of poker is not. We have enjoyed many a hand over the years. All I can say is that at his yippiest his putting is better than his poker!

My favourite Hobday story is a simple one illustrating his sense of humour and devil-may-care attitude. Speeding, as ever, to a US Senior Tour event, Hobday was doing more than 100 miles per hour on the freeway when he attracted the attention of a state trooper. This was not just any road cop but one straight from a movie with his wide-brimmed hat, dark glasses, gun, gleaming black boots, starched uniform and expression of utter contempt.

Hobday pulled over like a good boy and rolled down his window.

'God damn it boy, 'ave been waitin' all day for someone like you,' the trooper said.

Quick as a flash, smiling politely, Hobday replied, 'Well, I got here as quick as I could.'

When it came to speaking his mind, Hobday did not care for rank. Once, on the practice putting green, when a lengthy effort horseshoed around the hole and failed to drop, he looked to the heavens and roared, 'I'm only fucking practising!'

Another time during a round, while wearing a panama to protect himself from the sun, this notoriously poor putter missed a short one. He took off his hat, threw it to the ground and, again looking upwards, yelled, 'I didn't think you would recognise me.'

Another hat, another story, or it may be a version of the same story. That happens when people sit down in a clubhouse and recount tales from the past. Truth becomes twisted, fact becomes fiction. A good story remains a good story.

On this occasion Hobday's chosen headgear bore the name 'David Frost' clearly on top. Frostie, a fellow South African, was the putter Hobday always wanted to be, hell the putter everyone wanted to be. After perhaps not the first three-putt of the round, Hobday removed his hat, threw it to the ground and looked to the sky. 'I knew it wouldn't take you long to figure out it was me under here and not Frost,' he lamented.

Simon was easily recognisable. He was the one standing at the bar wearing only a grin. A lot of the time he did not wear much in the way of clothes. Some would say 'just as well' when you consider his colour clashes and aversion to dry-cleaning. He would never have been sponsored by Morphy Richards. They manufacture irons, don't they?

The story goes that he once wrote to a golf-clothing manufacturer in the following terms: 'If you don't send me a couple of hundred pounds a week, I'm going to start wearing your clothes.'

Sometimes, as I said, he wore nothing. Stripping down to the bare bones may or may not have had something to do with his spending a night in a Mexican jail. But he was mighty lucky not to have been locked up after removing all his clothes in a Swiss bar and then streaking through the streets of the ski resort in shrinking sub-zero temperatures.

Some say that I was instrumental in getting Hobday to remove his kit by betting him £5 he would not. I have no memory of that (it must have been a good night!). He had apparently arrived at the bar wrapped in layers of warm clothing. As the evening wore on and the brandy intake increased, he began to take off one garment after another. He was a man who never refused a dare. So, there he stood at the bar bollock naked. At least he acceded to a management request to put on some underwear, though I am not sure the owner was entirely satisfied with him placing his pants on his head.

I know of another occasion when, disappointed at missing the halfway cut, he sat down at a bar in the same Crans-sur-Sierre resort and asked the barman to bring him a pint and a repeat pint every fifteen minutes until told to stop. That proved another long night.

Who else but Hobday would locate a Viking hat and place it in his golf bag with the plan of donning it should he win the tournament, the Irish Open as it happened? Who else but Hobday would put it on anyway before playing his approach to the 72nd and final green? And who else but Hobday would hole the shot for an eagle 2?

Again, the detail may not be spot on, but you could imagine Hobday, as the story goes, reacting to unintentionally bouncing his ball across a lake, Barnes Wallis-style, by walking straight through the water hazard and on to the green. Oh, yes, the lake was snake infested.

He had several partners in crime in those days, characters like Jack Newton, Tertius Claassens, Vinny Baker, my very good friend and one-time travelling partner John O'Leary and Ian Stanley. Who knows if any of them was involved in a jape – and that's a charitable description – that nowadays would probably involve imprisonment for the perpetrator. History doesn't relate the name of the golfer.

The scene was one of those interminable flights to Australia where boredom can set in. The bad boys, as usual, were at the back of the plane. Our 'hero' thought he would entertain the lads. He cut a hole in his breakfast tray, pulled down the zip of his trousers and, carefully I presume, inserted his willy into the middle of his 'full Australian'. Sausage, bacon, scrambled eggs, the works, not forgetting what looked like a button mushroom.

'Miss,' he said, having summoned the stewardess, 'there is something wrong with my mushroom.'

Then there was the story of the golfer who once grabbed a waiter by the balls as he passed carrying a tray in each hand. Get out of that.

Hobday, for one, has never been entirely happy about being labelled crazy. His response was perfectly articulated when speaking to writer Lauren St John in her book *Fairway Dreams*. He pleaded, 'When I play I get angry sometimes. I get pissed sometimes. I chase women sometimes. Christ, what's so odd about that?'

An exhibitionist, a master of the quick quip, a humorist, a drinker, a womaniser and a very fine golfer, albeit occasionally an angry one, Hobday was also a fine executioner of the practical joke.

An exhibition match was staged in South Africa during the early 1980s involving Dale Hayes, Mark McNulty, Hobday and John Bland (though it may have been Tony Johnstone). McNulty well deserved his reputation as a demon putter who for years weaved magic with an old Titleist Bullseye putter, complete with blue grip. Simon had found and bought a used one from the professional shop. He exchanged it with the 'genuine' one from McNulty's bag when he wasn't looking.

There were 2,000 people gathered round the 1st tee. Dale, now an accomplished broadcaster and after-dinner speaker, introduced the players to the gallery. 'Now most of you know Mark for his incredible putting prowess,' Hayes said.

With that, Hobday interrupted, asking, 'Where is that bloody putter?' Then he walked over to McNulty's bag, whipped out the substitute putter and broke it over his knee. McNulty's eyes popped out of his head. He looked on in stunned silence at what Hobday had done to his favourite putter and was about to attack him when the author of the practical joke pulled out the genuine article from his own bag.

A free spirit like Hobday is always going to get into trouble with officialdom and he was often fined for his behaviour. Once, though, he escaped punishment.

Having been refused relief from a bad lie, Hobday politely asked the official if he would be fined if he called him an arsehole. (I have heard a worse version.)

'Absolutely,' the rules man replied.

'What if I called you a fucking arsehole?'

'You would be fined a lot.'

'OK then, what if I just think you are a fucking arsehole?'

'Oh well that's all right.'

'OK, I think you are a fucking arsehole.'

And that, ladies and gentlemen, is the one and only Simon Hobday.

John Bland

Sam on John: 'Not at all bland. A great character, a great storyteller and a great friend, Blandie still hits the ball very nicely despite being well into his sixties. Blessed with huge hands and fingers, the South African has always been a great striker of the ball and a brilliant putter. He was better value than his two victories in Europe, with most of his thirty-plus tournament wins coming in his native land.'

Back in the day, Louis Martin, the head of South African golf, got in touch with a few of us and asked if we would support a charity pro-am for the first lady, wife of President F. W. de Klerk. We were delighted to be involved.

It proved a wonderful day of golf and bonhomie. We played at Kyalami Country Club, a parkland course halfway between Johannesburg and Pretoria. 'Out in the country but close to home' as its slogan states. Some of you will know Kyalami – Zulu for 'my home' – as the name of the racing circuit that used to stage the South African Grand Prix.

There followed a black-tie dinner and prize giving at the Presidential Palace. It was all very grand and very stylish. The women, including my then wife Helen, donned their finest gowns. Little did she know what master prankster Tony Johnstone had in store for her.

(Not So) Simple Simon

Unbeknown to Helen, Johnstone – it is always him – slipped the silver salt and pepper dishes into her handbag late on in the evening. Most of the guests seemed to be in on the 'joke'. As we were leaving the security guards, who had been tipped off, insisted on having a look inside Helen's bag.

'But why?' she asked, quite reasonably in the circumstances. 'You are not searching anyone else.'

They went ahead, checked the bag and, of course, pulled out the 'stolen' goods. Helen was mortified for the few seconds it took till everyone, including the president and first lady, to start laughing. If looks could kill, I would have been a dead man. But she took it in good part. Considering . . .

Tony Johnstone could be victim as well as perpetrator. I remember an occasion when he even managed to look like a person with murder in mind . . .

Like myself, Tony is a keen gardener. The lawn at his English home in Sunningdale is his pride and joy, every blade cared for with loving attention. Walk on it at your peril. Well, OK, you can walk on it but woe betide anyone who does not treat the manicured surface with the greatest respect. I knew that. Actually, I felt pretty much the same about my lawn.

That was how I had the idea for a bit of devilment. Traditionally, the South African players on the European Tour would always host a barbecue during the PGA Championship at Wentworth, usually at Tony's home. These were great nights, often glamorised by South African cabin crew who would help with the occasion.

Anyway, I arranged for one of the stewardesses, as they used to be called, to go behind a hedge and start swinging a club. Divots began to fly. All Tony and others could see was the top half of the woman swinging away with a wedge and dislodging great clumps of grass and earth.

Tony, thinking that his precious lawn was being savaged, went ballistic. He ran upstairs and reappeared with the gun he used to fire at targets. He looked like one of those settlers about to warn cowboys off his land. Of course, Tony would never have pulled the trigger.

What he did not know at the time was that I had positioned myself out of sight flat on the ground behind the hedge. Every time the stewardess swung the club I threw a divot into the night air.

I had gathered some divots from the Wentworth practice ground earlier that day. All good practical jokes require preparation and planning. It worked perfectly. Tony blew a gasket and everyone else nearly burst their sides laughing.

Perhaps the biggest joker of our era was Simon Hobday, a live-life-to-the-full character whose sharp wit and eccentricities kept everyone amused, sometimes horrified. Most of the European Tour players of that generation have a 'Simon Hobday story', especially his fellow South Africans. A favourite of mine, probably less meaty than most, offers an example of his quick-thinking humour.

He was playing in a Seniors event with those two giants of American golf, Hale Irwin and Raymond Floyd. At one hole he found himself shortest from the tee, about 10 yards behind the other two. It was, therefore, him to play first to the green.

'What's the yardage?' he asked his caddie.

'One hundred,' came the confident reply. Whereupon, Hobday dumped his shot into the bunker short of the green. He gave the caddie a look but said nothing. Instead he turned to Floyd.

'What yardage do you have, Ray?' he asked.

'One hundred and ten,' Floyd replied.

'I am sorry, Ray, I played out of turn,' he said to Floyd quick as a flash before smiling menacingly at the caddie who had mucked up the yardage.

Tony Johnstone

Sam on Tony: 'One of the slowest players on the planet, but we love him. A very, very funny man and a natural storyteller. His 1992 victory in our flagship PGA Championship at Wentworth represented the most important of his six Tour successes. But I know he was most proud of his triumph in the 2008 Jersey Seniors Classic, coming as it did after multiple sclerosis had earlier forced a retirement. A prolific winner on what used to be known as the Sunshine Southern Africa Tour with seventeen victories, Tony also represented his native Zimbabwe in seven World Cups and the same number of Dunhill Cups. Tony is great fun. Just don't make a wrong step in his precious Sunningdale garden! '

Since I'm pretty sure he will have carved me up somewhere in this book let me tell you about my mate John Bland. For twenty years on the Tour he was my dining companion every night. That was before he took his wheelbarrow to the US Seniors Tour and filled it up with money, leaving me to order room service!

Blandie, as everyone knew him, was the straightest driver on the course and the worst driver in the world when at the wheel of a car. Or a boat, as you will discover later on. When I say the worst, I mean the worst. Without exception or exaggeration.

There was, for example, the occasion when he went to the main Ford factory in South Africa to pick up a new car. He managed about 5 yards before wrecking it. Somehow, he reversed the vehicle the wrong way off a ramp and it fell 6 feet before landing with a crash on to the concrete floor. Undeterred, he marched positively towards the open-mouthed salesman.

'I love that car, man,' he said. 'But it's a shit colour!'

He kept writing off cars, fourteen of them at last count. Two bit the parched dust in the Kruger National Park, with one of the crashes resulting in his mum breaking her collarbone.

My great friend Bland owned a smallholding with heavy metal gates. For some reason known only to him and his maker he delighted in driving up to the gates and pushing them open with his front bumper. He would return his sponsored cars every year looking as if they had been through a crusher. One year he got through the entire golf season without a scratch and went to trade it in for a new one. So, what did he do? He filled the petrol car full of diesel and it lasted about a mile before conking out.

One day at Fancourt, that delightful resort on the Garden Route in the Western Cape, we watched him reverse into an oak tree. Result? Bent bumper, of course.

'What happened to the car?' I asked, feigning ignorance as I surveyed the damage a few hours later.

'That was not me,' he replied. 'Somebody must have bumped into me while it was parked.' Somehow, he was never to blame.

(Not So) Simple Simon

Only once do I remember his being blameless. A few of us were involved in filling his hubcaps with stones. Christ, what a racket the car made as he drove off. It sounded like a Sherman tank. Did Blandie notice? Never heard a thing apparently. And he arrived back at the golf club the following morning with his car making the same tank-like noise.

Maybe his cavalier disregard for cars was not just a question of bad driving. In his early days as a professional he never much bothered about the make of the car or, as it happened, its condition. He drove an old banger for a while that had no floor on the passenger side. He started the engine either with a screwdriver or a teaspoon that he stuck in the ignition and turned. That worked.

The trail of vehicular destruction extended beyond cars. He was quite the celebrity when moving to a new community at Knysna near George on the Western Cape. So much so that a party was held in his honour attended by the mayor, no less. They got on immediately. Before the end of a highly successful evening the mayor offered John carte blanche to use his boat that was moored on the quayside specially built for the development.

A few days passed and Blandie thought he would take advantage of the mayoral generosity. He climbed aboard, sat on the captain's seat, revved it up to full power and reversed into the quayside, pretty much destroying the boat and the landing stage.

Sheepishly, he telephoned the mayor with the bad news.

'My boat, you say, that's strange,' the mayor replied. 'My boat is not there at the moment.'

I first met John at the Victoria Falls Classic in 1979. I had just turned pro. We played a practice round together, with Blandie proclaiming at the end that I would never beat him as long as I lived. I had been that bad. I beat him the very next day, of course. He gave me an old Rhodesian two-dollar note on which he wrote the words 'You got lucky'. I kept it in my wallet for the best part of thirty years until sadly I lost it a couple of years ago.

The thing about John is you can never get one over him. He is so sharp, so quick, a great practical joker and a master of the put-down.

There was, however, one memorable occasion when I did him in cold blood. John had been a good friend of the then president, F. W. de Klerk, for many years. They played golf together. He gave the president golf lessons. When a First Lady's Golf Day for charity was held, there was only one pro going to be paired with F. W. As it happened, I played in the group ahead with Pieter Koornhof, who held many prominent political and diplomatic roles throughout his career including being ambassador to the United States.

An idea came to me as we were nearing the halfway house where the golfers would stop for refreshment. I asked Piet to confirm if F. W. had a good sense of humour. This he did.

We were sitting in the hut when in came the president followed by Blandie. Introductions were made.

'This is my old friend, Tony Johnstone,' Blandie said to the president.

'Sir, it is a pleasure to meet you,' I replied. 'I would just like to say that none of the other golfers share John's view that you have sold the country up the river with all this Nelson Mandela and one man, one vote stuff.'

(Not So) Simple Simon

The president twigged immediately. He spun round to John and said, 'Call yourself a friend. You are an absolute disgrace.'

John froze to the spot, speechless for once and white as a sheet. I left with Piet ready to tee off at the start of the back nine.

Within minutes Helen, John's late wife, came up to me and asked what I had done to her husband. He was in a terrible state, sitting in the halfway house shaking and muttering about 'that bastard, Johnstone'.

I got him – thanks to the president of South Africa.

Blandie said he would never forgive me and he never has!

Chapter Sixteen

Captain Torrance

I was standing beside the practice putting green in front of The Belfry hotel on the morning of the singles in 2002 when my good friend David Feherty emerged from a door carrying a pint of Guinness. He had brought it for me in the not unreasonable assumption that I would be feeling nervous and could do with a drink to calm down.

In fact, I was pretty relaxed and confident about what lay ahead. That did not mean I did not fancy a glass of something. I was about to accept his kind offering when a warning light flashed in my head. Let's say I had knocked it back where I stood and a photographer had captured the moment; let's say that Europe had lost and a picture of the captain drinking alcohol appeared in a newspaper the following day. Not the way I would have wanted my captaincy to end. So I stepped inside the door and, away from any prying eyes and lenses, took a couple of good gulps.

Compare that with the behaviour of Walter Hagen, the US playing captain in 1931. He went in for intimidation in a big way when about to tee off against his opposite number, Charles Whitcombe, the second of the three golfing brothers.

Hagen was standing on the 1st tee with a coat thrown majestically over his shoulders when a waiter appeared carrying a tray on which stood, just as proudly as Hagen himself, the 'perfect' Martini. Hagen took a sip or two from the stem glass and nonchalantly swung his driver a couple of times with his other hand. As if adding to the grandeur of the occasion, he swapped drink and club to show he could drink and swing with either hand. The announcement of his name prompted him to drain the glass and take aim. The records show that he smote a beautiful drive down the middle of the fairway.

It couldn't happen now, not with the way the media seek out negative stories.

There's also another reason why it couldn't happen now. Since 1961, when a change in the format doubled the number of matches and points, only once on either side has there been a playing captain. Arnold Palmer survived the strain of attempting both roles by leading the US to victory at East Lake Country Club, Atlanta, in 1963 and accumulating a personal haul of four points out of six.

Prior to 1961 the playing captain was very much the norm. The aforementioned Hagen, for example, retained a monopoly on the playing captaincy from the first match in 1927 until the sixth ten years later, when he restricted his duties.

The great Hagen did not always live up to his billing. The second Ryder Cup contest at Moortown in 1929 produced a story of overconfidence on one side and motivation on the other.

'We need to get off to a good start and I'll play George Duncan,' Hagen told Gene Sarazen in a locker-room conversation.

Unbeknown to both men, Duncan, one of the fastest swingers and quickest players ever seen at the highest level, overheard the American's cocky words. Remarkably, Duncan whipped Hagen 10 and 8, winning 10 of the last 19 holes in the two-round contest. 'This is the happiest day of my life,' Duncan declared.

Every captain approaches the task differently or at least tries to put their own mark on proceedings. J. H. Taylor, a grunter at the point of impact long before Monica Seles and the noisy tennis brigade came along, was a remarkable sixty-two years old when selected as non-playing captain in 1933. He was asked to professionalise the GB&I team and to that end ordered early-morning runs along Southport beach for his team. They may not have liked it but a home victory followed.

The legendary Ben Hogan ruled with a rod of iron in a non-playing role in 1949. He instituted a schedule of early wake-up calls and long practices, a combination anathema to Jimmy Demaret, though he probably wasn't the only one. 'Hey, Hawk!' he declared. 'We training for golf or the army?'

Hogan was captaining his country for the third and final time in 1967 when he made his notorious introduction at the official dinner. 'Ladies and gentlemen, the United States Ryder Cup team – the finest golfers in the world.' The strict disciplinarian, in charge of a team including Arnold Palmer, Billy Casper and the colourful Doug Sanders, decreed no late nights and imposed a 10.30 p.m. curfew. You can't argue with his record, though. He won all three matches as captain and all his matches as a player.

GB&I had not won the Ryder Cup for twenty-four years until Dai Rees led the home team to a memorable victory at Lindrick in Yorkshire in 1957. Rees, who used to train with his beloved Arsenal FC, proved the inspiration for a convincing 7½–4½ success. There was one moment of rancour within the triumphant ranks, however. Harry Weetman's reaction to being dropped for the singles was to declare that he would never again play in a team captained by Rees.

A Rees masterstroke was to promote that great Scot Eric Brown to number one for what promised to be – and turned out to be – an explosive encounter with Tommy 'Thunder' Bolt. Eric was a rough, tough character who put the fear of God into everyone he met. I am glad to say he became a good friend. It was obvious that Bolt, a notoriously bad-tempered man, and Brown disliked each other intensely.

When the two adversaries arrived late on the 1st tee, the wise-cracking Demaret joked that the last time he had seen them they were standing at fifty paces throwing clubs at each other. Both men practised gamesmanship. Knowing Brown to be a fast player, Bolt slowed to an agonising pace. His strategy backfired, though. Brown whispered something to his caddie who sped off towards the clubhouse before returning with a lounge chair. Brown sat on the chair while Bolt fiddled. At the end of the match, which Brown won 4 and 3 in morale-boosting fashion, Bolt snarled, 'I can't say I enjoyed the game.' Brown had a ready reply. 'That's because you don't like getting stuffed.' Bolt reputedly snapped a wedge in half in the locker room and failed to appear at the closing ceremony.

Dai Rees was understandably ecstatic at the surprise victory. 'It's wonderful,' he said. 'This is the greatest shot in the arm British golf ever had. My team should receive the freedom of nearby Sheffield.'

American excuses were long and somewhat undignified. Captain Jackie Burke said his American players were overtrained and over here too long; the small British ball did not suit them; they putted horribly; the pins were of variable height and thickness, making it difficult to chip the ball into the hole and to see the target from the fairway!

Royal Birkdale in 1969 proved notable for the famous final-green putt concession by Jack Nicklaus, which gave his opponent Tony Jacklin a half point and the home side a share of the Ryder Cup. It was regarded pretty much universally as one of the finest examples of sportsmanship and did much to revive the health of the then one-sided competition.

Not everyone was happy, however. Sam Snead, the US captain, spoke for many members of his team when he subsequently revealed, 'When it happened, all the boys thought it was ridiculous to give him that putt. We went over there to win, not to be good ole boys. I never would have given a putt like that – except maybe to my brother.'

By 1977, after another twenty years of American domination, the Ryder Cup was struggling. I always remember the late Peter Dobereiner, one of my favourite writers and dining companions, describing American public reaction to the event as somewhere between 'the Tennessee Frog-Jumping Contest and the Alabama Melon-Pip Spitting Championship'.

Something had to change. Two years later, not least because of the urging of Nicklaus, Europe joined the party. The effect was not instant, but in 1983 I was a member of the European team that went agonisingly close to registering what would have been a stunning victory over an American team captained by Nicklaus at Palm Beach Gardens in Florida.

Captaining for the first of four contests in a row, Tony Jacklin said in defeat, 'One thing is certain, these matches are going to be as close as this from now on. There will be no more American walkovers.' He never said anything about European walkovers!

Since then, and starting in 1985 at The Belfry, the list of victorious European captains has grown and grown – Jacklin twice, Bernard Gallacher, Seve Ballesteros, Bernhard Langer, Ian Woosnam, Colin Montgomerie and, of course, yours truly.

As you might expect from strong-willed men in such a normally individual sport as golf, each captain presented his own style and approach.

I concentrated on my own players and paid not the slightest attention to what the Americans were doing. There was no second-guessing on my part over pairings and order of play. I was determined to treat everyone the same in terms of equal importance, albeit taking a slightly different approach according to personality and character. I went into the event with definite – though flexible – plans that could be changed should the need arise.

My most difficult moments came a year before the match. Only after much agonising soul-searching and a lot of thought did I plump for Jesper Parnevik over Jose Maria Olazabal to join Sergio Garcia as my captain's selections. Telling the Spaniard he had not made it was one of the worst experiences of my life. No more need be said about 9/11, the attack on the twin towers of the World Trade Center that caused the Ryder Cup

– insignificant in the grand scheme of things – to be postponed a year to 2002. The disruption to my captaincy was minimised by the professionalism of the European Tour.

One of my favourite moments, which demonstrated the enduring camaraderie between the two teams despite the intense rivalry, came after the match as a few of our vanquished opponents visited our team room. David Duval, always a welcome guest, sat down beside me and noticed that we were showing one of the motivational videos I arranged to be prepared showing a series of fuck-ups by the Americans. There on the screen, almost on cue, blazed a bit showing Duval taking four attempts to extricate himself from Road Bunker in 2000, an aberration that ended his challenge to Tiger Woods in the Open Championship.

I put my hands over his eyes and said, 'Don't look, David.'

'Don't worry,' he replied, quick as a flash, 'I got my name on the trophy.'

Only the Ryder Cup can produce memories like that.

Paul McGinley

Sam on Paul: 'McGinty, as I like to call Paul, is a good friend and neighbour and occasional playing partner at Sunningdale. He gave me my finest moment when holing the putt that clinched victory for Europe in my 2002 captaincy. I think he is a nailed-on future Ryder Cup captain. There is a passion within and a permanent glint in his eye, a great lad to have on your side. Paul

has won four European Tour events and has a perfect three from three in his Ryder Cup appearances. Despite his seven knee operations it is still impossible to keep up with him on the course. I think you would call him brisk.'

As a Manchester United fan – and even if I were not – I would not lightly compare anyone with Sir Alex Ferguson. He is the best. And part of what makes him a great football manager is his man management, an area in which he has no equal.

Not for him the widely accepted belief that in team sport you must treat each player the same way and equally. Ferguson believes that everyone has to be treated differently, according to character and status. Eric Cantona, for example, was always afforded special treatment. He needed to be.

Sam had the same philosophy and that is a big reason why his Ryder Cup captaincy in 2002 was so successful. He was never going to treat Sergio Garcia and Colin Montgomerie, to give two examples, the same as a couple of rookies like Phillip Price and, er, Paul McGinley. He knew everyone had to be handled in different ways. Not better, just different.

I want to tell you about how Sam captained me in 2002. He was brilliant.

If you remember, the match against the United States should have been played in 2001. As it happened, I was on a high at the time. I had just won the Welsh Open in what had been my most successful season. Everyone looks forward to the Ryder Cup, but I could not wait to make my debut such was my rich vein of form.

Then it happened. Terrorists struck the twin towers in New York in a horrific atrocity forever known by the date – 9/11. The eleventh day of the ninth month. There was, of course, no way the Ryder Cup, due to take place a few weeks later, could go ahead. The match was put back twelve months.

A week is a long time in golf, as it is in most things. But a year . . . Everything can change in a year. Twelve months on, my game was not nearly as good. My confidence was not as high. Here we were in the unique situation of having qualified for a match on the strength of 2001 form and not playing until a year later.

The week before the match the Amex, one of the big World Golf Championship events, was held in Ireland. Two of our team had not qualified – Lee Westwood and myself. So, Sam arranged for us to join him for a round at The Belfry. Chubby Chandler, our manager, made up a four.

The day arrived. Sam picked me up in a very flash chauffeur-driven BMW and we drove to the Midlands. The Belfry looked a picture. The course was ready. I felt pretty much ready. And Sam, as I discovered that day, was clearly ready.

We played our round and had a quick sandwich in the hotel. Then, with a flourish so typical of the man, Sam asked the waiter for a bottle of pink Laurent Perrier champagne and two glasses. Carefully clutching the bubbly as if it were his firstborn, he guided me to the car for what proved to be the most fascinating and illuminating return journey. Sipping champers, we spoke for two hours solid, though, in truth, Sam did most of the talking.

He told me who would be playing five matches and who would be playing three. He told me all the planned pairings with the roles each player would have. He made it sound very special; he made me feel very special. He said that as a rookie I would be one of those playing three matches. His plan was to pair me with Padraig Harrington in the Friday and Saturday foursomes. I would sit out both fourballs and, of course, play a third time in the Sunday singles. That sounded fine. I was quite happy.

So, after sitting out the Friday-morning fourballs, I teed off in the afternoon with Padraig, a fellow Irishman and a good mate. We ran into a brick wall. The pairing of Stewart Cink and Jim Furyk produced the best golf of the day to beat us 2 and 1. I actually played really well and from a personal point of view was delighted with my performance. Though beaten, I was looking forward to the next day. Not for long. Sam wanted a word.

'I have some bad news for you,' Sam said, as everyone relaxed back in the team room.

'Paddy feels he let you down and he has gone to practise. He is insistent that he does not want to play in the foursomes tomorrow morning. He says he would be much better spending the morning practising to ready himself for the rest of the match. I am afraid that means you do not have a partner because I don't want to split up any of the other pairings.'

There was nothing I could say. Suddenly, from being reasonably happy, I felt utterly disconsolate. I had played so well. We had been beaten by the best of the Americans on the day.

Worse was to follow, however. Sam told me that because I did not have a fourball partner I would have to sit out the whole day. Talk about a double whammy. I now faced the prospect of missing out completely on the Saturday and with the singles playing only two games in the entire match. Again, there was nothing I could really say.

'I want you to get up in the morning, see the guys off in the foursomes and go and play nine holes. Get ready, keep loose.

You never know, you might be needed in the fourballs,' Sam added.

You never know, all right. I was walking down the 9th fairway the following morning when I saw Derrick Cooper, one of Sam's helpers, charging towards me in a buggy. There was no time for niceties.

'Thomas [Bjorn] did not play well this morning,' Derrick told me, 'so you are going out with Darren [Clarke].'

The adrenalin was pumping through my veins when I arrived at the team room. I knew I would be very comfortable with Darren. We had known each other since we were boys. We went to play World Cups together. He did not muck about either.

'You tee off first at every hole,' he declared. 'I want you to smash it down the middle, confident in the fact that you've got me coming straight after you.' That helped a lot. Darren has always been one of the straightest drivers of a golf ball. It was just the boost I needed.

We were last match out, against Scott Hoch and the in-form Furyk. And we found ourselves one down with one to play, that famous closing hole at The Belfry that always seems to produce such drama. We were feeling the pressure. We knew that if we lost we would go into the singles a point down. We knew all about America's great record in the singles. It seemed as if the whole Ryder Cup was resting on this game.

I managed to hit the longest drive of the four. Darren did not hit a good one. He was short of the right bunker in the rough, furthest away of the four. Suddenly, Sam was right beside me, putting his arm round my shoulder.

'I want you to play out of turn,' Sam said. (You can do that in match play when your partner is furthest away.)

'I want you to hit one on the green and put pressure on the Yanks.' The idea had come from Bernhard Langer but Torrance knew when to accept advice and when not to.

I was 200 yards away. This was the last hole at The Belfry, the last game on the second day of a Ryder Cup. Darkness was falling. It seemed that the entire crowd had gathered behind the green. Every cameraman, every photographer, all eyes and all lenses seemed to be looking at the shot facing me. Two hundred yards over the water with a right to left wind.

I hit a great 4-iron and found the putting surface. Neither of the Americans managed a par 4. I rolled my ball in to win the hole, halve the match and ensure that Europe were tied going into the singles. It was a huge psychological boost.

Everyone went wild. The cheering was amazing. Back in the team room, music was blaring and everyone was hugging. I was not alone in downing a pint of Guinness. Darren had played extremely well and I held my own. I was on cloud nine.

All of a sudden, Sam comes over and whispers in my ear. 'McGinley, you showed so much balls there. You're my man. I am putting you out at number twelve in the singles. If it comes down to the last match, I know I can count on you.'

For a rookie to hear that. Wow. I don't know if you can get higher than cloud nine. But I grew a foot, always something a short-arse like me can do with. A quick shower and it was back for dinner.

'Have you seen the draw?' Bjorn asked me.

I played it cool. I said I would look in a minute. I knew. Sam had had a word. I could afford to be casual. Eventually, I looked at the bottom of the sheet and there was the name of Jesper Parnevik. I was 'hidden' at number nine. I could not help but feel deflated. Almost before I had time to take it in, though, Sam was beside me.

'I know what you are going to say. But I had a think. You are still playing that role. The winning of the Ryder Cup has invariably come down to matches eight to ten. You are bang in the middle at number nine.'

I grew a few more feet. I am now feeling 12 feet tall.

The next day, I am coming down the 18th fairway again, knowing the position. I could be the man that holes the winning putt.

Sam places an arm round me and whispers in my ear. 'This is what we talked about. You're my man.'

The rest is history.

Colin Montgomerie

Sam on Colin: 'My Ryder Cup hero. I heaped pressure on him by putting him out first in the 2002 singles and he responded magnificently with a crushing defeat of Scott Hoch that inspired everyone coming behind. Monty became the same strong man that Seve Ballesteros had been for first Tony Jacklin then Bernard Gallacher. Every successful captain needs a Seve or a Monty.

But for the absence of a major championship, his record reflects his exceptional ability: eight Order of Merit successes, including seven in a row; forty tournament victories, featuring thirty-one on the European Tour; eight Ryder Cups as a player without ever losing a singles match; a winning Ryder Cup captain in 2010.

My fellow Scot finished in second place five times in majors and might have filled in that hole in his CV but for a tendency to be his own worst enemy on occasions. He was certainly good enough.'

The final day of a Ryder Cup, a no-hiding-place occasion when Europe's finest dozen take on the twelve best Americans in the singles, can be more nerve-racking than anything else golf has to offer.

Yet, with the overnight score tied at 8–8, there I was alone on the practice ground, apart from caddie Andy Prodger and coach Denis Pugh, in front of an audience of 7,000 excited spectators, so relaxed that I started larking about with the gallery. (By the way, it must have been the only time in my life that I was the first man on to a practice ground. I have never been, shall we say, the most assiduous practiser in professional golf. But my opponent, Scott Hoch, never warmed up for more than half an hour.)

It must have been an hour before my tee-off time. The gates had opened a couple of hours earlier and already the atmosphere of anticipation and expectation was amazing. I was hitting sand wedges in the general direction of a 100-yard distance board without particularly trying to hit the target. But the ball struck the marker at my third shot, by luck rather than by design.

'Hey Monty, it took you three attempts to hit it,' a voice from the stand shouted, prompting much laughter all round.

I don't know why but I spun round and shouted back, 'OK, who said that?'

The people sitting around the heckler all pointed the finger. 'You try it,' I cried.

And down he came. It took him a couple of minutes to get from his seat to the range where, of course, he received a tremendous ovation. You should have seen the faces of Messrs Pugh and Prodger. I could see them thinking, 'What the hell is he doing? This is the crunch day of the Ryder Cup and Monty is mucking about without a care in the world!'

Anyway, there he was and, judging by his practice swing, this was at best an 18 handicapper. He was not very good. He thinned his first shot and did not do much better with his second. If memory serves me correctly, Dennis stepped in to suggest that was enough. There was some serious work to be done. But the guy held on to the club and, bold as brass, declared, 'Monty had three shots.' More laughter.

So, he took his third attempt, a complete duff with the divot travelling further than the ball.

By this time Sky Sports had spotted what was going on and the antics were being broadcast live, viewed, of course, by my teammates in the European room and by the opposition in the US room. Nothing had been planned but I think it helped with confidence levels for everyone to see how relaxed I was.

That in no small measure was down to Sam Torrance, the most positive of captains and a real inspiration to his players. Sam never doubted for a second that Europe would win and that conviction spread throughout the team. He certainly helped me play the golf of my life that week.

And the previous evening he had produced his masterstroke.

Paul McGinley and Darren Clarke had secured a vital half point at the conclusion of the Saturday matches to ensure that we did not start the singles in arrears. You do not want to give any American team a lead going into the singles. Padraig Harrington and I had defeated the pairing of Phil Mickelson and David Toms to maintain my unbeaten record.

I may have been relaxed and in top form but I was not entirely without worry that week. My back had been pretty bad all year, so much so that it was only the week before that I could confirm to Sam that I would be fit to play. To help me survive the week, however, and to play five out of five matches as Sam asked of me, I arrived at the Belfry with my own personal masseur. That meant a two-hour massage every evening.

As a result, I was late into the team room for dinner, still oblivious to the order of play for the singles, still unaware of my position and the identity of my opponent. Just how the names are matched can be crucial. You can sometimes have a good idea of the outcome just by looking at the sheet.

I got the sheet and looked at the 8, 9 and 10 spots where matches are nearly always decided and where I had been placed in the past. I could not find my name. Then I looked for the longest name. I could not see it. For a split second – and this was all done in a few blinks of the eye – I thought I had been missed out. I thought there had been a terrible mistake.

But there I was, not 'Montgomerie' but 'Monty' at number 1. Sam, the gambler, had taken a punt on top loading his order, placing his strongest and most experienced players in the vanguard and ignoring the accepted practice of locating strength in the lower half of the draw. Sam's plan was to be blue on the board early – blue for Europe – and blow the Americans away.

US captain Curtis Strange, as it happened, had done precisely the opposite by listing Jim Furyk, Davis Love, Phil Mickelson and Tiger Woods at 9, 10, 11 and 12. The danger of that tactic was that the contest might be over by the time his big guns came into play.

I took my seat at the table and begun studying the match-ups. It looked fantastic for us. I will never forget Sam looking towards me.

'I have done it, haven't I?' he said.

'Yes, you have,' I replied.

Eight years on, when it came to my captaincy in 2010, I adopted pretty much the same tactic. Good enough for Sam, good enough for me, I thought, though I did keep Padraig Harrington and Graeme McDowell back as a couple of tail gunners.

Just as well, really, since the top four of Lee Westwood, Rory McIlroy, Luke Donald and Martin Kaymer yielded only one and a half points out of four. That just shows you that best-laid plans 'gang aft agley', as Robert Burns wrote. You always need a bit of luck because you never really know what is going to happen.

I had a pretty good idea, though, when I marched from a buzzing practice ground that Sunday morning in 2002 to the noisiest 1st tee I ever heard.

I smashed the ball down the middle of the fairway a distance of over 300 yards. Long for me. Adrenalin, I suppose.

Sam walked 25 yards with me off the tee and just said, 'You're my man. Go get the point.'

Happily, I did. And a few hours later Paul McGinley, 'batting' at number 9, completed business.

Chapter Seventeen

The Fame Game

Just in case there is someone out there who does not know the urban myth (or is it merely a joke?) about Frank Sinatra and the high-school kid in a restaurant, let me remind you.

Sinatra was dining with some friends when a young man – let's call him Rory – approached the table and introduced himself to the great man. 'Would you please do me a favour, Mr Sinatra?' he asked respectfully.

'What kind of favour?' the legendary singer replied.

'I'm here with my girlfriend and I want to impress her. It would be great if you could drop by my table and say "Hi, Rory".'

'OK, kid, I'll try.'

Sure enough, on the way back from what Americans call the restroom, Sinatra stopped by the teenager and his friends. 'Hi, Rory,' he said.

'Don't bother me now, Frankie, can't you see I'm busy?' the young man said.

Well, there I was on the practice range at West Kilbride, conducting a clinic as part of a company day. My mobile rang. A voice I recognised immediately said hello. I put my hand over the phone to speak to the assembled guests. 'Sorry, it's Michael Douglas,' I said, with a big grin on my face.

What happened next? Well, I didn't return to my call and tell the son of Spartacus and husband of Catherine Zeta-Jones not to bother me when I was busy. Douglas, with whom my son Daniel and I had played in the Dunhill Links Championship the previous week, was phoning to say how much he had enjoyed playing with us. A class act. And Catherine Zeta-Jones is not too bad either!

Sinatra, incidentally, was a keen golfer. As I mentioned, Ol' Blue Eyes spent the entire week watching Ben Hogan win the 1953 Open Championship at Carnoustie and in 1959 he, Bob Hope and Bing Crosby were famous spectators at the Ryder Cup at Eldorado Golf Club in Palm Desert, California. No wonder Dai Rees and his GB&I team felt intimidated.

The first time he played a round of golf with Arnold Palmer, a struggling Sinatra spent most of the day in the Palm Springs rough. 'What do you think of my game?' he asked Arnie rather bravely.

'Not bad but I still prefer golf,' a deadpan Palmer replied.

Golf and celebrity have always gone together. However, it was golf and notoriety in the case of Al Capone, who played twice a week in the Chicago area, sometimes at Olympia Fields Country Club, a venue for major championships, and sometimes at Burnham Woods. The latter was the reputed burial ground for the guns and police uniforms used by Capone's gang in the 1929 St Valentine's Day Massacre.

The Fame Game

Capone, who could shoot in the 80s – balls and bullets – would walk down the fairways surrounded by twenty wise guys with names like Banjo Eyes and Killer. Capone wore a monogrammed silk shirt, plus fours and a diamond-studded belt. The whisky flask on his hip would be passed around his playing partners, who included Jack 'Machine Gun' McGurn.

One day, according to one report I read, a revolver Capone kept in his golf bag went off injuring its owner in the leg. It could not have happened to a wiser guy.

Golf and celebrity were a good fit long before Bing Crosby and Bob Hope came along with their high profile, obvious talent and desire to create their own tournaments. The AT&T Pebble Beach National Pro-Am began life as the Crosby Clambake in 1937.

Over the years there have been celebrity-sponsored tournaments such as the Glen Campbell Los Angeles Open, the Sammy Davis Jr Greater Hartford Open, the Dean Martin Tucson Open and the Andy Williams San Diego Open. More recently the Justin Timberlake Shriners Hospitals for Children Open took place at TPC Summerlin in Las Vegas. Outside the PGA Tour is a Celebrity Tour in which celebrities play competitively for prize money in what are regarded as corporate hospitality entertainment events.

Pro-celebrity golf – as distinct from pro-ams – began in Britain in 1974 with the Peter Alliss-fronted television programme *Pro-Celebrity Golf* on the BBC. These were recorded first at Turnberry then Gleneagles, with various combinations of professionals including Johnny Miller and Peter Oosterhuis, Lee Trevino and Fuzzy Zoeller. I remember watching the early programmes, which featured stars such as Sean Connery, Bobby Charlton,

Telly Savalas, Bing Crosby, Bruce Forsyth, Jimmy Tarbuck, Ronnie Corbett and Henry Cooper. I have played with most of them over the years.

I have to confess I have never been embarrassed by being star struck. I was playing in the Kenyan Open in the early 1970s and staying in the InterContinental Hotel. One day I was walking across the lobby when I recognised a well-known figure coming towards me. 'Holy shit, it's James Bond,' I thought.

'Morning, Sam,' 007 said, before heading off for a take or two.

I was overwhelmed that James Bond knew who I was. Connery had an aura, as did Clint Eastwood, who joined a group of us chatting at Pebble Beach. He might have been attracted by the presence of a few stunning wives of amateurs. They were certainly attracted by him! It was like flies round shit.

Sean and I have since played many rounds of golf together. He stayed in my old house in Largs when being taught by my father. Dad taught Sean so well that he carded a 3 under par 69 on the Old Course one year to win the R&A Autumn Medal.

Fly 1,000 miles or so south from Kenya and you will arrive at Zambia, scene of one of my earliest tournament victories as a professional. Victory in the 1975 Zambian Open earned me a game the following day with President Kenneth Kaunda. He was not a great golfer, I have to say, but he never lost a ball!

As I've said, the president and Brian Barnes became great friends, what with Barnsie winning in Zambia twice and competing there frequently in what was known as the Safari Tour. This was around the time that Barnsie was being lined up for an acting career. To explain: Brian's manager was the larger-than-life Derek Pillage who, as it happened, was a friend and associate of the actor Stanley Baker, himself a keen golfer. That connection earned the ebullient Pillage a few scenes in the classic film, *Zulu*, starring Baker and Michael Caine. When I say a few scenes, I exaggerate. The only part of Pillage that survived the editing room was his considerable rear emerging from a window and descending a ladder.

'Saw yer arse last night,' I would say to him when we met.

Barnsie was later lined up to appear in the prequel, *Zulu Dawn*. Pillage, who entertained grand ideas of his charge starting a new career when his playing days were over, arranged for acting lessons. This was long before Vinnie Jones made his first tackle never mind his first film. However, the project was postponed on Baker's sad death and his chance was gone.

Golf often attracts the most unlikely people. If Chris Evans in spikes is an incongruous marriage, then what about that heavy-metal icon Alice Cooper in cashmere? Yet Evans is a bona fide golf nut and Cooper has become almost as well known shooting birdies as spilling (fake) blood on stage. How unlikely a golf addict is country and western singing and songwriting legend Willie Nelson, with his T-shirt, jeans and ponytail? But his passion led to him building his own course at home in Austin, Texas.

I loved his attitude about it being his own course, so he could do what he wanted, wear what he wanted, drink what he wanted and play with whomever he wanted. 'I have got one hole that's a par 23 and yesterday I damn near birdied the sucker,' is his familiar refrain when interviewed about his passion. In June 2012 he launched the inaugural Willie Nelson Celebrity Golf Tournament at his own Pedernales Cut N Putt Golf Club in Texas.

The Bob Hope Desert Classic in California began in 1965, not least because of a desire on behalf of the comedian to match his mate Bing Crosby in his patronage of golf and charity work. It took fifteen years to cross the Atlantic, though the Bob Hope British Classic lasted only four years under that name. The Four Stars – so-called, according to the joke, because it attracted only four stars – carried the baton under various sponsors and for the most part at Moor Park in Hertfordshire until its demise in 1990. Apart from a few American celebs, including Telly Savalas, the tournament relied for its broader appeal on the usual suspects of Tarbuck, Corbett, Cooper, Forsyth and Terry Wogan. I was beaten in a play-off by Mark McNulty in 1987 while Scotland's greatest footballer Kenny Dalglish, a keen and very useful player, took the celebrity prize in 1989.

The Dunhill Links Championship now flies the flag for pro-celebrity golf in Europe. Academy Award nominee Bill Murray, of *Ghostbusters*, *Groundhog Day* and *Lost in Translation* fame, probably the most pre-eminent celebrity golfer in the world, is a regular at St Andrews, as is Hugh Grant. There are many more actors and singers attracted to the Scottish event, as well as an increasing number of sportsmen such as footballers Jamie Red-knapp, Johan Cruyff and Ruud Gullit; cricketers Michael Vaughan and Andrew Strauss; rugby union's Gavin Hastings and Zinzan Brooke; and, of course, my good Sunningdale friend, tennis player Tim Henman.

Henman is by a long way the best celebrity golfer I have ever seen. He could have easily been a professional golfer. Among the other sportsmen, Gary Lineker is pretty good. Sean Connery at his height was right up there among the golfing actors. Christopher Lee has a lovely swing but behaves in the most extraordinary fashion. I will say no more.

The Dunhill retains a special place in my heart because my son Daniel and I won the Pro-Am in 2003 with a better ball score of 251, 37 under par. Daniel, who was fifteen at the time, put together rounds of 73, 70, 68 and 67 from the amateur tees at Carnoustie, St Andrews, Kingsbarns and St Andrews respectively. The sight of Torrance and Torrance at the top of the leader board made me choke back the tears. Remember, I cry at the drop of a stitch.

I can't remember if that was the year I nearly ran goalkeeping great Peter Schmeichel off the road. I was driving back to St Andrews from Carnoustie near the Tay Road Bridge at Dundee. This big black Mercedes would not let me get into the left lane. I let rip with a bout of road rage that would make Tony Soprano look like a kitten. I hate idiots on the road. I went mad, peeping the horn, shouting and swearing at the driver. Then I saw the placid smiling face of the big Dane. I was mortified.

The eccentric Bill Murray is the subject of perhaps the most bizarre story to emerge from the Dunhill. Murray had arranged to spend the evening with the European Tour's resident practical jokers Mark Roe and Robert Lee. A bit of a pub crawl was to be followed by a spot of dinner. The plan had not been to attend one of the many student parties in St Andrews. But Murray, like a Scotsman at Hogmanay unable to resist the sight of an open door, walked into the flat and made himself at home. So, feeling right at home, he went into the kitchen and washed the dishes, pausing only to grab a snack from the fridge. Can you imagine the face on the first-year divinity student, let's say, who walked into the kitchen to find a Marigold-gloved Murray doing the dishes?

That would not have been the style of the late, lamented Frank Carson, one of the funniest men I have ever met. He could never have slipped quietly into any room. I remember arriving at La Duquesa, a hotel on the Costa del Sol with which I used to have an attachment, to find the place pretty much in uproar. Frank had been hosting a group of twelve corporate guests for a long golfing weekend. I was told he had not stopped to breathe once in four days as he cracked joke after joke without ever repeating the same story. The golfers were sore with laughing. He was fantastic, the stuff that he stored in his head.

The Ryder Cup captaincy opened many doors for me – for example the door to Buckingham Palace. I found myself one of ten guests invited to have lunch with the Queen and Prince Philip. There were people there from all walks of life. I was the only sportsman. My God, it was intimidating. You just hope someone else speaks. Jokes are my style – but you can't start telling jokes to the Queen. Golf was not really her thing. I did say to her that my daughter, Anouska, had wanted me to bring one of the corgis home.

Tim Henman

Sam on Tim: 'The Tim Henman I know is quite different from the Tim Henman who was willed to win Wimbledon by just about everyone in Britain throughout a distinguished tennis career. For a start he pretty much detests the Tiger Tim nickname that was given to him by the media. And he much prefers to be called by his

new nickname (see below) rather than Tim when playing golf at Sunningdale. The Tim Henman I know is an exceptional golfer, one of the finest amateurs I have ever played with and certainly by a long way the best celebrity. He could definitely have made it as a professional had he chosen golf when a youngster. I have no doubt about that. But he enjoyed a wonderful tennis career with eleven ATP tour successes, a world ranking high of number four and six semi-finals in major championships. A gifted sportsman, he is also great fun and a very popular member of our club.'

Hardly a week goes by without the phone ringing and a distinctive Scottish voice crying out, 'Ping Pong, how are you?'

This is Sam Torrance getting in touch with yours truly to arrange a game of golf at Sunningdale. It might be Sam and Paul McGinley, for example, taking on me and Jamie Redknapp.

'Ping Pong' was, as usual, the work of Queenie (Michael King), a stylish player in his day on the European Tour and an inveterate inventor and distributor of nicknames that stick. Ping-pong, table tennis, take away the table – you get the drift. I quite like it. A welcome change from Tiger Tim.

Golf has been a passion of mine for years. I couldn't play all that often during my tennis career for obvious reasons, there just wasn't time. But I have caught up since retiring by playing two or three rounds a week during the golf season and keeping my hand in during the winter. At the time of writing my handicap is scratch, plus 0.4 to be exact. If I get any lower I will have to add strokes to my round when taking part in the Dunhill

Links Championship, always a highlight of the year for us amateurs.

Golf tends to be popular with tennis pros. Rafael Nadal is keen but I have never had a game with him. I have been out a few times with Roger Federer who, as you might expect, is fairly decent. I played most with Pete Sampras, who since his retirement has virtually set up home on the golf course. Pete, fellow American Todd Martin, Yevgeny Kafelnikov and myself were a fairly regular four. The last time I heard Pete was playing off a handicap of 3.

Before Pete there was Ivan Lendl, who had ambitions to become a professional golfer. That's not for me. I have had my top-class professional sports career. Now I just want to enjoy myself, play with my friends and get my competitive buzz from our modest money matches. That keeps the juices flowing. Some have said very kindly that I am good enough to enter top-class amateur championships, but why would I put myself through that?

Lendl, who teamed up with Andy Murray as his coach at the start of 2012, seems a very different beast. I remember reading that he played 250-plus rounds of golf in his first year out of tennis. He was as obsessive a practiser on the range as he had been on the courts when winning eight Grand Slams. He declared himself determined to play pro golf and he did to the extent that he took part in two European Tour events and three Nationwide Tour events. Not with any success. However, he did win a celebrity players event in the States. I doubt if he matched his high aspirations, though he has passed on the golf bug to his daughters who, last I heard, are on track to be professionals. I met Lendl in 2011, when he claimed to be playing off plus 3.

That seems an amazing handicap except that the Americans have a different system.

The most extraordinary story of a tennis pro turned golf pro is that of Australian Scott Draper, so much so that there has been a lot of talk about making a film out of it.

Draper, very much a contemporary having been born within three months of me, won the junior doubles championship at Wimbledon at the age of eighteen, by which time he was already suffering from an almost paralysing obsessive compulsive disorder. I have read that at its worst he could scarcely leave his room. He would repeatedly make and unmake his bed. He was fixated by the number three, meaning, for example, that he would tap the table or clap three times. I have also read that he suffered from an obsessive fear of regurgitation and vomiting. His mother once said that she thought acne medication had unbalanced his brain chemistry. But he managed to overcome all that.

There is so much more in this amazing tale. Scott married his childhood sweetheart, Kellie, who was suffering from cystic fibrosis. While her health was deteriorating rapidly in 1998, he won his only major professional singles title at The Queen's Club in London. Sadly, she died soon afterwards.

It was at this time, while grieving for Kellie and locked inside a deep depression, that he began playing golf. Somehow, golf became his therapy. In tennis, he was identified as the quickest walker in the game. I remember beating Scott in the second round of the Wimbledon singles in 2002, an unremarkable match but for the fact that prior to our coming on to Centre Court two heavily lunched jokers managed to breach security for a knock-up. The crowd loved it; the officials were apoplectic.

Scott's story moves on to 2005 and an amazing week at the Australian Open. Scott made his professional golf debut while competing in – and winning – the mixed doubles title with fellow Australian Samantha Stosur. Honest, I am not making this up. On the Friday morning he shot 79 in the first round of the Victorian Open before rushing to the tennis arena in Melbourne to win his mixed doubles semi-final in the afternoon. Saturday saw him card a second round 74 to miss the cut in the 54-hole tournament.

On Sunday he and Sam won the tennis title. And just to round it off Scott teed off at 7.50 a.m. on Monday trying to qualify for the Heineken Classic.

Within a few months of that, Scott was forced to retire from tennis because of a knee injury. There was a short spell in 2007 when he became Lleyton Hewitt's coach, but the golf bug had bitten deep and he decided that was where his future sporting career lies. I doubt if Tiger or Rory need to worry.

As you might imagine, his life spawned a fascinating autobiography entitled *Too Good*.

Bob Torrance

Sam on Bob: 'My father is the hardest worker I have ever known. He can – and does – spend all day standing on the practice range at a tournament or in the bays at the National Sports Training Centre in Largs, now known as the Bob Torrance School of Golf. Or the "salt

mines", as he likes to call them. There he stands, a cigarette cupped in his hand, underneath a flat bonnet, spreading swing wisdom with that distinctive gruff voice of his.

I call him my greatest asset, the only person who has ever coached me. He and my mother are my greatest fans, and during a break from teaching at an event the two of them sit in the press area following my every stroke on the scoreboard or, if televised, on the box.

Dad was the professional and greenkeeper at Rossendale in Lancashire when he took me under his golfing wing. I hadn't really played much golf before then. I was eight, maybe nine, when I came in one day and told my parents I had scored 37 for nine holes.

'You're a bloody liar,' Dad said. 'Show me. Let's go out there and have another nine holes.'

I shot another 37. That was when he became aware that I might have the talent and the desire to become a decent player. And when I left home as a teenager to make my way in golf he gave me my first car, a Vanden Plas Princess 1100. That left him car-less.'

The most famous person I ever taught was not my son and not Padraig Harrington, the twice Open champion; his name was Bond, James Bond, 007 himself.

Sean Connery's first ever visit to Largs for a lesson proved a bit of a bunfight. Word got around. Hundreds, if not thousands, turned up with their cameras and their autograph books. Television arrived to do some filming. I was apologetic.

'Don't worry, Bob, it's fine,' he said.

Later, he stayed the night with Sam in his big white house on the hill. But that morning he paid a visit to my house where my wife June had invited 'the girls' around for a cup of tea. She did not let on the real reason for the invitation. When there came a knock at the door and James Bond walked in, there was pretty near a mass outbreak of fainting by June's friends.

'Don't kiss me, Sean, I've got a cold sore,' June said as she opened the door.

'I don't mind at all,' he replied, giving her a smacker, the dream of most women at the time, and probably even now.

Anyway, I gave Sean a lesson. It quickly became obvious he had talent. I reckon he could have become a scratch golfer had he started at a younger age. I could tell that first time that he had studied method – and I don't mean method acting – and one method in particular.

'Have you been reading the Hogan book?' I asked, referring to Ben Hogan, my all-time hero, the greatest there has ever been in my opinion.

'Yes, I've got it at my bedside,' he replied.

'Throw it away and get Sam Snead's book.'

My reasoning was simple. Hogan was a smallish man with a swing suitable for players of a similar size. Snead was tall and athletic, like Sean. I believe firmly that you teach the man and not the method. In other words, what worked for Hogan might not work for some, especially bigger golfers.

I like to think that Sean benefited from my lessons. I think that I heard he shot 69 over the Old Course in an R&A Medal after we did some work. We got on well. Sean likes a laugh and a joke. But he is very competitive and does not suffer fools gladly. Sean was a regular in the Showbiz Eleven football team during the late 1950s and 1960s. There was an occasion when at 0–0 the Showbiz Eleven won a penalty in the final minute. Sean grabbed the ball and placed it on the spot. As he was preparing to take the kick, Dave King, the comedian, ran up and struck the ball nearer the corner flag than the goal. Those present swear that Sean looked like he was going to strangle him to death.

The first thing I look for when someone comes to me for a lesson is the swing. Is it free and flowing? You want it to be what I call 'oily'. Then I look from the ground up, not from the head down. Feet and legs are the most important. But I also look to see if the golfer is a leg–body or a hand player: Nicklaus was the former, Henry Cotton the latter.

I have several mantras. For example: never weaken a strength to strengthen a weakness. In other words, never take away what they are good at in order to improve what they are not so good at. You can do five things wrong in a golf swing and one thing right and play superbly; equally you can do five things right and one thing wrong and play crap. You must strive for perfection; you will never reach it but you must strive for it.

Timing is less important than it used to be when the clubs were whippy. More important now is coordination with everything working together.

The two most important areas are the takeaway and the start of the downswing. Everything outside that doesn't matter. Sam still works on trying to get his takeaway right. He always had a great leg action. Sam also had a pause at the top of his swing right from the start. A pause is good. Snead had a pause but Hogan did not and no one has been better than Hogan.

Peter Thomson said of Hogan that he was three or four shots a round better than anyone else technically.

It is funny. I saw Hogan win the Open Championship at Carnoustie in 1953. I did not rate him. I changed my mind. He became my idol. Just about the greatest day of my life was when I accepted an invitation to visit him at Shady Oaks Golf Club in Fort Worth, Texas, the place with which he was always associated. He took my wife, June, and I to dinner at his private table in the club.

We drank a couple of bottles of wine and later had a malt whisky that I brought from Scotland. I had been tipped off about his liking for a good malt. I also took him some cashmere socks in his favourite colours – caramel, grey and navy blue – and a few cardigans.

We talked golf, of course. We spoke about technique. Then he took me aside, away from June, for a little chat.

'I am going to tell you the secret of golf,' Hogan said. 'But you mustn't tell anyone. I am going to write it down some day, so, as I say, I don't want you to tell anyone.'

He took it to his grave, as I will do.

June is a sharp cookie. She was always saying to me you need to find someone talented who is prepared to work ten hours a day. Like Hogan. The first day I was with Padraig from early morning until nine at night.

'You've got one,' June said when I got home.

Then there was the time Paul McGinley came for a lesson. He was the last of the day and it was pretty cold, dark and wet when we neared the end of our work. A couple of bystanders had been watching. Eventually, they summoned up the courage to come across and speak.

'Excuse me, I am an England selector,' one said. 'If you don't mind me saying I think your right elbow is too close to your side.'

'So was Hogan's,' I said.

'He ain't no Hogan,' the man countered.

Maybe not, but like Sam, Paul holed the putt that won the Ryder Cup. And he is a great guy.

Chapter Eighteen

A Decent Punt

It was the great Lee Trevino who said about gambling in golf: 'You don't know what pressure is until you play for five bucks with only two in your pocket.'

He knew. He had been there, done that and worn the worried look on his face. But only when he was bluffing.

Then there is the kind of pressure felt by a professional trying to win a tournament or by an established player seeking to win a major championship. The club handicapper cannot know what that is like.

There is a story credited to Harry Vardon in which he attempted to give a club member a taste of the pressure. Vardon won a record six Open Championships, but it is his development of the Vardon grip (aka the overlapping grip), used to this day by the vast majority of professionals, that has sustained his name in the modern game.

Vardon finished runner-up to Ted Ray in the 1920 US Open

at Inverness Country Club in Toledo after missing a 3-foot putt on the final hole. One of those enthusiastic, if misguided, members asked Vardon how such a great player as him could miss so short a putt. Vardon replied with a challenge. He bet the man $100 that exactly one week on the member couldn't make the identical putt that Vardon had missed. He said that the guy had all week to practise the putt.

The man jumped at the bet. Vardon made sure the newspapers knew what was going on. Come the appointed hour, a huge gallery had turned up to watch events. The member missed the putt by a margin. His ball did not even touch the hole. That lesson about pressure cost the man $100.

When I started gambling at golf the stakes were no more than a shilling, the equivalent of 5p these days. Mind you, I was only ten years old and my victims were Brother Nicholas and the rest of his clerical fourball. That was at Routenburn Golf Course on the roof of my hometown of Largs, where I would sit on the wall beside the 18th green waiting for the arrival of the golfing priests with their shillings. A bit of a contrast to the $1.25 million that basketball legend Michael Jordan was reputed to have lost in ten days.

From there I moved on to the money matches with members at Sunningdale, from which I supplemented my meagre income as an assistant professional at the club. My winnings in that first year at the old Surrey club in 1971 provided me with enough of an income to open my first bank account.

As an assistant at Sunningdale you would play a member for your fee. If you won, you received double; if you lost, more often than not you still picked up your fee. The members were very kind. We would play singles or fourballs. The big matches were the goal. Everyone knew they were going on and everyone was desperate to gain access to them. Some members playing for a few grand would choose an assistant as a partner and give him a percentage of the winnings.

The next step was full-time tournament golf. I used to love the money matches we would have on a tour, usually on a Tuesday. To me, the most fun you can have on a golf course is two professionals against two other professionals for a couple of hundred quid. Just go for your life. I think that's fantastic. It's something that definitely improved me as a golfer and improved my competitive capability. I regarded a practice round on my own, just me on the golf course hitting balls, as a form of slow torture. I would play six holes and walk off. Give me a £200 match and I am in heaven. The amount actually doesn't really matter. I have always believed that you practise more sharply if you have got something on the game. You are playing for pride, not pounds.

There was never any harm in it, though I remember Greg Norman, partnered by fellow Australian Stewart Ginn, getting very angry at losing a match against John O'Leary and me at Portmarnock in 1980.

O'Leary was happy that day. However, he was less so on one occasion at Sun City, the gambling capital of South Africa. I was hitting the ball beautifully and backed myself to win at very attractive odds. John also had a bet on me. Sure enough, I was one stroke off the lead coming to the end of the third round on a day of energy-sapping high temperatures. Suddenly, I was overcome by the heat. I was absolutely gone, on the point of collapse. My attempted chip shot from the side of the 16th green saw the ball move barely a foot and I did not even fluff it.

So I picked up, staggered to the clubhouse without playing the final two holes and collapsed straight into the pool – clothes, golf shoes and all.

'That's our money gone,' was all O'Leary, oblivious to my welfare, could say.

Playing golf for money is as old as golf itself.

The 'hustle' forms part of the relationship between golf and gambling. Not a dance, as the word suggests, but a misrepresentation of the situation, shall we say. I hustled the priests in Largs; Trevino hustled Ray Floyd, another legendary money player, on their first meeting when pretending to be a Mexican handyman who would fetch the cart, carry his clubs into the locker room and clean his shoes.

The most notorious golfer–gambler–hustler was Alvin Clarence Thomas, known as Titanic Thompson because of his ability to sink everyone with his outrageous bets and scams. The so-called Man Who Bet On Everything, he was reputed to have taken $500 off Al Capone and lived to tell the tale. He could play to scratch right handed or left handed, fire pistols, shoot pool and pitch horseshoes with his incredible hand–eye coordination. But his best wheezes involved that formidable combination of skill and cunning.

One of his favourite hustles was betting he could make three out of five lengthy putts. His victim never knew that Thompson would go out on the course the night before to position a heavy water hose from the cup to the edge of the green. This created a pretty much invisible furrow for Thompson to roll his putts easily into the hole.

Thompson was nothing if not ingenious. Once while in Illinois for a tournament he stopped a farmer driving down a road

A Decent Punt

with a truckload of watermelons. He asked the puzzled man if he could count the melons before buying the entire load. There was one stipulation: the farmer was required to drive past a hotel in town where known gamblers hung out. The deal was done. At the agreed hour, as the farmer drove down the road, Thompson bet the gamblers that he could guess the exact number of watermelons. The wager was set and he cleaned up. Genius.

Another of his wheezes, which he took from state to state, involved Thompson betting 'suckers' that he could throw a peanut over a tall building. Impossible you would think except that Thompson had loaded the peanuts with lead.

There is a story that sounds somewhat fanciful but is credited to the legendary Sam Snead. Snead was propositioned by a wealthy club member, who suggested they play for $1,000 a hole. Snead said he was too busy. The rich guy persisted.

'What's your handicap?' Snead asked. Remember that the most important part of any money match is before a ball is struck when the terms are established – number of shots, type of bets, any other conditions, etc. A game can be won or lost in these negotiations.

'No handicap,' the mysterious man replied. 'Head to head, no strokes, but I want two gotchas.'

Snead – and this is where I have to suspend belief a little – had never heard the expression. But he agreed. The match began. Snead had a birdie putt on the 1st green while his opponent, clearly a bit of a hacker, could do no better than a bogey.

Snead was crouching over his birdie putt when the member approached from the rear, reached down and grabbed Snead's balls shouting 'gotcha'.

The member went on to win a few thousand.

Well, you try playing 17 holes not knowing when the second 'gotcha' was going to come.

The aforementioned Trevino and Floyd became a great American money pairing. We had the Yorkshire duo of Lionel Platts and Hedley Muscroft, who may not have enjoyed the most stellar of individual records but together in big betting matches were at times unbeatable. Like Thompson, their scams were not restricted to the golf course. Muscroft once relieved Welsh actor Stanley Baker – of *Zulu* fame – of £100 after giving him a 50-yard start in a 100-yard race. The only condition was that Baker would first have to drink a glass of water. He was never told that the water would be boiling hot.

Platts possessed a bag of 7-irons, in that he had a special set of irons made all stamped with the number 7. This was designed to confuse the opposition in match play. I am given to understand that Platts tried this out in the 1965 Ryder Cup match at Royal Birkdale. It must have equally baffled his partner Peter Butler – the pair didn't win a match!

Once Platts and Musgrove had had their day, Torrance and O'Leary gained a certain reputation. Ian Woosnam and his mate D. J. Russell were also pretty useful on a Tuesday.

Seve Ballesteros also loved a wager, and not just on the course. I remember once being in a hotel room with him at the French Open when he insisted on betting on his ability to throw a coin into a tiny square in the carpet. But that wasn't enough for Seve. He wanted to do it by throwing the coin beyond the target and spinning it back into the exact spot. He failed every time but every time he believed he was going to do it. That was Seve.

Laura Davies

Sam on Laura: 'Probably the best woman golfer Britain has ever produced. Certainly, Laura boasts the best record with four major championship victories, twenty tournament successes on the demanding LPGA Tour and eighty-one wins worldwide. What is more, she has played in all twelve Solheim Cup matches, from the first to the most recent victory by Europe over the United States. Laura still hits a long ball and remains competitive in a professional career that dates back to 1985. Her competitiveness goes beyond golf, though. Everyone knows Laura's love of all sport and her love of a bet, something she shares with me. One thing I would say about her: I would not fancy playing her for money in a triathlon of sports – golf, pool and darts – which I rate myself pretty highly at. And I would not say that about anyone else in the world, man or woman.'

P art of the pleasure of winning a golf tournament comes from the messages of congratulation that you receive from friends and relatives. The telephone would ring more than usual. There might be letters and cards, maybe even a bunch of flowers. Nowadays, it is a text message or an email or a tweet, or perhaps something on Facebook. It is the thought that counts.

That was very much the case some years back when I received a text from Sam. I was sitting in a tapas bar in Spain with my caddie and a few other people having a drink and something to eat.

'Congratulations on your terrific win,' he wrote with all his characteristic enthusiasm and warmth.

This was a bit out of the blue. I had never played golf with Sam. We did not really know each other that well.

There followed almost immediately a phone call that began with Sam and, it transpired, Christy O'Connor Jnr, singing – more like shouting – a familiar refrain heard at football grounds up and down the country. Only the words were different. 'One Laura Davies, there's only one Laura Davies, one Laura Davies, there's only one . . .' You get the drift. Then more congratulations from two men who had obviously been enjoying their day off. Drink had been taken, as they would say in Scotland and Ireland on such occasions.

This was all very well and gratefully appreciated except for a few little details. I had not just won a tournament. In fact, I had not won an LPGA tournament for over three years. And this was not a Sunday afternoon when events finish but a Tuesday night!

Even allowing for their inebriated state, I was puzzled. We were all puzzled. But we worked it out. Sam and Christy, at that time both in their fifties, were obviously in America for a Champions Tour event. The Tuesday of the week was traditionally the time to let your hair down. They had been in a bar – not hard to work out – and had been watching a rerun of my victory in the Wegmans Rochester International in 2001. Only this was 2004 and in their condition they had not realised they were watching an old recording. We had a good laugh about it. We laughed about it for days afterwards and any time I am in a tapas bar the story is trotted out.

Only recently I discovered that Sam has no memory of the incident. He probably swears blind it never happened. But I know – and now you know – different.

Anyway, it is the thought that counts.

As I said, Sam and I have never played golf together. But we have a few things in common. We have the same management company, IMG, and the same manager, the lovely and efficient Vicki Cuming. We also share a love of a bet. Unlike Sam I don't get involved in too many money matches on the course, but I have pretty much bet on anything over the years.

I used to spend a lot of time in casinos but I have given that up. I don't like the atmosphere any more. Football is my big thing. I love betting on football. I take it very seriously indeed, spending a lot of my spare time studying scores, statistics and trends, and reading up on everything I can on the game. You should not really gamble on anything without being as informed as you can. I like to think I am pretty knowledgable about football.

I certainly work at it. I will give you an example from a few days before writing this early in 2011. I worked out that Liverpool – my team – were statistically due a penalty taking into consideration the venue, the opposition and other variables. I knew that Steven Gerrard, their normal penalty-kick taker, would not be playing because of injury. I knew that Dirk Kuyt was in the starting eleven and that he would be a likely replacement for Gerrard should Liverpool be awarded a penalty. So I bet a few bob that Kuyt would score with a penalty.

Sure enough, Gerrard did not play; Kuyt did; Liverpool won a penalty; Kuyt took it. And just to show what can happen when betting, Kuyt missed! Such is life.

I have had the pleasure of playing in pro-ams and charity events with many famous footballers throughout my career – Kevin Keegan and Glenn Hoddle, for example, both brilliant players and both former England managers. I played three rounds in China once with Ruud Gullit, the great Dutch footballer. It's not just footballers, either. I enjoyed a wonderful day with Hugh Grant, the famous film star, who turned out to be a lovely man, very down to earth, nice and straightforward. He played half decently, too. Michael Phelps may be a stunning swimmer but he is no golfer.

Probably the best celebrity in terms of golfing ability was Nigel Mansell, F1 motor-racing champion. A scratch golfer at the time, he pretty much played like one.

It will not be too long before I hit the big 5-0. But I have no plans to stop either competing or supporting Liverpool!

Chapter Nineteen

Amateur Dramatics

I was once hit by the mayor of Bournemouth. That can happen in a pro-am when balls fly around in all directions. I call it my Spiro Agnew moment.

Agnew, a former vice president of the United States, was notorious for firing balls into spectators at pro-am events, such as the Bob Hope Classic. President Gerald Ford was another gallery scatterer, who featured prominently in the hilarious routines Bob Hope would deliver during his tournament.

'Gerry Ford is easy to spot on the course. He drives the cart with the red cross painted on top.' 'You don't know what fear is until you hear Ford behind you shouting "Fore!"' 'Gerald Ford is the most dangerous driver since Ben-Hur.' 'It's not hard to find Gerald Ford on a golf course – just follow the wounded.' 'Shortly after I started playing golf with Gerry Ford I thought it was time to take some lessons – not golf lessons, first aid.' 'When Agnew bellowed "Fore!" you never knew whether he was telling someone to get out of the way or if he was predicting how many spectators he would hit with the shot.'

The mayor of Bournemouth got me smack in the middle of my tummy. I was perhaps 30 yards from him and standing well to the right. You could read the make of the ball on the imprint on my stomach. This was during the pro-am for the old Sumrie Fourball Tournament in Bournemouth. I love a fourball, when you tee up with your mate and go for every shot. I played with my late, great friend Ronnie Shade, whose initials from his first and middle names could not better sum up the player: RDBM – right down the bloody middle.

On one occasion during the filming of a pro-am for television, a Henry Cooper drive flew right and struck a BBC continuity girl on the chest. You have never seen so many people volunteer to massage the injury. There was less of a rush when our 'Enery split his trousers down the arse.

Pro-ams can be difficult for a professional. We all know how important pro-ams are for the finances of a tournament and how attractive they are for sponsors. There are some who enter into them wholeheartedly, they make friends and contacts for life and treat the whole thing as a bit of fun. There are other pros, however, who regard the day as a monumental pain in the arse. Rounds can last forever – up to six hours – and you can be lumbered with not just the worst golfer in the world but a real tool.

Like the Italian businessman I was drawn with who knew best about everything, including how to play golf. He would not have broken 100. I could scarcely hide my glee when at one hole he missed a putt and smashed the ball off the green into a bunker. I had to inform him that two scores counted at every hole and since two of us had already picked up he would have to play on from the sand.

Lee Trevino used to be great in pro-ams, with both his amateur playing partners and the spectators. Once at the Benson and Hedges at Fulford in York, Trevino came straight off a plane – a bit jet-lagged – to the 1st tee for a practice round. This was not actually the day of the pro-am.

'Can I join you?' he asked.

I explained to him that I had promised a game to Steve Robertson, the tournament doctor and a pretty ordinary 24 handicapper. That was no problem to Trevino who, unlike some prima donnas, was perfectly prepared to play with a complete rabbit.

Trevino could not have been more brilliant. Steve was a danger to shipping and we were a long way from the sea. Eventually, we had him tee off 50 yards in front because he was killing people. A huge crowd had gathered to see Trevino in action. He had the spectators in stitches with his wisecracking and in awe with his shot-making. He even caught a ball in his hat, pitcher-style, that Steve had nailed with his 3-wood and was heading straight for me. The crowd went bananas.

As they probably did at Cypress Point in the early 1950s when Johnny Weissmuller, the best known of all the Tarzans, famously hit his ball into a tree during the aforementioned Clambake. He climbed up to play the shot and on the way down could not resist hanging from a branch by one arm, beating his chest with the other and yelling his immortal 'yea-ya-ya-ya-ah'. Well, you try spelling it.

Pro-am day is now Wednesday on the main Tours and Thursday on the Senior Tours. Back in the 1970s, though, they were staged not on the eve of the tournament but on the Sunday, the day after the final round, at a course near to the event. Crowds often as big as 20,000 would come from all around to see all – and I mean all – the top pros from number one Peter Oosterhuis down, playing with celebrities such as Sean Connery, Ronnie Corbett and Bruce Forsyth, as well as the sponsors' guests.

Ronnie Corbett played in the same group as me on the occasion of my all-time favourite pro-am day for reasons that are obvious. It was the day I shot 58! The round of my life, at least in terms of the lowest.

Sixty remains the magic barrier in golf. It still happens so infrequently that television commentators become extremely animated when any golfer gets in sight of golf's Holy Grail. But I skipped the 59 and went straight for the even rarer 58. According to official records there have been three 58s in tournament golf: Shigeki Maruyama in a US Open qualifier in 2000; Jason Bohn at the Canadian Tour Bayer Championship in 2001; and Ryo Ishikawa in the Crowns International on the Japan Tour in 2010.

My 58 happened in July 1992 and went almost unreported outside my native Scotland. The occasion was the Centenary Pro-Am of Bathgate Golf Club, a club between Edinburgh and Glasgow proud for having produced two Ryder Cup captains, Eric Brown and Bernard Gallacher.

I flew north on the Monday of the Scottish Open at Gleneagles in the company of Messrs Gallacher, Corbett and Forsyth. We were running late, arriving just half an hour before our tee-off time. No time to hit a ball, no time to have a practice putt, no time for lunch, but time, however, for a couple of swift pints of the black stuff.

The Guinness obviously took a little while to kick in as I missed a 10-foot eagle putt at the opening hole and a 3-foot putt for birdie at the 2nd. After that I went, as they say, 'nuts', playing the next seven holes in 7 under par to reach the turn in 28. The inward half produced birdies at the 10th, 12th, 15th and 16th, leaving me requiring just a par 4 at the last to break 60.

My drive at the 18th was perfect. It left an easy 90-yard sand wedge to the pin, my bread-and-butter shot as a pro. I am pretty hot from that range. There was a bunker to the right and another to the left, though neither could be said to be protecting the pin. An easy shot, but boy did I feel nervous. The thought of a 59 suddenly got to me. I pushed my shot 10 yards right of where I intended and close enough to the bunker for concern. But the ball bounced on the back mound of the bunker, received the friendliest of kicks left and rolled up to the flag. I was left with a tap-in for a birdie 3 and a 58. Little Ronnie could hardly contain himself with excitement.

For the record, my 13 under par score read: 4, 4, 3, 2, 3, 3, 3, 3, 3, (28), 3, 3, 4, 3, 4, 4, 3, 3, 3, (30) – total 58.

As Tarzan would say, 'Yea-ya-ya-ya-ah!'

Gordon Brand Jnr

Sam on Gordon: 'Sometimes Junior, sometimes Gordy, always a good friend. We played Ryder Cups, World Cups and Dunhill Cups together and always had a great time. Although born in Kirkcaldy, where former prime

minister Gordon Brown went to school, Junior grew up
in the Bristol area as the son of a golf professional. He
won twice in his rookie year of 1982 and went on to collect eight victories on the European Tour. He is an
inveterate prankster who used to chum around with the
Three Jokers – Mark Roe, Robert Lee and Russell Claydon. The stories they could tell, and, if you look
elsewhere in this book, have told.'

It was 1982, the Bob Hope British Classic at Moor Park and me
and Mark James found ourselves playing with Bob Hope himself for the last round of the tournament. There would have been
a fourth – and forgive me if you are reading this and you are the
person – but neither of us can remember who it was. I asked Mark.
When Bob Hope is around no one else gets a look-in.

Modesty forbids me from saying that I won by three strokes
from Mark with rounds of 65-73-65-69. I had turned professional the previous year.

But that's not the point.

The point is that we played with a legend, one of the world's
most famous comedians who, as it happened, played off 4 in his
younger days when a competitor in the Amateur Championship
at Royal Porthcawl. That was in 1951, so he would have been
forty-eight at the time.

Hope and Bing Crosby were renowned for their 'Road' pictures
and for their love of golf. For forty-six years, and long after his
death at the age of 100, Hope gave his name to the Bob Hope
Classic (the original American version), with the name changing
only in 2011 to the Humana Challenge. In 1995, the tournament's thirtieth anniversary, Hope teed it up with Bill Clinton,

then the sitting president, Gerald Ford, George Bush Sr and Scott Hoch. Three US presidents, a living legend and, er, Scott Hoch.

Hope always saved his best quips for Ford. 'Whenever I play with him,' he said of Ford, the curse of spectators with his wild shots, 'I usually try to make it a foursome – the president, myself, a paramedic and a faith healer.'

The Bob Hope British Classic was played four times under that name from 1980, with Bernhard Langer winning it the year prior to me and Spaniard Jose Maria Canizares winning the other two.

So, there we were, Hope, James, Brand Jnr and another geezer. We walked, Hope rode in a buggy. It was a particularly foul day, which is always possible in an English autumn. By the 2nd hole, we were soaked. Hope's glove was already too wet to use. He took it off and tried to put it into the pocket of his waterproof trousers. But he missed. He stuffed it between his waterproofs and his trousers and soon it worked its way down to the ankle, poking through the bottom of the legs. Mark and I both spotted this. It looked as if a hand was holding his foot. Mark, a dry individual, and I could scarcely putt for giggling. If we sound now like a couple of schoolboys, give us a break. It was bloody funny.

Not content with lashing down, the weather turned even nastier. Thunder and lightning forced a suspension in play. This was before the requirement for players to leave the course. In those days it was just a question of sheltering somewhere waiting for the storm to pass. Mark and I took cover.

Bob disappeared. We did not know where he had gone. But when it was time to resume, there he was. We asked where he had been.

'I spotted a house a couple of hundred yards away and knocked at the door,' he replied.

267

'Did you know the people living there?' one of us ventured.

'No, I just knocked.'

It turned out that a woman had answered the door, recognised the visitor as Bob Hope and invited him in. Before long he had taken off his sodden socks and shoes, dried his feet at the fire and been served with tea and cakes.

Can you imagine the chat in the local grocer's shop the following day?

'Oh, I had that Bob Hope round for a cup of tea yesterday. Nice guy but he had such smelly feet.'

The pro-am can give you the opportunity to come into contact with such diverse people in somewhat surreal circumstances. Shakin' Stevens, who I played with in the 1980s at a time when he was the biggest-selling artist in Britain, came complete with a noisy and loyal band of groupies dressed in leopard-skin outfits. He was an OK player.

Meat Loaf, another singer–celebrity with whom I found myself partnered, was no dead ringer for a golfer. He was basically a chopper. But he had not begun playing until the age of forty and did not get the bug until a few years after that.

I remember reading that he had partnered Lee Trevino in a pro-am in what was only his second ever round of golf. He did not own a set of clubs at the time, something he apparently remedied with a trip to his local Walmart store. He stuck them on a trolley and left them outside the clubhouse at Half Moon Bay in California. They were gone upon his return. Trevino introduced himself.

'Somebody took my clubs,' Meat Loaf said.

'It was me,' Trevino replied. 'I'm not going to play with anyone who's got those kind of clubs.'

As if by magic, Trevino handed over a brand new set of Callaway's.

My memory of Meat Loaf concerns his unusual method on the 1st tee. Prior to taking his stance he asked the gallery to shout as loud as possible when he was about to hit the ball. He swung and no one uttered a sound. We are proud of our respectful golf fans in this country.

He insisted. They duly obliged in a complete reversal of golf etiquette and we proceeded to have a great day. Pro-ams are different!

Daniel Torrance

Sam on Daniel: 'My firstborn, Daniel has either given me – or shared in – three of my proudest moments. He was at my side when I captained Europe to a great Ryder Cup triumph in 2002; he and I were playing partners when winning the Dunhill Links Championship Pro-Am in 2003; and he caddied for me when I won the London Seniors Masters event in 2007. They were all very special in their different ways.

Daniel is a very laid-back young man. A big Manchester United fan, he was almost as good a goalkeeper in his younger days as his father was. Lee Westwood will laugh at that one. He saw how bad I was. Daniel clearly has the ability to be a fine golfer. We shall see. Whatever he does, I will support him fully.'

I am the proud possessor of a Titleist 41, a golf ball I know I will never play with.

The '41' stands for the 41st American president, President George Bush Sr. His name is stamped on the ball, as is the presidential seal. He gave it to me when I was introduced to him during my father's Ryder Cup captaincy in 2002.

I have a bone to pick with Dad. He wrote in his autobiography that I lost the ball in the shrubbery in our garden when using it to practise my chipping. Not true. I still have it and it still looks brand new.

As the son of such a high-profile golfer, there was every chance that I was going to play. I was not born when he holed the putt to win the Ryder Cup in 1985 but I remember being at Valderrama in 1995 when he was pipped by Colin Montgomerie to the Order of Merit title. I must have been six years old. I remember him being very upset.

I did not start playing properly until I was twelve. That summer I reduced my handicap from 18 to 5. Later I got down to scratch briefly and recently I have started working at my game after a break. Like my father, I have had only one coach – he called his 'Dad' and I call mine 'Granddad'!

I caddied for Dad on the Seniors Tour in 2007 and was on his bag when he won the London Seniors Masters. That was special. But the best times have been playing golf with him, even when one or other of us would walk in after a row. That happened quite often. He can be pretty moody on the course and I can be quite stubborn. I wonder who I get that from? It used to madden him when I would hit a driver as hard as I could and not really care where it went.

We must have played hundreds of rounds together and quite often as partners in fourball matches at Sunningdale. I would always play with Dad unless one of my own friends was involved. I would collect any winnings from opponents while Dad always paid my losses. That was good.

Our most memorable partnership was our victory in the Dunhill Links Championship Pro-Am in 2003. I was fifteen and had just tied in the Gold Medal at Sunningdale. The Dunhill is such a popular tournament with professionals and amateurs, many of them famous sportsmen and celebrities, that there is a lengthy waiting list every year. Dad had been working hard with his contacts to get me in.

'Trying 2 get u in Dunhill' he texted me at my boarding school.

'What r chances?' I replied.

'80%.'

Within five minutes, I received another text. 'Sorry not 80%, u r in.' Then another. 'Have u picked yourself off floor?'

Dad received the following reply. 'No he hasn't. This is Daniel's maths teacher.'

That prompted Dad to send a gushing apology. I did not tell him until a phone call that evening that I had pretended to be my maths teacher. Got him.

The whole week proved fantastic. One practice round with Lee Westwood and Thomas Bjorn and another with Nicky Price. Then three rounds of competition in the company of Gary Lineker, who is a family friend and member at Sunningdale, and his professional Mark Roe. It was such a thrill.

Everyone was really nice. Bjorn said some very flattering things about my golf. And since I used to love driving the ball as far as I could I was particularly pleased to hear Roey asking, 'Bloody hell, is that 'is drive?' after one of my specials. We managed a 37 under total of 251 to win by three strokes. Dad calculated my rounds – played off forward tees for the amateurs, it has to be stressed – to be 73, 70, 68 and 67. It was really brilliant to score 5 under par 67 over the Old Course, a place I love, as does Dad. I once shot 52 there and not in my dreams. On my PlayStation, actually. It becomes easy when you play it a lot.

Dad gets very emotional on these occasions, on most occasions in fact. He is a right blubber. He was almost embarrassing in his gushing praise of me at the press conference. 'A year ago I had a lot of help from twelve great men at The Belfry and today I had a lot of help from one great young man,' he said. That was lovely, if a little over the top.

Mind you, I chipped in with my own bit of father worship. 'As much as I respected him before, it's doubled now,' I told reporters. He played great that week, especially the final day, and made a lot of birdies, which is what you need.

We played together the following year and did quite well. We were drawn for three rounds with Michael Douglas, who was really friendly. The famous Hollywood actor played much better than I thought he would. His handicap was 15, if I recall. Douglas, who was partnering Frenchman Thomas Levet, hit the ball down the middle and putted decently.

We also played one of the rounds with TV pundit Alan Hansen. We had a lot of fun and talked a lot about football. There was a bit of teasing going on as well. Dad and I are Manchester United daft while Hansen, of course, is one of Liverpool's best ever defenders. As you can imagine, we did not agree about much!

The 2002 Ryder Cup was also another memorable highlight. Dad was captain and he insisted that I stayed pretty close to him all week. We would walk round a green together after the players had finished and the spectators would be chanting 'Europe' and 'There's only one Sam Torrance'. It was awesome.

But the starts were very early for a lad who loves his bed. I remember on the Monday of the Ryder Cup Dad burst into my bedroom at The Belfry and gave me a right rollicking for lying in my pit. 'What the hell's going on?' he shouted. 'Get out of bed, this is the Ryder Cup.'

It was the Ryder Cup all right. And it was fantastic. And I slept for about three days afterwards.

Chapter Twenty

A Golfing Disaster Is
Only One Shot Away

Every golfer knows the story of go-for-it-good-guy Roy McAvoy and play-safe-bad-boy David Simms battling it out for the US Open title. How it goes to the last hole when Simms lays up and McAvoy takes on the long carry over water only to see a 'little gust from the gods' cause the ball to roll back into the pond.

How McAvoy keeps attempting the shot and keeps failing until succeeding with the final ball in his bag. His 12th stroke clears the hazard and, with the spectators going potty, his ball rolls into the hole. 'Five years from now,' McAvoy's girlfriend Molly tells him, 'nobody will remember who won or lost, but they're gonna remember your 12.'

This, of course, is the plot of *Tin Cup*, the 1996 movie in which Kevin Costner plays McAvoy and Don Johnson takes the part of Simms. Peter Jacobsen, the veteran US Tour player with a nice line in mimicry, is himself.

Fiction, of course, but fiction based on fact and reality. Gary McCord, American broadcaster extraordinaire and listed in the film credits as a golf adviser, carded a 15 in similar fashion.

Not that such behaviour is the preserve of the eccentric or John Daly. Arnold Palmer, no less, came to the 18th in the second round of the 1961 LA Open at Rancho Park needing a par 5 for a 69. His drive duly found the fairway. The lay-up was reckoned to be the percentage shot because of the length and the tight nature of the line to the green. Palmer opted for a 3-wood and pushed his ball out of bounds into the practice range. He reloaded and did exactly the same.

He reloaded again and this time hooked his ball on to the road. The same fate met his eighth shot. A fifth attempt landed on the green and two putts gave him a 12. How on earth did he manage a 12, reporters asked? 'I missed a putt for an 11,' Arnie replied with a smile.

The golfing disaster can happen at any time to just about anyone. Greg Norman had a penalty shot-sprinkled 14 at Lindrick's 17th in the final round of the Martini International in 1982. To John Daly, disaster seemed to arrive more frequently.

His most notorious *'Tin Cup* situation' took place at Palmer's Bay Hill Invitational event in 1998. Daly repeatedly tried (and failed) to make the 320-yard carry over water at the C-shaped 6th hole on the way to an 18. 'I've been working on my patience all year and I guess my patience ran out,' Daly said afterwards. 'But I'm not ashamed of what I did. I didn't quit.' He did pack in after an 11 in the 1999 US Open at Pinehurst No 2.

Billy Casper was no quitter but, as it happened, he was taking part in his final Masters at the age of seventy-three when registering a 14 at the par 3 16th in 2005. Five balls in the water represented the majority of the carnage.

There is undoubtedly an element of *schadenfreude* and black humour in the way the public react to sporting calamity. You would never find me as a professional clicking on to YouTube and laughing at a colleague's misfortune! But they invariably generate so-called water-cooler moments as workers gather on Monday morning and trade 'did you sees?'

Did you see, for example, that poor South Korean woman I. K. Kim miss a 12-inch putt on the 72nd hole that would have won her the Kraft Nabisco Championship, one of the majors, in 2012? A mere tap-in but the ball horseshoed round and stayed out. Almost inevitably, she lost the play-off.

Do you remember Hale Irwin in the third round of the 1983 Open Championship at Royal Birkdale whiffing a 2-inch tap-in at the par 3 14th? He eventually lost to Tom Watson by one stroke. 'I guess I lifted my head because my club bounced over the ball,' Irwin reflected.

I was tickled to discover that 'Tommy' Nakajima's proper first name is Tsuneyuki, meaning 'always happy'. I wonder how happy he was after putting into Road Bunker at the notorious Old Course 17th when in contention during the 1978 Open. It took him four to effect his escape on the way to a 9. Road Bunker will always be Road Bunker, but for more than thirty years it has also been the Sands of Nakajima.

That 9 was not even his worst single score in a major championship that year. The same Nakajima fell foul of Augusta National's 13th hole in the Masters a few months earlier. Trying to pinch a bit from the dogleg left, his tee ball struck a tree and dropped into Rae's Creek. The Japanese player wisely took his penalty stroke and, again sensibly, laid up with a 5-iron leaving himself a comfortable 100 yards from the green. However, he dumped his wedge shot into the creek and tried to play it where it lay. The ball popped straight up and landed on his foot. That cost the hapless Nakajima a two-stroke penalty. Then he handed his muddy club to his caddie who allowed it to slip from his grasp into the water. That landed him another two-stroke penalty for grounding the club in hazard. I wonder if he was still happy. The rest proved routine. He pitched over the green, chipped back and two-putted for a 13. 'I don't like to recall unpleasant occurrences,' he said when asked to detail his catalogue of mishaps.

From the Sands of Nakajima to Two Chips Chen, which sounds like a particularly Scrooge-like school-dinner server in Beijing. Tze-Chung Chen from Taiwan, originally known as TC, held a 2-stroke lead going into the final round of the 1985 US Open at Oakland Hills. He had doubled his advantage after four holes when disaster struck. From a good drive, he pushed a 4-iron second shot into the trees. His third shot landed in the greenside rough. He could only pop the ball up with his next and somehow the head of his sand wedge hit the ball twice sending it sideways in mid-air. The end result was a quadruple 8, a run of subsequent bogeys, a single-stroke defeat by Andy North and a new nickname, Two Chips Chen.

Numerically at least, nothing has exceeded the 19 of club pro Ray Ainsley at the 1938 US Open at Cherry Hills. His problem seemed to be slashing away at a ball drifting with the current in a stream as he stubbornly refused to take a penalty drop.

Much more recently – in the wake of Rory McIlroy's collapse at the Masters in 2011 – Kevin Na produced five minutes or so of

YouTube gold in Texas when thrashing his way through the undergrowth to a 16. 'How are we going to count all the shots?' the miked-up Na was heard to ask his distinctly unamused caddie.

So far I have kept myself out of all this mayhem. In fact, I don't remember ever carding double figures in a tournament. There was, however, a 9 at St Andrews that Alan Fraser, who helped me with this book, and I laughed about in the aftermath. Not at the time, definitely not at the time.

Scotland were playing Sweden on the Saturday of the 1993 Dunhill Cup. Fraser was wandering about, probably nursing a hangover. We bumped into each other and had a quick chat. He told me that Joakim Haeggman had just had a 9 at the 12th, at just 316 yards the shortest par 4 on the course. Since it was downwind that day, a number of players had driven the green.

'How in the world can you make 9 at that hole?' I observed.

Then I played the hole. I hooked my drive into some pretty impenetrable gorse. That's lost, I thought. So I hit another ball in roughly the same direction. I found my second drive in an unplayable lie and was forced to take a penalty drop. My fifth finished short right of the green with a big mound between myself and the flag. I chipped on to the green and three-putted for a 9!

Fraser was standing beside the green looking paler than any morning after the night before could explain.

'I guess that's how you make a 9,' I said, walking past him to the next tee.

I should have known not to tempt fate. There had been the occasion at Fulford in York when I was drawn with my old mate Des Smyth. We were playing the 9th, a short par 4 dogleg right. Smyth was in the trees, 50 yards short of the green, and completely blocked. He hit a fantastic shot through a tiny gap just a yard short of bunker and green.

'Fuck it, I would rather be in the bunker.'

'Well, chip it in,' I said.

And he did. Christ, I felt terrible. But we had a good laugh about it.

'Nobody will remember who won or lost . . .' Molly says in *Tin Cup*. Well, plenty of folk know that Paul Lawrie won the 1999 Open Championship at Carnoustie but a whole lot more are aware of how Jean Van de Velde contrived to lose the championship in the style of a French farce.

Needing a double-bogey 6 to clinch victory at the final hole, Van de Velde took 7 in what turned out to be the most tragicomic finale in Open history. Except that it turned out not to be the end. Van de Velde's implosion resulted in a four-hole play-off won by Lawrie.

Van de Velde's drive way right was sensible enough in that his ball avoided the burn that snakes across the fairway. But instead of then laying up in the fairway short of the burn in front of the green, he hit a 4-iron. His logic was to take enough club to clear the burn and it did not matter where it went after that. But his ball rebounded from the grandstand to the tee side of the burn into heavy rough.

The lie was so bad that his third shot landed in the burn. The sight of him removing his socks and shoes and standing in the water to assess the possibility of playing the ball from the burn got cameras clicking and mouths clacking. But he took his penalty drop, played his next into a bunker and eventually holed a 10-foot putt to make the play-off.

By then his brain was fried.

But that's what happens with golfing disasters.

Jane James

Sam on Jane: 'Mark and Jane James are just a great, fun couple. Jesse has been a good friend for years, as has his wife, Jane. I love them both. We have enjoyed many a drunken evening together.

Jesse and I have been through a lot. We played in five Ryder Cup teams together and were closely involved on the management side in both 1999 and 2002. I was Jesse's vice-captain at the Battle of Brookline and Jesse, in turn, was at my side for the next match at The Belfry. Jesse won eighteen times on the European Tour and achieved four top five finishes in the Open Championship. In 2004 he became the first European to win a Champions Tour major when taking the Seniors Player Championship.

Mark has struck Jane three times with a golf ball, giving lie to his claim not to be an accurate driver! '

Sam is exaggerating greatly, as usual. Jess only ever hit me twice!

The first time was at Fulford in York, when he struck me in the middle of the back while I was standing with a group of mates miles away from the fairway in the middle of a clearing.

'It is a good job the ball didn't end up in the bushes,' was his only comment.

The second occasion happened at Royal Dublin during a torrential downpour. I can't remember which hole it was, but I was standing up the fairway hiding behind my brolly. I heard him hit at least two balls off the tee (I think), so I turned round to see what the hell was going on. His ball bounced once and hit me right between the eyes.

You need danger money being a golfing WAG. These football WAGs have it easy. Their only risk of injury is falling off a pair of Louboutins.

My eyes refocused in time to see Jess and his caddie, John 'More Cash' Moorhouse, walk all the way up the fairway killing themselves laughing. I assume that was out of relief that I wasn't lying unconscious in the mud!

Talking about lying unconscious, we have indeed shared many a lively evening over the years. The best have tended to be the impromptu ones, the unplanned spur-of-the-moment sessions that have begun innocently and ended in mayhem.

The place is Rome, the year 1984. We were all in Italy for the World Cup. Sam was representing Scotland in partnership with Gordon Brand Jnr; Jess was playing with Howard Clark for England; and Woosie had teamed up with Philip Parkin in the Welsh corner.

The opening ceremony had just finished and there was a problem with the courtesy cars, so we settled down in the clubhouse bar. Howard was there with his then wife, Beverly. Brand Jnr was there. So was Sam, of course, Woosie, Jess and myself. A few drinks and one thing led to another. Someone got out the cards and suggested we play strip poker. Beverly and I cheated for England. I'm pretty sure that Jess also cheated. The upshot was that Sam and Woosie were pretty quickly down to their underpants. Sam was even forced to remove his Rolex watch.

Still the courtesy cars didn't appear. Time for more high jinks, only this time outside, as Sam jumped into a buggy and started careering around the car park. People jumped on and people fell off. I seem to remember Beverly whooping and hollering like a youngster on a dodgem car at the fair. The officials were not amused and players were identified. Beverly blamed it all on the driver whose name she incorrectly gave as Craig Stadler from the United States. Well, he has a moustache.

The morning after the night before brought the usual recrimination, apologies and guilt. Sam missed his tee-off time for the pro-am, perhaps because he was in a right state looking for his Rolex. He had forgotten – or simply did not know – that Gordon was looking after it.

The Irish were being blamed. They were innocent, as it happened, and Sam went to the organisers and owned up. That went down well with the officials, the Italians and, particularly, the Irish.

On another occasion – Jess and I think it was in San Remo – the usual suspects gathered for a bit of bonhomie. The place was pretty much closed for the winter and they had to open up a few restaurants and bars to accommodate the golfers. They might have wished they hadn't bothered.

Jess was doing his yoga, showing off the strength and agility that he proudly displays on the ski slopes, his second home. His third home is his garden. Woosie, in good spirits shall we say, was not impressed. The former boxer in him threw down a challenge.

'Hit me,' Woosie said to Jess.

'Don't be stupid,' Jess replied.

'Hit me here,' Woosie repeated, pointing to his solar plexus.

'No.'

'Look, I can take any punch. Hit me as hard as you like.'

Jess gave him a tap that far from satisfied Woosie.

'Punch me as hard as you can.'

Which is what Jess did. Now he may not look it but Jess is a powerful guy with strong arms. He knocked Woosie across the room with tables and chairs scattering all over the place like a scene from a saloon bar in a cowboy film. I looked over at Woosie on the floor in the corner of the room. He looked dazed and you could imagine birds twittering around his head as in a cartoon.

But Woosie just grinned and said, 'It didn't hurt a bit.'

Chapter Twenty-One

We Should All Be Sponsored by Advil . . .

The older I get the more convinced I become that Tom Watson's challenge for the Open Championship at Turnberry in 2009 was the finest sporting achievement of all time.

How can that be, you would be entitled to ask, when it ended in glorious failure rather than the most spectacular victory by any sportsman or woman in any sport in any era? Second place can never be the ultimate superlative. Point taken.

But the evidence for my belief stems from what precisely he did achieve. Watson, just two months away from his sixtieth birthday and less than a year after undergoing a hip replacement operation, went within a few inches of beating all the best players in the world – most half his age – in the toughest and most prestigious tournament in the world.

Let us remind ourselves further. Watson needed a par at the 72nd and final hole to win his sixth Open. He struck a glorious drive and a fine approach shot that would have finished in the heart of the green but for a hard bounce. It can always happen in links golf. His ball ran through the green. But he was still left with maybe a 10-foot putt for sporting – never mind golfing – immortality.

Here's the point. I am certainly no Tom Watson. But I am fifty-nine, as he was in 2010, and I have been a pretty decent golfer over a long career. Like Tom, I play Seniors golf. But to place things in perspective, put me at my age in a regular European Tour event on a course set up for tournament golf and I would not beat anyone. That week Tom was whipping everyone, the best in the world, and on a course set up for a major championship.

What he did was utterly beyond me and my imagination. I met Tom the following week at the Senior Open and I said to him, 'You made me proud to be a golfer.'

A golfer is what I remain, and I will for a few more years yet. I am far from being finished. Seniors golf has given people of my age the opportunity to be competitive. The great thing is the prospect of winning. I can be in contention every week, something that tournament players live for. It is difficult to get into contention between the ages of, say, forty-five and fifty. Then Seniors golf comes along and it is like starting all over again. It is the competition. The hardest 'club' in the bag is the pencil. I can play brilliantly in bounce matches at Sunningdale pretty much every day but in a tournament there are consequences for each shot.

Of course, as I approach sixty, nothing is as natural as it once was. When I was playing great on the regular Tour, I just went out and played. It just happened. You have to work at it more now. You have to work harder over every shot. The body is less flexible, more fragile. You are just not as good as you once were. Mediocrity is hard to stomach.

There was never any doubt that having played well over 700 tournaments around the world up until my fiftieth birthday I was going to carry on into a second career. And since everyone talked about the great riches that were available in the States I thought I would have a stab at the Champions Tour.

I went through four rounds of regional qualifying and managed to gain one of the seven cards available from final qualifying. I was in. I found myself joining – or being joined by – old pals from the European tour like Mark 'Jesse' James, Des Smyth and Rodger Davis.

It was a great Tour. They could not do enough for the players in absolutely every aspect, from transport and accommodation to food and laundry. Cars, prime parking places, meals, haircuts, computers, telephones – they were all laid on. Put your laundry in a locker, play your round and it would be clean by the time you finished. You wanted for nothing.

Every pro-am was a shotgun start and 4 hours 45 minutes later another shotgun would fire to indicate end of play. You were pulled off no matter where you were. Done. Four amateurs and one pro, only one score to count in a scramble and par was your friend. The prize-giving doubled as a party with great food and entertainment. Over by 8 p.m. Attendance not compulsory but it was so good all the pros turned up.

And it was buggy golf. I loved it. I had been walking for forty years – it was time to sit doon, as we say in Scotland. The rules stipulated either player or caddie and clubs on the buggy at any one time so as to control the speed of play for the spectators. Otherwise they would struggle to keep up. And the prize money was fantastic.

Despite all that I lasted four months!

Despite the money and the mollycoddling, I could not take it. I could not bear finishing a tournament on the Sunday and not getting home that same night. All my tournament life, other than a few weeks in Africa or wherever, I got home on a Sunday night.

I just could not settle in the States. I found it very difficult to fill in the gap between the end of one tournament and the start of another. I could not go on the piss – I was too old for that. I also found the jet lag terrible on the occasions that I did fly home to see the wife and kids. And because I did not settle I never played well. I was always struggling with some aspect of my game. Maybe I was overawed; maybe I was not good enough.

So, I decided to concentrate on the European Seniors Tour. It might not be as flash and has less fringe benefits – you even have to take your own balls – but I prefer it. The ambience is better. There is rivalry but no animosity. We have all gone down the same road and done what we have done. I just like being able to get home to my family.

There are still characters, maybe more than there are on the regular Tours these days. But the late nights and wild parties have long gone. It is just a hell of a lot quieter. I am sixty in 2013. I play golf, return to the hotel, have a spot of dinner and go to bed.

You have to look after yourself and watch out for those back injuries. Take Carl Mason, for example. What a player and what a Seniors career. Sometimes, though, he can't move never mind walk or play golf.

I hurt my neck the other day putting eye drops in. We should all be sponsored by Advil.

We share more than our aches and pains. We share a love for golf.

David Feherty

Sam on David: 'First things first, don't believe any of that shit about him having trained to be an opera singer. He might be a tenor with the noises that come out of his arse but not from anything that comes out of his mouth.

Feherty is simply the funniest guy I have ever met. His witticisms and one-liners are repeated throughout clubhouses around the world. "I'm sorry Nick Faldo couldn't be here. He is attending the birth of his next wife", is a particular favourite of mine. But there are many, many more.

Never mind the razor-sharp mind, he could play all right. You just had to see the 4-iron second shot at the Road Hole 17th at St Andrews to win the Dunhill Cup for Ireland to know the extent of his ability.

Now he has forged a brilliant television career as a golf commentator for CBS and interviewer for the Golf Channel. I love him to bits and I miss him a great deal.'

I am in and out of a partial coma, staring at the ceiling, about four days from going back to TV work after four months off. The FBR Phoenix Open is almost upon me, yet it seems like yesterday I was in New Jersey doing the Barclays. I feel like a 50-something crash-test dummy, and the vehicle of my life, which on this occasion is my beloved battered recliner, appears to be gathering speed towards its inevitable immovable obstruction. I don't know if everyone my age feels like this, but the years slip by so quickly these days, sometimes I wonder if I've accomplished anything.

The other day I heard the mailman drop something heavy on the front doormat. I hate the mail, and make a point of never opening any of it in case it's for me, but there was something alluring about the 'whumpf' that this particular package emitted as it hit the 'Bugger Off' bristles on the front step that made me stretch luxuriously (resulting in an alarming, involuntary and dangerously damp fart of the sort that might normally afflict an octogenarian). I slid gingerly out of my recliner and cautiously made my way to the door, listening all the time for signs of movement outside. I hate my neighbours, and the last thing I needed was to accidentally make eye contact with any of them, giving them the chance to wave cheerily or yell some inane greeting to which I might feel obliged to respond. No thank you. During the winter months I don't ram a plug of mud, grass and twigs up my rectum, but that's pretty much the only difference between me and a Kodiak bear.

I opened the front door a crack, squinted out furtively and scooped up the package, whipping it inside like a lizard's tongue. I yawned as I made my way back to my still-smouldering throne and noticed it was from Tour HQ in Jacksonville, but against my better instincts again, I tore it open. It was the *Official Guide to the PGA Tour*. Bollocks. I'd been hoping for something to drool over from Victoria's Secret, so this was a major disappointment. Still, I'd made such a huge effort to get it. What the hell I thought – I'd take a look.

You see, in my captivity as a course reporter, I have no need for the kind of information I imagined would be between these pages. After all, I am merely required to describe the action as I see it in the present, or at worst make a prediction, so I can hardly prepare for something that has yet to happen. That's my story anyway, and I'm sticking to it. But as chance would have it, I opened the shiny volume at page 231, and lo and behold, there was a picture of my personal self, under the heading 'Other Prominent Members'. I had no idea my member was considered prominent by anyone other than me, so naturally I was delighted! I noted that the photograph made me look fat, but despite this irritating accuracy, I read on.

Apparently at one time I had told someone I was 5 foot 11 and 200 pounds, and my 'special interests' were all sports, and golf course design. This was a load of crap, as at the time of enquiry, many years earlier, the real answer was 5 foot 10, 215 pounds, and I was especially interested in self-destruction by drugs and alcohol, and the music of Wagner. Over on the other half of the page, I noticed Nick Faldo, at 6 foot 3 and 195 pounds (huh), whose special interests were much more glamorous – flying helicopters, photography and fly-fishing for women in their twenties, probably all of them simultaneously. The swine.

For the purposes of this book, someone else investigated the European Tour website to check my comparable entries. There I was 5 foot 10 1/2 and 182 pounds, (shorter but thinner) and my 'interests', not special apparently, were writing.

Moving on. Under 'Other information' I discovered that I played in sixty-one events, made the cut in thirty-one and my highest finish was second behind a man about whom, despite my best efforts, I cannot find a single attribute to dislike. It was Kenny bloody Perry in the 1994 New England Classic, a tournament I was too hungover to win, even though there were more Irish people in our final-round gallery than I'd had in twenty years of playing the Irish Open. My career earnings were $329,903 and my highest world ranking was 65.

(Back to the European listing. I played 306 events in Europe between 1979 and 1996, won money at 228 of them, managed a stroke average of 72.63 for total earnings of €1.94 million. Maybe so, but I spent a hell of a lot more. I won five times, in chronological order: the Italian, Scottish, BMW International, Cannes and Madrid Opens.)

But that day I was not thinking about European tournaments where I might have staggered (sometimes literally) over the line. Suddenly, it hit me. Right at that point, I realised the answer to the question that had been nagging me earlier. I have accomplished bugger all. (But I've done it in a stylish and windswept manner.) In fact, I now pass for an expert in a game at which I clearly sucked. Maybe the Official Tour Guide needs a new category – 'Other Flatulent Members'. Talk about a breeze! I could have won the money list in that one.

The 'fat one' would have run me close. I am referring to Sam, of course, my great buddie. I think back to my one and only Ryder Cup appearance at Kiawah Island in 1991 when Sam, already a veteran of five previous matches, made me feel bigger and better and more important than I ever had.

He was always going to be a great captain. Sam never lectured his team unless you consider a lecture to be telling dirty jokes over a cold beer or playing cards in a hotel room. More than anything else he made them feel special because now, numbered among their friends, is Sam Torrance.

I love the man. I know him so well, but then if you are a golf fan, so do you.

Acknowledgements

To Simon & Schuster for persuading me that this book would be a good idea!

To Sarah Wooldridge at IMG for turning that good idea into reality.

To my old pal Alan Fraser for bringing all the wonderful contributions together into an acceptable format.

To my friend and manager, Vicky Cuming, for keeping us all on schedule.

Most importantly, to all those that have generously given their time and their stories. Without you, it would never have happened. A donation has been made to the Seve Foundation by way of thanks.